IRON INDIGNATION

The Evolution of Canadian Artillery Tactics and the Victory at Vimy Ridge

IRON INDIGNATION

The Evolution of Canadian Artillery Tactics
and the Victory at Vimy Ridge

Colonel David W. Grebstad, RCA

Library and Archives Canada Cataloguing in Publication
Grebstad, David W. author
Iron Indignation / David W. Grebstad

Issued in print and electronic formats.
ISBN: 978-1-990644-52-8 (soft cover)
ISBN: 978-1-990644-55-9 (e-book)

Editor: Jennifer McIntyre
Cover design: Pablo Javier Herrera
Interior Design: Winston A. Prescott

Double Dagger Books Ltd
Toronto, Ontario, Canada
www.doubledagger.ca

Dedicated to all the men and women of the Royal Regiment of Canadian Artillery who have served their nation in peace and war, and to my wife Colleen – understanding, supportive, and, above all, patient.

CONTENTS

The cannons have their bowels full of wrath, and ready mounted are they to spit forth their iron indignation 'gainst your walls.
— William Shakespeare, King John: Act II, scene 1.

At 0530 hours on the morning of April 9th, in the damp, cold and gray pre-dawn light, a hailstorm of iron such as nobody had ever experienced fell on the German positions. Its racket equalled the roaring and raging of a hurricane-lashed sea. Everywhere rose huge fountains of earth. The ground seemed to shake.
— *Generalleutnant* Alfred Dietrich, Commander, 79th Reserve Infantry Brigade, Vimy Ridge

INTRODUCTION

Dante never imagined an inferno such as the Vimy Ridge was when hundreds of guns were turned loose upon it on the morning of 9 April 1917. Had he been able to look down through the ages with prophetic vision upon the tortured earth, and the men who it engulfed in its writhings, the great Italian would have added a new horror to hell, a horror in which the victims were subject to unending shell-fire, and were forced to endure forever its agonies and apprehensions.[1]

In the early morning hours of April 9, 1917, thousands of Canadian soldiers emerged from dugouts and trenches into the cool, snow-filled air of the western slope of Vimy Ridge. Months of planning, preparation, and rehearsal had led to this moment as the four divisions of the Canadian Corps moved steadfastly eastward up the gentle slope behind a rolling barrage of artillery fire furnished by thousands of guns and mortars. Over the next several hours, the Canadians methodically worked their way across the shell-pocked terrain, and by late morning they were masters of most the ridge that dominated the Douai Plain of the Arras region of northeast France, a feature that had been in German hands since 1914.

What the Canadian Corps achieved on Vimy Ridge has become, rightly or wrongly – there is substantial debate about this – a key event in the Canadian historical narrative. Sovereignty over the terrain upon which the Canadians advanced was transferred by France to Canada in 1922, and the site of the battle now boasts the largest Canadian war memorial in existence, the Vimy Memorial, erected in 1936. Despite the subsequent mythologizing of the battle in the decades that followed, there was nonetheless a sense even among contemporaries that something important had happened. Even Sir Arthur Conan Doyle, the creator of

Sherlock Holmes, was moved to write only two years after the battle that "the whole might of Canada was drawn together in the four fine divisions which lay facing the historic Vimy Ridge... Nothing could have been more magnificent or more successful than their advance... Sweeping onwards with irresistible fury, they overran three lines of German trenches."[2] In the years since, while debate has swirled as to whether or not Vimy Ridge was truly a "nation-building" experience, from a purely operational and tactical perspective, historians have celebrated the Canadian Corps' operation for the ingenuity in its planning and the effectiveness of its execution. No less an esteemed military historian than the late John Keegan referred to the Canadian Corps' success on Vimy Ridge as "sensational."[3]

Consequently, the Canadian Corps' operation at Vimy Ridge has been one of the most closely studied and historically scrutinized events of Canadian military history. Indeed, one could be excused for thinking that there can't be much more to say about a battle so thoroughly gone over. The aim of this book is to challenge that assertion by diving into the technical and tactical details behind the artillery bombardment of Vimy Ridge in support of the Canadian Corps and, more importantly, the vast, interconnected fire support network that made it happen.

The role of the artillery in the historiography of modern warfare is often overlooked: it often finds itself in the historical penumbra, overshadowed by the much more exciting and admittedly crucial narrative of the manoeuvre arms. It is true that the manoeuvre elements of warfare, namely the infantry and the cavalry, including their descendants in the armoured branches of modern militaries, are essential components of the historical narrative; it is they that force the issue that, in the end, secures the victory or results in defeat. The intense and intimate nature of their combat easily overshadows the less sanguine and sometimes mundane tale of gunners and guns pounding away for hours or days at a time at targets they can't see. Lamentably, this leaves huge swaths of the historical narrative of major engagements untapped and unexplored.

That the artillery bombardment of Vimy Ridge was devastatingly intense is undeniable; the thunderous cacophony and concordant earth tremors produced by thousands of tonnes of high explosive epitomize Shakespeare's prosaic phrase: *iron indignation*. By April of 1917 enormous, destructive bombardments preceding infantry assaults had become de rigueur among the Allied armies of the Western Front. Before then, during the opening chapters of the Great War, there were insufficient guns, artillery ammunition, or men available to the combatants to prosecute such enormous bombardments, some of which lasted weeks at a time. In fact, it wasn't until the Allied offensives of spring 1917, of which the Battle of Vimy Ridge was a part, that the men, guns, ammunition, and doctrine, as well as the myriad of other essential elements of the fire support organization, had been built, trained, and deployed to enable such massive bombardments. The enormity of the Allied fire support network in Northwest Europe is staggering: during the Franco-Prussian War of July 1870 to May 1871, the belligerents deployed one gun for every 350 soldiers; at the outbreak of the Great War in 1914, that ratio had dropped to one per 200, but those numbers climbed significantly when the war adopted a static nature during the period 1916–18; at its crescendo on the Western Front there was, on average, one gun fielded for every sixty soldiers![4] The blood harvest reaped by the artillery was a bumper crop; the French estimated that 67 per cent of its casualties were caused by artillery fire, while the Germans attributed 75 per cent of their losses on the Western Front to the artillery.[5] Even though the Americans were late to the party, 87 per cent of their casualties were inflicted by German artillery.[6]

As a consequence of this expansion of the artillery branch, the fire support network at Vimy Ridge and the bombardment it unleashed were massive. Indeed, the sheer size of the bombardment is well known and has been written about in detail by both academics and popular historians since the guns fell silent, but very few have taken the effort to drill down into the ways and means of the enormous, intricate, and integrated fire support system. This book will address that.

The idea for this book began during the run-up to the centenary celebrations of the Battle of Vimy Ridge. I undertook this endeavour with the best of intentions, hoping to have the book written and published in time for the actual celebration in April of 2017. Unfortunately, as is the case with many of us in the twenty-first century, life got in the way. Working full time didn't lend itself to writing an in-depth historical-technical-tactical analysis of a major battle – perhaps THE major battle – of Canadian military history. The situation was exacerbated, ironically, when I volunteered to help organize a week-long commemorative battlefield tour from the Normandy Beaches to Vimy Ridge for 100 members of the Royal Regiment of Canadian Artillery, called Gunners Return to Vimy. The tour culminated at the centenary commemoration event at Vimy Ridge in 2017, which came and went without the book being finished, yet alone published; sadly, thereafter it fell on the back burner, as I felt that the moment had passed. Eventually, however, I realized that the story of the gunners' contribution to victory at Vimy Ridge, and the years-long path of doctrinal evolution that preceded it, was a story that needed to be shared. Consequently, I redoubled my efforts, and the product of my labours is the book you now hold in your hands.

I undertook to write this book in an effort to fill what I think is a lamentable gap in this narrative of the battle: a historical-technical analysis of the artillery's contribution to the assault that is more than simply a rehashing of *what* happened; it is also an analysis of *why* and, most importantly, *how* it happened – all taken from the artillery's perspective. Between the opening salvoes of the war in August 1914 and the beginning of the Vimy Ridge fire plan, new tactics, techniques, and procedures had emerged as leaders at all levels, and in all corps, worked to solve the tactical and operational problem posed by the German army. The result was an artillery branch that was markedly different than the one that marched to war. Therefore, to fully understand Vimy Ridge, one must understand the numerous components of the massive interconnected and devastatingly effective fire support network that was the result of nearly three years of doctrine and equipment development, evolution, and refinement; a result that was achieved at immense cost in terms of both blood and money, the former in particular.

And to fully understand how the artillery enabled the victory at Vimy Ridge, it is important to understand all the nuances of the artillery, both tactical and technical. How did shrapnel rounds work? How did a battery move from one position to another? What did a forward observation officer (FOO) do, and how did he do it? These are but some of the questions that I will answer in this book, and by doing so, I aim to provide a much broader appreciation of artillery than would be possible simply by commenting on the enormity of the bombardment of March and April 1917. In fact, through this approach, Vimy Ridge becomes a case study that exposes how the artillery and the men who served the guns fought and lived in the Great War. Perhaps historians Shelford Bidwell and Dominick Graham put it best when they observed that "by grasping the working methods of the soldier, the historian may lay his hands on the continuous thread of reason that was real to his subjects at the time and led them through the noise and the confusion."[7]

This book will answer those questions through an historical-technical analysis of the development, implementation, and execution of the fire support plan for the Canadian Corps' assault on Vimy Ridge. It will start by providing a primer on the nuances of artillery in general, followed by a brief survey of the history of the Royal Regiment of Canadian Artillery to establish the culture and background of the Canadian gunners who went to war in 1914. Thereafter, in order to establish a firm foundation from which to discuss the strategic, operational, and tactical situation in the spring of 1917, this book will conduct a brief overview of the war from its outbreak to the period of the Allies' 1917 spring offensives. Having laid this groundwork, the book will then describe how strategic goals shaped the operational- and tactical-level objectives that culminated at the crest of Vimy Ridge. It will then illustrate the means by which the bombardment was executed, which is to say the artillery tools that were available to the Canadian Corps in the form of equipment, personnel, resources, doctrine, and procedures. Finally, it will describe the ways in which the gunners of the Canadian Corps employed these tools to aid in the successful assault on Vimy Ridge.

I have based my research on official and primary sources as much as possible. I have conducted extensive research on personal accounts of the battle as well as official documents. As there are extensive analyses available of the assault from an operational perspective, I have relied on secondary sources to provide the meat of the framing narrative, particularly with regard to the operational and strategic machinations that shaped the development and execution of the assault.

You, the reader, are perhaps wondering what qualifies me to add to the historiography of the Battle of Vimy Ridge, a path upon which many more luminous and renowned military historians have already trod, and whose footprints remain so visible. It's true, I'm not a professional historian, nor do I have PhD. I do, however, bring several skills to the table that might make this a worthwhile history. First, I have a passion for military history in general, and artillery history in particular. I have also been published in several peer-reviewed academic historic and professional journals including the *Canadian Army Journal, Canadian Military History*, the journal of the University of Laurier Centre for Military and Disarmament Studies, *The Canadian Military Journal, Manitoba History* (now *Prairie History*), the journal of the Manitoba Historical Society, and, finally, the *Journal of the Society for Army Historical Research*.

But a passion for history, of course, even the history of the artillery, is not in itself sufficient qualification for such a study. I also bring a level of technical expertise to the table, having served, at the time of writing, over thirty years in the Canadian Forces as a member of the Royal Regiment of Canadian Artillery (RCA). I first joined the Regiment in November 1990 as a private in the Primary Reserve, serving in the 116th Independent Field Battery, RCA. I spent nine years in that unit, being promoted to the rank of gunner, then taking my commission, and eventually achieving the rank of captain. I transferred to the Regular Force in 1999 and have now served over twenty years as an officer in the regular component of the Canadian Artillery, achieving at the time of writing the rank of colonel. I have served in the 1st and 2nd Regiments, Royal Canadian Horse Artillery, and the Royal Regiment of Canadian Artillery School, and I have commanded at both the troop and battery levels.

Perhaps most important to this study, I am a graduate of the Instructor-in-Gunnery program at the Canadian Artillery School. This course, sometimes referred to as a "Masters of Artillery" among its graduates, is a challenging, in-depth program aimed at allowing its students to truly master the technical and tactical nuances of the artillery. Thus, beyond a simple passion for the history of the artillery, I also bring to bear thirty years' experience and technical artillery knowledge to the following historical analysis. To be sure, some aspects of artillery have changed since the Battle of Vimy Ridge, but much has stayed the same. And, of course, from a purely scientific perspective, the laws of physics to which the ballisticians among the artillery are subject have not changed at all.

Thus, what follows is a historical-technical-tactical analysis of the fire support provided to the Canadian Corps' assault on Vimy Ridge aimed at addressing not just *what* happened on April 9, 1917, and the weeks leading up to it, but *how* and *why* it occurred as well, from the perspective of the artillery. The efforts of the men who made up the Canadian Corps artillery organization at the Battle of Vimy Ridge were a critical element of the success of the operation. The artillery organization was vast and intricate. It involved hundreds of guns and thousands of shells, and thousands of men and horses working toward a common end in the face of inclement weather, challenging terrain, and a well-ensconced and efficient enemy. The moving pieces of this symphony of fire were practically innumerable, but despite these challenges the Canadian Corps artillery provided the battle-winning fire support that allowed the Canadian Corps to achieve its objective and secure the operationally important Vimy Ridge for the Allied forces. This book will tell their story, from the gunner loading the howitzer to the general who pulled it all together, and in the process, it will shed light on a tremendous tactical and technical victory that all Canadians can rightfully be proud of.

A PRIMER ON ARTILLERY

Legend has it that Napoleon Bonaparte quipped to one of his subordinate commanders to "leave the artillerymen alone, they are an obstinate lot." As with many historical witticisms, there is no way to know whether Bonaparte, himself a gunner, actually did say such a thing. Despite its tenuous veracity, the statement, with its charming deprecation, is worn now as a badge of honour by the men and women who serve the guns, among whom Bonaparte's comment is an accepted fact. Accurate or no, at the very least it serves to highlight that the artillery is a martial arm in its own right, differing in organization, traditions, and ethos from the various other branches and arms of modern militaries: the infantry, cavalry, armoured forces, engineers, and the various support elements necessary to feed, house, equip, and care for land forces.

Artillery soldiers may not all be obstinate, of course, but they are most certainly unique. They serve machines of war that are a testament to the unfortunately efficient technological evolution of humankind's ability to kill one another. Over the centuries, artillery has evolved from simplistic machines designed to hurl rocks to modern-day ballistic missile launchers. Consequently, viewed holistically and over a broad swath of time, that which constitutes *artillery* is indeed a wide spectrum. The confusion is exacerbated by the use, in modern infantry and armour, of armament that would have been considered in past ages the exclusive domain of the artillerist, such as mortars, anti-armour rockets, and missiles. These tools seem to be the evolutionary descendants of ballistae, catapults, and Napoleonic field guns, and even modern main battle tanks have, in many ways, arguably more in common with nineteenth-century horse artillery cannon than the cavalry-turned-tank regiments that currently employ them.

In a very general sense, artillery is that arm in which destructive projectiles that are too large to be individually launched are propelled toward their target by some type of crew-served equipment. The simplicity of such a broad definition means there is a bond among artillerymen that spans centuries – perhaps millennia, if one accepts Roman catapults and ballistae as early forms of artillery. True, the differences between a Canadian artillery soldier loading a 98-pound high-explosive (HE) projectile into an M777 howitzer of 155mm calibre to destroy a Taliban position nearly twenty kilometres away and a Roman soldier loading a 25-pound stone onto a torsion-powered ballista to break down a stone wall are stark. Nonetheless, there is an intuitive commonality.

A singularly important characteristic of modern artillery is the use of an explosive chemical reaction within a confined space, a chamber, to propel a projectile toward a target. This form of projectile delivery emerged in the thirteenth century through the use of large, unwieldy, and mostly immobile cannon charged with an early form of gunpowder. Their targets were normally city walls or battlements against which the kinetic energy of the projectile was applied in order to smash the obstacle. Not long thereafter, the provision of fire support, which is to say the use of artillery fire to assist tactical manoeuvre by infantry or cavalry units, is first recorded as occurring during the Battle of Crecy in 1346. In the centuries since, artillery has evolved considerably and its scope of practice has broadened beyond simple surface-to-surface fire support to include air-defence, anti-tank, and locating artillery. Indicative of the common philosophy and ethos among the members of the artillery, in armies that have inherited British traditions the lowest rank of those serving in the artillery are known as gunners, equivalent to private in infantry battalions, regardless of whether they actually work on a gun, a rocket system, or weapon-locating radar. While the title is a proper rank in its own right, it is also used colloquially to describe all personnel, regardless of rank, who serve in the artillery.

Let us turn now to a discussion of some of the technical aspects of artillery fire. Hereafter, the focus of this chapter will be on these technical issues of surface-to-surface fire support, and we will leave the discussion of tactics, organization, and the command and control of artillery during the Great War to later chapters.

To begin with, artillery fire can be delivered *directly* or *indirectly*. In the former, artillery fire is delivered directly against a target that the gunners can see, often referred to as *firing over open sights*. This was the de facto means of delivering artillery fire for much of the history of artillery support. Conversely, indirect fire involves artillery pieces firing at a target indirectly, either from behind an intervening feature or at a distance from whence the gunners manning the piece are unable to observe their target. As a consequence, the gun engages the target by applying aiming data such as barrel elevation and azimuth, among other technical applications, which are computed trigonometrically.

Artillery fire can also be either *adjusted* or *predicted* when it is fired indirectly. In the case of the former, the fire of the artillery piece is adjusted by an observer of some sort who provides the coordinates of the target location, which in turn is used to make trigonometric calculations to produce gun-aiming data. The observer then adjusts or *ranges* the impact of the shell, also known as the *fall of shot*, by ordering corrections to range and bearing of fire until the projectile strikes the target. The term *registered* is also used from time to time to describe fire that is adjusted onto a target. In the case of predicted fire, the fall of shot is not registered or adjusted, but rather is simply fired at grid coordinates using data that predicts it will hit the target, by incorporating certain allowances for naturally occurring "errors."

One should not equate the use of the term 'error' in this regard as a mistake or omission. Rather, the term should be understood to mean all the myriad environmental conditions that exert some influence on the performance and accuracy of the projectile. To help explain, let's employ a theoretical model. Imagine an immense dome that is long enough and high enough to accommodate the range and vertical elevation of an artillery round throughout its trajectory. Let us also imagine that this dome has been sealed in such a way as to create a perfect vacuum, and we have deployed in this dome a gun with a quantity of ammunition, all of which has been perfectly machined to exactly similar specifications. In this theoretical vacuumed dome of ours, gravity is the only force affecting the flight of the projectile. Consequently, when our gunners fire several of their perfectly machined rounds through their perfectly machined barrels – which, for theoretical argument's sake, do not wear from the firing and maintain an exact temperature – each of the rounds will follow exactly the same trajectory, which would be a perfect parabola, and each would land in precisely the same place.

Of course, such a dome does not exist, and our theoretical model defies several laws of physics; hence the effect of *errors*, which, as mentioned above, are not mistakes but deviations from standard conditions. These deviations are extensive and include, but are not limited to, factors such as air density, wind speed and direction, humidity, the temperature of the propelling charge in use, minute differences in the weight of shells, human error in laying the gun, and, at extreme ranges, even the rotation of the earth.

None of these conditions will be exactly the same at two different moments in time. For instance, wind is rarely steady but flows in gusts that cannot be perfectly compensated for. Barrel temperature is another example: when one round is fired, the heat of the chemical explosion and the friction of the round travelling down the tube will heat the metal of the barrel, causing it to expand, which reduces the internal diameter of the barrel to a minute degree. If a subsequent round is fired, the reduced barrel diameter will not only produce more friction, slowing the projectile, but will also seal more of the propellant gas behind the round, imparting greater pressure and thus increasing the velocity of the projectile. Naturally, the muzzle velocity of the second round will be different from that of the first. Consequently, if a gun fires 100 projectiles, given these innumerably changing conditions inside and outside the barrel, no two rounds will experience exactly the same conditions even when using exactly the same elevation and bearing of fire, and so no two rounds will land in the same place. Instead, the effects of the errors will cause the rounds to form an oblong *beaten zone* about the target. The length and width of this beaten zone will be dictated by a number of factors, such as range to the target and the nature of the shell itself, and of course the fluctuating meteorological conditions not only at the gun and the target, but throughout the whole of the trajectory of the projectile. These errors can be reduced by compensating for environmental conditions through the collection of meteorological data, crew training, and the rigid adherence to common industrial production standards, but they can never be completely eliminated. In fact, in certain circumstances, such as when one intends to suppress a large area, the elongated beaten zone may be beneficial to the tactical situation. In other circumstances, such as when one is attempting to destroy a pinpoint target like a bunker or a machine-gun nest, the naturally occurring dispersion of the elongated beaten zone demands a high volume of fire in order to achieve the effect.

The term *effect* is one of extreme importance to the employment of artillery fire. When fire is delivered against a target, it is done to have some sort of effect upon it. When discussing the use of HE kinetic artillery fire, these effects are categorized as *suppression*, *neutralization*, and *destruction*. Suppression prevents an enemy from moving, manning his post, or operating his equipment. It is fleeting and mostly psychological. The duration of the effect is directly related to the duration of the fire used to suppress him, and can be mitigated, to a degree, with experience and training. Neutralization fire is similar, although a heavier weight of fire is used with the intent of causing casualties and destruction to material. Consequently, the rate of fire required for neutralization is substantially greater than that used for suppression, and the amount of time required for the enemy to recover from the neutralizing effects is longer. Destruction, as the name implies, focuses on the physical destruction of men and materiel. To destroy a target with artillery requires long, sustained bombardments that are costly in time and ammunition.

We will close with a brief review of the taxonomy of the various types of artillery pieces we will encounter in this book. There are several terms that are often used interchangeably but nonetheless have a very specific definition: these include gun, cannon, howitzer and mortar. The term *gun* has come to be used synonymously with all artillery pieces. From a purely technical perspective, a gun was essentially a *cannon* that fired a projectile at a high muzzle velocity and generally flat trajectory, although some degree of elevation of the barrel was possible to allow for greater range. A *howitzer* was defined by Great War contemporaries as "a gun capable of throwing a heavy shell at angles of elevation up to 45 degrees and capable of being drawn at a trot by a six-horse team."[8] This ability to fire at higher trajectories allowed the howitzer to provide plunging fire behind intervening crests. Notwithstanding these differing characteristics, for the remainder of this book the term *gun* can be understood to mean an artillery piece, regardless of technical type, and we will stipulate whether an artillery piece is a gun or a howitzer only when this is absolutely necessary for technical reasons.

A mortar, however, is something similar but substantially different from a gun. A mortar, simply, is a weapon that usually consists of a barrel and a stabilizing stand that holds the barrel in a very upright manner, over 45 degrees. Mortar rounds are thus fired with very steep angles of elevation, which results in reduced range but produces a very steep angle of fall at the target. This type of trajectory is ideal for firing into trenches or against targets that are nestled behind a large intervening feature.

The preceding text was an admittedly brief and simplistic overview of the technical nature of artillery fire, but it should be sufficient for our present study here. It will set the context for the narrative that follows in this book by allowing the reader to understand the nuances of the artillery fire support system during the Great War, which of course profoundly affected the planning, implementation, and execution of the fire support plan at Vimy Ridge. Before delving into that, however, we will first conduct a brief overview of the history of the Royal Regiment of Canadian Artillery leading up to the Great War.

CANADIAN ARTILLERY

The Royal Regiment of Canadian Artillery has a long and very successful tradition of serving Canada and Canadians. It comprises batteries and regiments of Canadian soldiers, both regular and reserve, that can be found in nearly every region of the country, from sea unto sea. Its units have long and glorious histories, and indeed some of the units predate even Confederation itself. What follows in this chapter is a brief historical survey of the Royal Regiment of Canadian Artillery from its early days until the outbreak of the war. This chapter will investigate the Regiment's roots in the British Royal Artillery and survey how the Regiment was formed, its historical accomplishments in Canada and abroad, and how it ultimately evolved into the massive fire support organization that contributed so much to the victory at Vimy Ridge.

One cannot have a fulsome investigation of the efforts of the men of the Royal Regiment of Canadian Artillery in the spring of 1917 without reference to the Royal Regiment of Artillery in Great Britain. It is from the British Artillery that the Canadian Artillery draws its customs, its traditions, and, in both the First and Second World Wars, its doctrine and tactics. One could argue that of all the regiments of the Canadian Army, the Royal Regiment of Canadian Artillery has most unabashedly adopted the customs and traditions of its British forebear. For instance, the Royal Regiment of Canadian Artillery has adopted the cap badge and flag of the Royal Artillery, as well as the tradition of using its guns as the regimental colours. The Canadian Artillery has also adopted the birthday of the Royal Regiment of Artillery as "Artillery Day" and, like their British counterparts, recognizes the sovereign as the "Captain General." Even the twin mottoes of the Royal Artillery – *Ubique* (everywhere) and *Quo fas et Gloria ducunt* (whither right and glory lead)

– have been adopted wholesale by the Canadian Artillery.[9] Pertaining to this present study, during the Great War, the Canadian Artillery, like other dominions of the British Empire, employed only slight alterations to customs and identifying titles in order to emphasize nationality. For example, Canadians used the term Canadian Field Artillery (CFA) instead of Royal Field Artillery (RFA) to identify their artillery brigades, and the term *Canadian Divisional Artillery* instead of simply *Divisional Artillery*, as the British did, to denote the artillery assigned to an infantry division. These were simply minor changes in appearance, however; in terms of organization, tactics, techniques, and procedures the Canadian and British artilleries were essentially one. Thus, any investigation of the Canadian Artillery at Vimy Ridge must begin with the Royal Artillery.

The Royal Regiment of Artillery has a long history, one that is beyond the scope of this book to delve into in depth. Suffice to say, the modern Royal Artillery appeared in regimental form under a Royal Warrant issued by King George I on May 26, 1716, which authorized the formation of two batteries of artillery, each comprising one hundred men. It is important to note that May 26 is now recognized as Artillery Day in the armed forces of both Great Britain and Canada. The structure and size of the Royal Artillery fluctuated over the next several centuries until July 1, 1899, when the organizational structure that would exist throughout the Great War was put into place.[10] As of that date, the Royal Artillery existed in two branches: the Mounted Branch, which consisted of the Royal Horse Artillery and RFA, and the Dismounted Branch, which consisted of the Royal Garrison Artillery (RGA). The division of the artillery into mounted and dismounted branches was an organizational schism that existed until 1924.[11] A third group, known simply as the Royal Artillery, was responsible for ammunition storage and supply. In the mounted branch, the field artillery consisted of those guns of smaller calibre that were employed in direct support of infantry manoeuvre, while the horse artillery carried lighter guns and used horse teams with additional mounts to support more mobile cavalry formations. The RGA, conversely, employed larger-calibre weapons and cumbersome siege pieces, as well as the coastal artillery's immobile emplaced guns. From the ranks of the RGA came the numerous siege and heavy-artillery batteries that became so crucial on the Western Front during the Great War.[12] Of the larger-calibre guns that were found in the brigades of garrison artillery during the war, 60-pounder guns and 4.7" howitzers were classed as *heavy batteries*, while all others, from 6" howitzers and guns up to the monstrous 15" howitzers, were called *siege batteries*.[13]

The differences between the mounted and dismounted branches went beyond calibre and mobility to include a psychological and philosophical difference as well. The fire support problem in the RGA was unique in that its members had to solve the question of engaging moving targets, such as ships at sea, with large-calibre weapons at extended range, necessitating a more mathematical approach than that which was used in the mounted branch. After the creation of the RGA in 1891, the officers of the RGA, who previously had been transferred in and out of the dismounted and mounted branches during their careers, remained solely in the dismounted branch. This afforded them the opportunity to focus exclusively on the particular technical challenges of garrison and coastal artillery, and, as a result, they developed a greater appreciation for measuring individual shell velocity and taking into account the effects of meteorological conditions on the accuracy of their fire.

The gunner officers of the mounted branch, whose bailiwick consisted of the fluid manoeuvrings of military formations on the battlefield, were far more focused on élan and speed, and generally spurned the plodding trigonometric calculations of their dismounted confreres.[14] Lieutenant-Colonel W.H.F. Weber of the RFA explained in 1919 that this pre-war school of thought emphasizing manoeuvre had come to Britain from France – "on the crest of a French wave from Calais" – and, according to this philosophy, "our methods were too slow and our policy of training too conservative. They cried for more haste, closer support of the infantry (which was interpreted into actual proximity and a very short range in the final stages of each battle), direct laying [aiming], a more rapid rate of fire, less complicated gunnery, less telephone, more tactical teaching at our practice camps."[15]

It would be one thing if this were simply a different way of thinking, but the proponents of this school went to so far as to spurn their opposites. As an example, in 1915 Colin Hutchison, a pre-war regular officer of the RFA, wrote to his uncle Duke Hutchison, who was considering enlisting in the British Army and was weighing the pros and cons of the various branches of artillery, and provided him with this advice: "The real field artillery officer, and I admit there are very few left now, looks with scorn upon anything mechanical. He claims to be able to hit targets without calculation for temperature, pressure and wind, and looks upon anything drawn by other means than horses as beneath contempt."[16] It is with this organization and professional outlook that the Royal Artillery began the

Great War.

The history and heritage of the Royal Regiment of Canadian Artillery is inextricably linked with the country itself, although the existence of Canadian volunteer artillery batteries actually predates the nation. As early as 1750, King Louis XV of France ordered the creation of an artillery battery among the *troupes de la marine* who were stationed in Canada. While not strictly Canadian in the sense of the modern nation-state of Canada, the battery was nonetheless created in what came to be known as Canada. As well, as early as 1793, the Loyal Company of Artillery was formed in Saint John, New Brunswick. Interestingly, this particular organization still exists and is perpetuated by the 3rd Field Regiment, Royal Canadian Artillery.

The size of the Canadian Militia artillery grew substantially throughout the second half of the nineteenth century. In the Province of Canada, which eventually became the provinces of Ontario and Quebec after Confederation, the Militia Act of 1855 created a 5000-man militia force that included seven batteries of field artillery. By 1860 there were five volunteer companies of artillery in New Brunswick, and later that same decade another five brigades of artillery were created in Nova Scotia.

It wasn't long after the young dominion had come into existence that its political leaders turned their attention to the defence of their new nation. In retrospect this is unsurprising, as one of the key impetuses that led to the creation of the Dominion in the first place was to present a unified front of defence in the face of a highly militarized, and decidedly belligerent, United States, which had just emerged from the bloodletting of the Civil War and harboured deep animosity toward Great Britain for its support of the South during the conflict. The Dominion government passed another Militia Act in 1868; this resulted in the creation of an active militia of 40,000 men that eventually included ten field and thirty garrison batteries among its order of battle. With the decision of the imperial authorities to call home their legions in 1871, the British military force in British North America was reduced to garrisons in the strategically vital Royal Navy bases of Halifax, Nova Scotia, and Esquimalt, British Columbia, leaving the inland fortresses at Kingston and Quebec City tenantless. The fortresses were handed over to the Dominion, which thereafter issued Militia General Order number 24 on October 20, 1871. This authorized the creation of A and B Batteries of garrison artillery in order to provide for the care and protection of Fort Henry in Kingston and La Citadelle in Quebec City and to serve as practical schools of gunnery for the training of all ranks of the militia artillery. With the creation of these two permanent batteries, the Dominion of Canada took the first tenuous steps to creating a professional army.

The Dominion government passed another Militia Act in 1883, which allowed for the creation of permanent corps, which is to say full-time, permanent forces. Consequently, in August of 1883, the Regiment of Canadian Artillery was formed as a permanent corps comprising A and B Batteries and the newly authorized C Battery. The latter, although authorized to be formed, was not manned until 1887 in Victoria, British Columbia. The Regiment of Canadian Artillery was granted the prefix *Royal* on May 24, 1893, and thereafter was known as the Royal Canadian Artillery. In 1898 the Permanent Force element of the regiment was reorganized into two divisions, not unlike the mounted and dismounted divisions of the Royal Artillery: the Royal Canadian Artillery (Field Division), into which fell the field batteries, and the Royal Canadian Artillery (Garrison Division), consisting of the Canadian Garrison batteries. Just three years later, in June of 1901, the nomenclature changed again to Royal Canadian Field Artillery and Royal Canadian Garrison Artillery.

Between Confederation and the outbreak of the Great War, the Canadian Artillery supported operations in a number of theatres across North America and even abroad. Its first exposure to warfighting came during the North-West Rebellion of 1885. After years of conflict between the Dominion government and the Indigenous peoples of the northwest, the Métis and several First Nations bands sought the leadership of Louis Riel, who was at the time living in exile in the United States, to attempt to redress their grievances with the government in Ottawa. When their efforts came to naught, the Métis and their First Nations allies rose up in rebellion against the Dominion government. Ottawa dispatched the Northwest Field Force, under the command of British General Frederick Middleton, which included the two permanent artillery batteries, A and B. In addition to the two permanent batteries, an active militia battery from Winnipeg, the Winnipeg Field Battery, also participated in the conflict. The gunners were decisively engaged throughout the conflict; A Battery and the Winnipeg Field Battery were particularly active and supported the militia assault during the culminating action at Batoche. In total, six men from the Royal Regiment were killed and eighteen wounded during the conflict.

Fourteen years later, the first overseas expeditionary operation was undertaken by the Canadian military. In 1899 the Boers of Orange Free State and Transvaal in South Africa rose up in arms against the British, who sent a call for support to her dominions. Canada answered the call, and dispatched several contingents to South Africa to support the British war effort. Three batteries were designated to participate in the conflict, C, D, and E, the men for which were drawn from the ranks of the Royal Canadian Field Artillery (Permanent Force) and various active militia batteries from across the country. The three batteries did excellent service in South Africa and established a solid reputation among the soldiery of both Canada and Great Britain. This was in spite of finding themselves fighting in a hostile climate against a determined enemy who, despite their appearance as disorganized insurgents, for the most part maintained a superiority in artillery firepower in terms of both range and weight of shell – a question we shall return to in greater detail later.[17]

The South African, or Boer, War was the last conflict in which the Canadian gunners were involved before the outbreak of the Great War. In 1906 the British decided to withdraw the last remaining garrisons of British troops from their bases in Esquimalt and Halifax. As their predecessors had done in 1871, the Canadian military created five companies of Royal Canadian Garrison Artillery in Halifax and Esquimalt to replace the withdrawing British troops.

Organizationally, the years leading up to the Great War saw substantial changes in the Canadian Artillery. Imperial and Commonwealth artillery units have a long history of emphasizing the role of the battery in the organizational realm. It was a relatively recent development, in the late nineteenth century, to group batteries together to form a larger unit – a brigade. This started early in the Canadian narrative – the 1st Provisional Brigade of Field Artillery was created in 1880 when batteries in Wellington and Guelph, Ontario, were 'brigaded' together. Five years later the unit was renamed 1st Brigade Division of Field Artillery. These two batteries were geographically close, but in 1898 the Canadian Militia brigaded three batteries from St. Catharines, Hamilton, and Toronto into the 2nd Brigade Division. The efficiency produced by brigading batteries was readily evident, and by 1905 ten such brigades had been organized for the Canadian Artillery. Two independent batteries in London and Winnipeg were left as such, as it was deemed impractical to brigade them.[18]

The year 1905 was a seminal one for the Canadian Artillery, beyond simply the reorganization of many batteries into brigades. The permanent element of the Canadian Artillery, known as the Royal Canadian Field

Artillery since 1901, was renamed the Royal Canadian Horse Artillery. Additionally, the Canadian Militia undertook to develop the tactics, techniques, and procedures of the Royal Horse Artillery, which is to say employing mobile batteries with lighter guns to support cavalry units who moved around the battlefield at a quicker pace than the foot-bound infantry.[19] Since the creation of the Royal Canadian Horse Artillery (RCHA) in 1905, the regular component of the Canadian artillery has maintained that designation.

Yet another milestone in the evolution of the Canadian artillery was achieved in 1905 with the creation of Camp Petawawa. The camp, which exists to this day, was developed to address the need of the Canadian artillery for a training area capable of accommodating the increased ranges that twentieth-century guns were able to achieve. Until that time, no ranges were available in Canada to facilitate artillery practice at ranges greater than three kilometres. North of the town of Pembroke, which lies in the heart of the Ottawa Valley about two hundred kilometres northwest of Ottawa, the Canadian Militia authorities found a picturesque stretch of terrain that they realized would be an excellent training ground for all branches of the Canadian military. The federal government purchased close to 20,000 acres from local residents and another 55,000 from the Province of Ontario and created Camp Petawawa. Its first use by the artillery occurred in the summer of 1905, when the permanent corps in the Horse and Garrison Artillery units conducted a practice camp. Over the course of the year, however, batteries from across Canada travelled to Petawawa to take advantage of the newly purchased training ground. The availability of such a training resource materially improved the professionalism of the Canadian permanent and active militia artilleries in the years leading up to the Great War. The exercises culminated in the summer training session of 1912, when the largest concentration of Canadian artillery up to that point occurred. A total of twenty-six field batteries and two heavy batteries, consisting of over 5,000 men and over 2600 horses, descended on Petawawa for a period of six weeks. [20]

The five years prior to the outbreak of the Great War were busy ones for the Canadian Militia and its artillery branch. In 1909, the result of the Imperial Defence Conference, which took place in May of that year, was to ensure a common organization among imperial militaries based on the War Establishments of the Home Regular Army. This led to a visit to Canada in 1910 by Sir John French, Inspector General of the Imperial Forces, who made recommendations for the organization of the Canadian Militia. Of the artillery, he observed that one-third of the batteries were sufficiently trained for war, that another one-third would require a few weeks training, and that the remainder would need a few months.[21]

Of the many recommendations made by French, the most profound was the suggestion to reorganize the ten military districts in eastern Canada along divisional lines. On April 1, 1911, those became six divisional commands. The artillery establishment to support the divisional model was large: each division had three field artillery brigades, each consisting of three 18-pounder batteries of four guns each; a howitzer brigade of three batteries armed with 4.5- or 5-inch howitzers; and finally, a heavy battery of four 60-pounder breech-loading guns or 4.7-inch quick-fire guns. Such an aggressive increase in the Canadian artillery required a massive reorganization of the branch. Indeed, to achieve the reorganization plan, a total of forty-two extra batteries were required for the force. A slow and deliberate attempt to achieve these lofty ambitions resulted in the gradual increase of guns and batteries to the Royal Canadian Artillery organization, but the Canadian Militia never fully realized the grandiose plan. Another inspection in 1913, this time by General Sir Ian Hamilton, the British Inspector General of Overseas Forces, found that the six-division scheme was still short 284 guns and howitzers.[22]

So, with an inadequate artillery park, albeit one with a modernized organizational scheme, the Canadian Militia and the Royal Canadian Artillery watched as events unfolded in Europe that would eventually lead them to war.

THE ROAD TO THE GREAT WAR

In the years leading up to the outbreak of the war in 1914, the great powers of Europe had grouped themselves into two principal alliances. The participating nations arranged to provide mutual support to one another, within their alliance, in an effort to act as a counterweight to their adversaries. The first was begun in 1879, when Germany and Austria united in a mutual defence alliance, to which was added Italy in 1882, an arrangement that has become known to historians as the Triple Alliance. In the face of this alignment, Russia and France entered into their own defensive alliance in 1894. A few years later, Germany openly moved to challenge British supremacy at sea, which revealed the stark reality that Britain's future adversary was most likely to be Germany. Consequently, in 1904 Great Britain and France entered into a defensive alliance known as the Entente Cordiale; a similar arrangement between Great Britain and Russia was agreed to in 1907.[23]

Most military leaders at the beginning of the twentieth century thought the eruption of a European conflagration to be only a matter of time. Indeed, several flare-ups in the young century nearly led to war prior to 1914, in particular in 1909 after Austria annexed Bosnia-Herzegovina the year previous, and again in 1911 when Germany dispatched a gun boat off the coast of Morocco to prod territorial concessions out of France in Africa. Wiser minds prevailed in both instances, but a greater confrontation loomed large in the minds of British military authorities. Thus, in the years preceding the Great War, the political and military leadership of Great Britain undertook a number of strategic appreciations to determine what its national strategy would be, should it be drawn into a war in Europe.[24]

The debate surrounding Britain's national strategy in a future continental conflict centred specifically around the question of whether the British army would be used to assist the French army on the continent in an expeditionary manner, or whether it would be used for defence of Great Britain while the Royal Navy alone provided the expeditionary element of the British war effort. A key milestone in this evolution came in 1908 as the result of an inquiry by a subcommittee of the Committee of Imperial Defence to consider the possibility of war, and even the threat of invasion of Great Britain. The subcommittee concluded that "so long as our naval supremacy is assured against any reasonably probable combination of powers, invasion is impracticable."[25]

Although Germany aspired to challenge Britain's naval supremacy, it never really produced a fleet that posed a legitimate threat to the Royal Navy. The British intended, therefore, to use the Royal Navy to maintain command of the seas during any continental conflict, and choke victory from the enemy through economic strangulation. While this became the strategic focus of the British in preparation for war, the question of the employment of Britain's land forces was constantly in a state of flux. During the close of the nineteenth century and the opening of the twentieth, a series of debates among the British politico-military leaders centred on whether the army should be used as an amphibious force in support of the Royal Navy's maritime operations, or whether it should be used alongside the French army on the continent. The debate culminated in 1911 and is excellently chronicled in the memoirs of Lord Hankey, the Under-Secretary of the Navy.[26]

At a joint conference to determine British military plans, Lord Kitchener, the lavishly moustachioed secretary of state for war who was responsible for British land operations, presented to the British leadership a compelling argument for the employment of a British Expeditionary Force (BEF) as the left flank of a joint Anglo–French force to be deployed somewhere in France or the Low Countries against an invading German army. Kitchener's presentation was juxtaposed with a complacent, almost morose, argument proffered by the Royal Navy contending that the BEF should be used in support of British maritime operations. Kitchener's argument was so well articulated, however, that the question of British army involvement in France during a future conflict became a *fait accompli*. From that point on, Hankey reported, it was decided that in the event of a continental war between France and Germany that drew Great Britain into the hostilities, the BEF would be deployed alongside the French as a complement to, rather than a departure from, traditional

British maritime-economic strategy.[27]

The shoe finally dropped in the summer of 1914. In a series of well-known events, German Chancellor Bismarck's prophetic utterance that "one day the great European War would come out of some damned foolish thing in the Balkans" became manifest. On June 28, a Serb nationalist in the Austrian province of Bosnia shot and killed Archduke Franz Ferdinand of the Austro-Hungarian Empire, along with his wife and driver, during their visit to Sarajevo. Austria delivered a severe ultimatum against Serbia, whose political leaders in Belgrade made no attempt to hide their support of Serb nationalists in Bosnia. The Serbian leadership could not accept Austria's demands without giving up complete sovereignty, and when they replied in the negative, Austria declared war on the small Balkan nation on July 28. Russia, seeing itself as the protector of Slavic nations, mobilized her forces two days later. Kaiser Wilhelm II of Germany demanded Russia demobilize her forces, and when Czar Nicholas II in Moscow refused, Germany declared war on Russia. This caused France to mobilize her forces, and on August 2, the German ambassador to Belgium demanded free passage through Belgian territory.

This seemingly strange demand was made in order to facilitate its war plan: the famous Schlieffen Plan devised by German Field-Marshal Count Alfred von Schlieffen, Chief of the Prussian General Staff from 1891–1905. The Schlieffen Plan was the German solution to the problem of a two-front war. Faced with the French armies in the west and the Russian armies in the east, the Germans sought to devise a way in which a sudden knockout blow could be delivered against the French army, after which the German army would turn eastward and rush to meet the advancing Russian forces which, it was thought by the Germans, would take much more time to mobilize than their French confreres. More importantly, to avoid the heavily fortified border between France and Germany and the delay this would produce, von Schlieffen envisaged a broad but speedy swing through the Low Countries of Belgium and the Netherlands. Here it was hoped the much smaller national armies could be overcome with relative ease and thereafter the advancing German armies could strike the French army on its less robust left flank and threaten an advance on Paris, all while a smaller force advanced against the French in the Alsace-Lorraine region in an attempt to hold them there and delay a westward reinforcement of the exposed flank.

While the "sweeping arc" portion of the original Schlieffen Plan called for an invasion of France by seventy-nine divisions, by the outbreak of the war Germany had only eighty-seven divisions for the whole of the Western Front. When the Schlieffen Plan was put into action in July and August of 1914, General Helmuth von Moltke, von Schlieffen's successor, committed a smaller force to the assault and reduced the overall frontage in an effort to avoid violating the neutrality of the Netherlands. This slight change to the concept of operations may have doomed the Schlieffen Plan's already audacious and risky goal to failure. When he launched his offensive, von Moltke committed twenty-five divisions to the holding operation in Alsace-Lorraine and only fifty-three divisions to the main assault, all of which were disposed in seven armies: two of these were arrayed against the French in Alsace-Lorraine, while the other five formed the sweeping German left wing.

The Belgians declined to permit German passage through their territory. In response, the German army crossed its border with Belgium on August 4, 1914. Up to this point, Great Britain had been diplomatically manoeuvring to avoid war in Europe, but with the German invasion of Belgium she was thrust onto the horns of a dilemma, having signed a treaty in 1839 with France and Germany guaranteeing Belgian neutrality. Great Britain demanded Germany cease its offensive operations, and when the Germans declined, Great Britain, and by extension Canada and her other imperial dominions, was drawn into the Great War.[28]

The Canadian military on the eve of the Great War was small. Its headquarters was in Ottawa, under the guidance of the minister of militia and defence, who in 1914 was the domineering Colonel Sam Hughes. Administration of the military was conducted by the Militia Council, presided over by the minister and assisted by the deputy minister. The senior military leadership included the chief of the general staff, the adjutant general, the quartermaster-general, the master-general of the ordnance, and the paymaster general. Although this council was meant to be an organ by which the Canadian military was administered and commanded, due to the sheer force of Hughes' bombastic personality and his position atop the hierarchy, the council had very little influence on military affairs and the minister's authority was paramount.[29]

The Canadian Army was known as the Canadian Militia until 1940 and was composed of two elements: the active militia and the permanent militia. The former were soldiers and units who paraded irregularly, focused mostly on annual training during the summer. In many ways the active militia of 1914 was like the modern-day army reserve. The permanent active militia, by contrast, were Regular Force units composed of full-time, professional soldiers.

The active militia had grown considerably in the decade before the outbreak of the war. Indicative of this growth, the number of men participating in annual summer training rose from 36,000 in 1904 to 55,000 in 1913.[30] For administrative purposes, these militiamen were organized into 226 active militia units that had been divided into divisional areas and military districts, based on French's recommendations mentioned in the previous chapter. Table 3.1 gives an overview of this organization.

Table 3.1 – Divisional Areas of the Canadian Militia, 1914		
Divisional Area	**Geographic Area**	**Headquarters Location**
1st Divisional Area	Western Ontario	London, ON
2nd Divisional Area	Greater Toronto Area	Toronto, ON
3rd Divisional Area	Eastern Ontario	Kingston, ON
4th Divisional Area	Western Quebec	Montreal, QC
5th Divisional Area	Eastern Quebec	Quebec City, QC
6th Divisional Area	Maritime Provinces	Halifax, NS

There was no divisional hierarchy in western Canada, only three military districts: Military District No. 10 included all land from Thunder Bay to the Alberta border and had its headquarters in Winnipeg, while District 11 comprised British Columbia and the Yukon Territory, and District 13 included the province of Alberta and the Territory of Mackenzie.[31]

The permanent active militia consisted of two cavalry regiments, the Royal Canadian Dragoons and the Lord Strathcona's Horse (Royal Canadians); a Royal Canadian Horse Artillery brigade of two batteries; five companies of Royal Canadian Garrison Artillery; an infantry regiment in the Royal Canadian Regiment; and assorted staff and support officers in the Canadian Engineers, Medical Corps, Veterinary Corps, Ordnance Corps, Pay Corps, and of course the Royal Military College of Canada. The authorized establishment of the Permanent Force was a paltry 3,110 officers and men, and 684 horses.[32]

The declaration of war was not a complete surprise. Canadians had been following developments in Europe in the media, and the imperial government was in continuous communication with Canada and the other dominions by messages and dispatches between the secretary of state for the colonies, and the governor general. In anticipation of the outbreak of hostilities, plans to raise a contingent of between 20,000 and 25,000 men for service overseas were discussed at a special meeting of the Militia Council on July 30, presided over by Colonel Sam Hughes. The next day, on July 31, all militia districts and divisional areas were ordered to start developing plans to raise troops for a possible expeditionary force to Europe.

A plan for the mobilization of the Canadian Militia had been in place for several years. While it was in the process of reorganizing, based on General French's recommendations, it also undertook to develop mobilization plans for use in the eventuality of a war in Europe. In 1910, a committee in Militia Headquarters began to develop a mobilization scheme. It took three years to complete, and by 1913 the Militia Headquarters staff had drafted a plan to transfer the six divisions of the Canadian Militia to war footing. The plan had many weaknesses, but in the end the staff had constructed an arrangement that would have facilitated the raising of a 25,000-man expeditionary contingent, consisting of an infantry division and a mounted brigade. When war erupted, however, Hughes all but abandoned the established plan in favour of his own mobilization scheme, consisting of new units, battalions, and brigades filled with volunteers and recruits from the long-established militia corps across the country.

At 8:45 p.m. Ottawa time on August 4, 1914, the governor general received a cable from the secretary of state for the colonies in Great Britain stating that the British Empire was at war with Germany. In response to the cable, the governor general replied:

> *Great exhibition of genuine patriotism here. When inevitable fact transpires that considerable period of training will be necessary before Canadian troops will be fit for European war, this ardour is bound to be dampened somewhat. In order to maximise this, I would suggest that any proposal from you should be accompanied by the assurance that Canadian troops will go to the front as soon as they have reached a sufficient standard of training.*[33]

The governor general was correct about the ardour for combat, especially among the ranks of the militia. Even before the declaration of war, forty-eight units of the active militia had offered their services in the conflict.[34]

News of the outbreak of war was greeted with patriotic fervour throughout Canada. In Ottawa, thousands gathered around the newspaper bulletin boards to follow every update. The Governor General's Foot Guards paraded through the streets, cheered by a throng of spectators. Across Canada, crowds surged into the streets to celebrate the news and join each other in rapturous, patriotic singing. In Toronto, the armouries and private drill halls were filled with potential volunteers.

While most of these examples of hyper-patriotism were exhibited in a celebratory fashion, in some circumstances they manifested themselves in a darker manner. In Edmonton, there were riots and one German citizen who denounced the British Empire was badly beaten.[35] In Regina, nine fires were started and an Austrian and a Russian were arrested by police.[36]

Two days later, on August 6, 1914, the cabinet authorized the creation of an Active Service Force for service overseas.[37] Ignoring district, division, and brigade chains of command, Hughes had the adjutant general of the Canadian Militia wire directly to the 226 commanding officers of militia units across Canada, asking them to forward lists of volunteers directly to Militia Headquarters. The commanding officers were informed that the Canadian Expeditionary Force, as it came to be known, would be imperial in nature and would be considered alongside British regular troops. Potential recruits for the artillery should stand no less than 5 foot 7, and artillery drivers no less that 5 foot 3, each with a chest of no less that 34.5 inches. Engineers less than 5 foot 4 were unwelcome, and prospective infantry soldiers should stand no shorter than 5 foot 3. Applications would be considered in the following priority: unmarried men, followed by married men without families, and finally married men with families. Rolls of prospective recruits who met all requirements and had passed the required medical examination were to be forwarded to Militia Headquarters no later than August 12, 1914, where the militia authorities would survey the rolls and establish the quota for each unit. The quotas would then be transmitted to the commanding officers for them to fill. Those volunteers who were accepted into the ranks of the Active Service Force were sent to Valcartier, Quebec, for training.[38]

Valcartier remains a military camp to this day. It is a bustling, busy base with a constant hum of activity, and is home to the 5e groupement du brigade mécanisé canadienne (the 5th Canadian Mechanized Brigade Group), but in 1914 it was but a small local training base. Two years earlier, the militia department had realized that it was necessary to secure a centralized training area for Quebec-based militia units to use. The site, located sixteen miles northwest of Quebec City, was found in 1912 and purchased in 1913. When the Canadian government arrived at the decision to send a force overseas, the minister of militia decided upon Valcartier as the Canadian staging area. The camp was originally designed to accommodate 5,000 militia volunteers on summer training, but in order to facilitate the concentration, organization, and training of the Canadian soldiers destined for overseas service, the base had to expand into neighbouring farmland, necessitating its expropriation from local owners. On August 8, 1914, construction began on the infrastructure necessary to support the concentration of the Canadian Expeditionary Force.[39]

On August 10, the Canadian government determined the size of the initial Expeditionary Force was to be 25,000 men.[40] In a thunderclap grasping of the obvious, Hughes realized that having the tiny staff of Militia Headquarters sift through what was bound to be a tsunami of volunteers was impractical. Consequently, he issued quotas to the divisions and districts regarding the form of the expeditionary formations and the units each was expected to furnish. District headquarters then determined how many volunteers each of their units was required to provide and issued quotas to the units' commanding officers to furnish the necessary personnel. This had the unsurprising impact of unequal distribution of quotas, charges of favouritism, discrimination, and nepotism, and of course much greasing of palms between determined volunteers and the commanding officers who held in their hands the fate of the applicant's future.[41] Up till this point, only recruits from the active militia were accepted as volunteers, but on August 11, perhaps in anticipation of the number of volunteers that would eventually be required when the war reached its zenith, non-active militia recruits were accepted and were to be enrolled immediately in the active militia for training. In a unique turn, on August 14 another caveat was enacted, stating that no married man was to be enlisted without the consent of his wife.[42]

During the first half of August, elements of the necessary support staff began to trickle into Valcartier. Starting on August 18, that trickle turned into a torrent from all points across the Dominion. Between August 18 and 21, 4,200 soldiers arrived in Valcartier. Just one week later, on August 27, 20,089 soldiers were on site, and by September 8, 36,665 soldiers had arrived. In a matter of weeks, Valcartier had transformed from a sleepy militia training camp to a bustling centre of activity.

Throngs of men, living under canvas, moved about. Arrangements for clothing, equipping, and attesting men to the Canadian Expeditionary Force were undertaken, and training was conducted to bring the force into some degree of readiness.

One of the key points in the new mobilization scheme was the abandonment of established militia units as deployable forces. On August 22, twelve provisional battalions were created and posted in Camp Orders – it was into these battalions that the volunteers would be placed for deployment to Europe, rather than in the militia regiments to which they belonged.[43] Nonetheless, the authorities did see the logic in grouping men from military districts into the same battalion, even if their original regiments were not to be used as deployable units.

The number of volunteers selected by Militia Headquarters was larger than the number required for the first contingent, so volunteers were aware that there was still a chance that they could be weeded out of the first contingent even after to deploying to Valcartier.[44] Fortunately for those determined to serve abroad, this policy was reversed on September 20, when the government realized that it would be necessary to have reinforcements close to hand in Europe when the contingent finally entered into the fray and started suffering casualties. Consequently, all volunteers who arrived in Valcartier and were found fit to serve were sent to England, although not necessarily all would be on the first wave of forces going into battle.[45] On October 3, at 3:00 p.m., the first ship of the armada of thirty transport vessels ferrying the Canadian Expeditionary Force moved out of the Gaspé Basin en route to England.

The fire support organization of the 1st Canadian Division conformed to the structure of a divisional artillery as laid out by the British military: three brigades of field artillery, each consisting of three 18-pounder batteries and an ammunition column; a heavy battery armed with 60-pounder guns with an ammunition column; and a divisional ammunition column. Although the British war establishment called for a howitzer brigade to be included in a divisional artillery, Canada had insufficient howitzers, as only seven of the twenty-seven 4.5-inch howitzers ordered by the Canadian Militia had been delivered. As detailed previously, the three field brigades were created anew from volunteers, although each battery had associated active militia batteries who were responsible for generating the men to fill its ranks. It was Lieutenant-Colonel Edward Whipple Bancroft (E.W.B.) "Dinky" Morrison, at the time filling the position of director of artillery, and who would later command the Canadian Corps artillery at Vimy Ridge, who decided which active militia batteries would furnish the men, horses, and guns for the artillery of the first Canadian contingent. The majority of these came from eastern Canada, as shown in Table 3.2.

Table 3.2 – Elements of 1st Canadian Divisional Artillery on Deployment, 1914		
Brigade	**Commanding Officer**	**Source of Personnel**
1st Brigade	LCol E.W.B. Morrison	Ottawa, Belleville, Gananaoque, Kingston
2nd Brigade	LCol J.J. Creelman	Montreal, Sherbrooke, Sydney, Moncton
3rd Brigade	LCol Mitchell	Toronto, Hamilton, St. Catharines, London, Cobourg
Divisional Ammunition Column	LCol J.J. Penhale	Montreal, Quebec City, Maritime Provinces
Heavy Battery	Major F.C. Magee	Montreal, Maritime Provinces

The artillery of the Canadian Expeditionary Force initially fell under the command of Lieutenant-Colonel Harry Burstall, who, until the outbreak of the war, had been commanding the Royal School of Artillery at the

Citadel in Quebec City. The 1st Brigade drew its headquarters personnel from Ottawa, including its first commander, none other than Morrison himself, while its three batteries were filled with men from Ottawa, Belleville, Gananoque, and Kingston. The 2nd Brigade was placed under the command of Lieutenant-Colonel J.J. Creelman; its headquarters staff came from Montreal, and its batteries from Montreal, Sherbrooke, Sydney, and Moncton. Finally, the 3rd Brigade was commanded by Lieutenant-Colonel Mitchell, who had been commanding the 2nd (Toronto) Brigade in the active militia. The headquarters staff was filled with men from Toronto, while its batteries came from Hamilton, St. Catharines, Toronto, London, and Cobourg. Lieutenant-Colonel J.J. Penhale assumed command of the divisional ammunition column, whose troops came from Montreal, Quebec City, and the Maritime Provinces, while the heavy battery, created from the men and equipment of the Montreal Heavy Brigade, fell under Major F.C. Magee, from St. John, New Brunswick.[46]

The first contingent had not even reached England when the Governor General of Canada telegraphed the secretary of state for the colonies to offer a second contingent of forces.[47] The imperial government replied favourably by the end of the month; thus, in November of 1914, the authorized strength of the Canadian Expeditionary Force was increased from 25,000 to 50,000 men.[48] That summer, the Dominion government increased its commitment again, this time to 150,000 men. The Canadian prime minister, Robert Laird Borden, visited the Canadian troops in Europe during the summer of 1915 and returned to Canada with the conviction that even more troops were required, and the number was once again raised, this time to 250,000. In the space of a year, the size of the Canadian contingent increased tenfold. [49] As astonishing as that seems, on January 12, 1916, an order in council authorized the minister of militia to raise the size of the Canadian Expeditionary Force to 500,000.[50] Such an undertaking was a herculean task for a nation of eight million, so recruiting became a critical undertaking among the populace at home.

Recruiting for the second detachment began in mid-October 1914. Quotas were quickly met, particularly in the west where the ranks were filled as quickly as clothing and equipment could be provided.[51] After the whirlwind generation of the 1st Canadian Division, the generation of the second contingent proceeded under expeditious, but much more practical, measures. Part of this was due to a shortage in materiel, particularly artillery pieces. The whole of the Canadian Artillery arsenal had accompanied the 1st Division to Europe, and there were insufficient guns available from imperial stocks to outfit the 2nd Division. Consequently, the units, once recruited up to strength, remained in their respective military districts until they embarked in the spring of 1915.[52]

The 2nd Canadian Division was created in May of 1915 and deployed to France in September of that year. This resulted in one other major event in Canadian military history: the creation of the Canadian Corps. The existence of two Canadian formations dictated the necessity of a higher headquarters to command, control, and administer the two organizations. Consequently, on September 13, 1915, the Canadian Corps became active under the command of British Lieutenant-General Alderson, and on September 22 the 2nd Canadian Division came into the line alongside the 1st Canadian Division near St. Eloi, where they would stay throughout the winter of 1915–1916.[53] Although this may seem of little importance, the creation of an operational Canadian Corps was unique to the Dominion forces, and certainly was indicative of Canada's increasing commitment of forces to the war effort. The Canadian Corps of two infantry divisions was augmented seven months later with the creation of the 3rd Canadian Division, raised in France in December of 1915, followed by the 4th Canadian Division in April of 1916, a question that will be dealt with in more detail in the next chapter. Although, initially, the divisions of the Canadian Corps would continue to be hived off and moved around individually to augment British formations, by 1917 the Corps would become a homogenous unit that Canadian military and political leaders would struggle tenaciously to keep together.

We turn now to a brief survey of the major actions of the Canadian military leading up to the Battle of Vimy Ridge in the spring of 1917.

PRELUDE TO VIMY RIDGE

The Battle of Vimy Ridge occurred thirty-two months after the war began. To cover such a period of conflict would be a historical work in its own right, and thus beyond the scope and purpose of this book. It is, however, important to understand the major events that unfurled during that period as they had a significant influence on when, where, and how the Battle of Vimy Ridge was to occur. What follows is a very brief historical survey of the opening thirty-two months of the war leading up to the spring of 1917, with a focus on operations in Northwest Europe.

In the previous chapter we surveyed the chain of events that eventually led to the German invasion of Belgium under the strictures of the Schlieffen Plan. While anyone with a passing acquaintance with the German scheme for offensive operations on the Western Front will be familiar with the Schlieffen Plan, its French counterpart is less well known. The French, under the leadership of General Joseph Jacques Joffre, arranged their operational plans in accordance with what they referred to as "Plan XVII," which, as the name implies, was the seventeenth iteration of French mobilization and operational contingency operations in the event of a war with Germany. The first sixteen iterations had come and gone over a period stretching between 1875, shortly after the Franco-Prussian War, and 1906, and the seventeenth and final version came into effect in 1907. Plan XVII called for a primarily offensive attitude on the part of the French army, focusing on attacks into the region of Alsace-Lorraine – which had been lost to the Germans after the 1870 war – and the Ardennes region. While it allowed for the possibility of a German advance through Belgium onto the French left wing, it nonetheless discounted the speed and severity of those attacks, focusing instead on the most direct route between French and German territory. Consequently, when the war erupted, the sixty-two divisions of the French army were arrayed in five field armies stretching from Alsace to Reims, the bulk of which were arrayed facing northeast toward the Alsace-Lorraine region.

Shortly after the Germans crossed into Belgium on August 4, Joffre had the French First Army advance slightly toward the present-day confluence of the French, German, and Swiss borders. A week later, the French First and Second Armies began to move into the Lorraine region, and shortly thereafter the French Third and Fourth Armies moved northeast into the Ardennes region. None of these offensives, however, succeeded in pushing back the German divisions that had been tasked to advance along this axis. While the front in Alsace-Lorraine remained stable thanks to the French fortresses and prepared defensive positions, the Germans were able to make substantial advances through the Ardennes, while their colleagues in the sweeping manoeuvre continued their advance through Belgium with only minor resistance from the defenders.

The BEF crossed the channel and by August 22 had taken up positions on the French left flank, along the Mons Canal near the border of Belgium and France. Just a day later, the German forces fell upon them. To the British right, the French army was forced to withdraw due to German pressure, leaving the British flank exposed. This prompted the British to withdraw to maintain symmetry and secure flanks with their French allies. This, in turn, resulted in what became known as the "retreat from Mons," a series of delaying defensive engagements carried out by the British and French as they slowly fell back toward Paris under continuous German pressure. Faced with widespread withdrawal along the whole of the French front, Joffre abandoned Plan XVII, which had proven to be unequal to the situation.

The British and French withdrawal continued throughout late August and September, and while some historians may have characterized this as a near-rout, the Allies generally withdrew in good order and in certain circumstances were even able to impose substantial delay and inflict major casualties on the advancing Germans. For their part, German frustration in Alsace-Lorraine and the extending lines of communication on the right flank, where the sweeping Schlieffen manoeuvre was being hampered by the Allies' dogged delay, slowly drained the energy out of the German army's advance. Confusion and competition among the German commanders caused several of them to deviate from the original intent of the Schlieffen Plan, and by early September the plan to outflank and encircle Paris was abandoned for a frontal attack against the British and French line. On September 4, 1914, as the German army crossed the Marne River, which drained out of the high ground south of Verdun and ran westward to join with the Seine in Paris, Joffre ordered his armies to take the offensive.

The Battle of the Marne began on September 6, 1914. The Germans, suffering from over-extended supply lines and poor communications, were unable to cope with the unexpected offensive push from the Allies. The German withdrawal started as a trickle on September 8, 1914. As one German formation withdrew, it left the flank of its neighbouring formation threatened, prompting another withdrawal to maintain cohesion and symmetry – a situation not unlike that experienced by the British and French after the attack at Mons. The trickle quickly became a torrent, and von Moltke was replaced by General Erich von Falkenhayn. The Germans realized their hope of defeating France in the west had quickly evaporated, so they withdrew their forces to a line running approximately from Soissons to Verdun, where they could establish defensive positions. On September 13, 1914, the Germans were finally able to halt the Allied counterattack, and both sides abandoned the principles of manoeuvre warfare that had hitherto been the prevailing doctrine that defined the opening phases of the war. The belligerents settled into an era of static, siege-like trench warfare that persisted until at least August 1918 and the beginning of the "last hundred days" campaign, which eventually brought the war to a close.

There was still some manoeuvre to be had, however. The British and French left flank, and the German right flanks, were exposed. What followed was the so-called race to the sea, as both sides attempted to outflank the other; this generally extended the front line of the Western Front northwesterly, culminating in mid-October 1914 at the Belgian town of Nieuwpoort on the coast of the North Sea. Although both sides had adopted the paradigm of siege warfare, neither side actually knew it at the time, and consequently both launched repeated frontal assaults in an attempt to penetrate the opposing line and restore manoeuvre to the battlefield. Each attempt failed miserably as thousands of young men on both sides were hung up on barbed wire or mowed down by machine guns. The winter of 1914–1915 gave both sides a chance to breathe and settle into static, trench warfare.

This situation, however, was seen as only temporary. The strategic goal of the Entente allies, particularly the French and British, was the 'rolling back' of the German interlopers. With this in mind, the Allied militaries remained focused on a return to offensive action.[54] As Kitchener articulated to the commander of the BEF, General Sir Douglas Haig:

> *The special task laid upon you is to assist the French and Belgian Governments in driving the German armies from French and Belgian territory, and eventually to restore the neutrality of Belgium…the defeat of the enemy by the combined Allied Armies* must **always be regarded as the primary object for which the British troops were originally sent to France**, *and to achieve that end the closest co-operation of French and British as a united Army must be the governing policy. [Emphasis added]*[55]

As the trench lines were established on the continent throughout the late fall and early winter of 1914–1915, the Canadians drilled and trained in Salisbury. There were many new tactics to be learned, as the first few months of the war had caused the British authorities to reconsider their method of fighting. Reflecting on the opening phases of the war, which had culminated in the strategic stalemate of trench warfare, the British leadership realized that, in order to re-open the front, many more guns and shells would be required.[56] And not just more guns and shells, but bigger guns and shells as well. Eventually, the imperial artillery park would include an upgraded 6-inch howitzer, a new 8-inch howitzer, and the introduction of 9.2-inch howitzers.[57]

The Canadians' sojourn in Salisbury was memorable, but for all the wrong reasons. While the first Canadian contingent tarried in England, the British Isles experienced the most disagreeable fall and winter weather that many local citizens could remember. Cold and rain made training difficult and proved to be a serious sap on the contingent's morale. Of their time in Salisbury, Morrison recalled that "those six months resulted in one of the most miserable and useless periods of hardship on which many look back."[58]

The first contingent was required to remain and train in Salisbury for a full six gruelling and inhospitable months, however, because it required significant training to bring it up to speed with the remainder of the imperial army. As most of the Canadian volunteers who found themselves on Salisbury Plain were either active militia men or civilians newly recruited into the Canadian Army, there was much for them to learn about the ways of modern warfare. While the annual summer camps in which the active militia participated certainly provided the bare minimum of military training, it was a far cry from what was required to prepare them to face the German forces bearing down on France and Belgium. Thus, it was not until February 7, 1915, that the 1st Canadian Division, under the command of British Brigadier-General Edwin Alderson, began crossing the English Channel for France. By February 16, the whole division was in France and ready to move into the line.[59]

For the first several weeks in France, each of the Canadian infantry brigades was attached to a British division near Armentières, a French town on the border with Belgium near Ypres, to acclimatize them to the war on the Western Front. Finally, on March 3, 1915, almost seven months after Canada had been drawn into the war, the 1st Canadian Division relieved the 7th British Division on the left flank of the British IV Corps in the line. The Canadians were now in the fight.[60]

Neuve-Chappelle

The advent of spring in 1915 brought with it the hope of a return to offensive operations for all parties concerned. Importantly for our purposes here, it also brought the introduction to the front line of the 1st Canadian Division on 8 March 1915. The first major offensive operation was launched by the Allies; the French planned to put in an attack in the Champagne region, coordinated with a supporting attack by the BEF. The French offensive was cancelled, however, and the British attack became a solitary effort known as the Battle of Neuve-Chappelle.

The 1st Division's first action came to pass on 10 March 1915 as part of the assault on Neuve-Chappelle, a town in northern France that lies about halfway between Armentières and Lens. The operation was initially very successful, but a firm victory was stymied by British reluctance to exploit both their own success and German counterattacks. The attack ended two days later, on 12 March 1915, and cost the 1st Canadian Division one hundred casualties, a rate generally on par with offensive operations at that point in the war. In general terms the Canadians' first exposure to war on the Western Front was well received.

Notably, the British artillery that supported the attack at Neuve-Chappelle introduced a new term into the gunner's lexicon. When the artillery laid down a curtain of fire in a straight line in front of their troops in an effort to isolate the Germans in their trenches, the British gunners used the French term *barrage*, meaning curtain, to describe the type of fire they witnessed. The barrage was to become a widely employed procedure throughout the First and Second World Wars, and it will be dealt with in much greater detail later in this book.

After Neuve-Chappelle, on 27 March, the 1ˢᵗ Canadian Division was marched out of the line and placed in reserve for rest and recuperation. The Canadians' first blooding was generally light, but a far more sinister confrontation, where the casualties would be much more severe, lay in their near future.[61]

Neuve-Chappelle is an important historical way-marker for another reason. It was at Neuve-Chappelle that it first became acutely obvious to the British and Canadian leadership that the amount of ammunition necessary to sustain offensive operations drastically exceeded what was available. This situation developed because no one had foreseen the awesome amounts of ammunition that would eventually be required in order to break the operational stalemate of the Western Front's trench warfare. In the month before the Battle of Neuve-Chappelle, the allocation of ammunition to imperial armies was a paltry ten rounds per gun, per day for the 18-pounders and eight rounds per gun, per day for the 4.5-inch howitzers. Neuve-Chappelle didn't improve the situation, and afterwards the allocation dropped to three rounds per gun, per day for both weapon systems.[62] Much ink has been spilled over the causes and the results of the "shell crisis" of 1915, and we needn't delve into it in any great detail at this juncture. It is sufficient to say that a lack of skilled workers on the home front in Great Britain, due to massive recruitment into what was termed Kitchener's New Armies, which is to say the vastly increased BEF, contributed to the inability of British industry to meet the need for ammunition resupply.[63] The crisis was so acute that, in the end, responsibility for munitions production was moved from the War Office to a government department run by a cabinet minister. Moreover, the widespread publication of the situation in the media of the day, and the reciprocal accusations of incompetence between military and political leaders, ultimately contributed to the downfall of Prime Minister Asquith's government in 1916.

The Second Battle of Ypres

Returning now to the service of the Canadian Army on the continent, in April 1915 the 1ˢᵗ Canadian Division moved northward to the Ypres Salient in Belgium. Ypres is an ancient town in the west of Belgium, not far from the French border. It sits astride the Ieperlee, or Ypres-Ijzer, Canal, which connects the town with the Yser River and the sea. Ypres had remained in Allied hands during the opening phases of the war. In the spring of 1915, the front line sat to the east of the city and formed a bulge in the line facing east-northeast, which became known as the Ypres Salient. After Neuve-Chappelle and some time for rest and training, the 1st Canadian Division relieved the 11th French Division in the line between April 14 and 17, 1915, deploying the 2nd and 3rd Canadian Infantry Brigades in the middle of the line of the salient, with the 45th Algerian Division to their left and the 28th British Division on their right. The 1st Canadian Infantry Brigade was in in the rear, conducting training for possible action elsewhere. As the troops of the 1st Canadian Division occupied the trenches and outposts of the departing French soldiers, the Germans emplaced 5730 gas cylinders filled with chlorine gas to their north, along the northern edge of the salient near the Belgian town of Langemarck, and waited for a favourable wind.[64]

The German chlorine gas attack during the Second Battle of Ypres in the spring of 1915 is a relatively well-known event in Canadian military history, but a short summary is worthwhile here. On April 22, the French troops to the Canadian left came under intense bombardment shortly after 4:00 p.m., after which the German artillery fire gradually shifted onto the Canadian positions. At 5:00 p.m. the Germans opened their gas cylinders for six to eight minutes and released more than 160 tons of chlorine gas.[65]

The results were atrocious. Although the Canadians were not completely spared the effects of the gas, they were nevertheless fortunate enough to escape the worst of it, which, due to the location of the cylinders and the prevailing direction of the winds, was concentrated to the left of the Canadian positions. As the chlorine gas struck the unprepared Allied soldiers, the French and British forces almost immediately began to withdraw, leaving the Canadian left flank exposed for a distance of approximately 7300 metres.[66] The attacking Germans exploited the gap created by the withdrawing forces and moved forward into an area known as Kitchener's Wood, a wooded area deep within the former Allied territory and not far from the town of St. Julien, which lay behind the Canadians and which was a major communications node. The withdrawal of the French and British left St. Julien ripe for capture by the attacking Germans. The batteries of the 1st Canadian Divisional Artillery were concentrated near St. Julien but oriented north-easterly to fire over the lines of the 2nd and 3rd Canadian Infantry Brigades. In the face of the German advance, the gunners switched their fire almost ninety degrees to the left to support the withdrawing French forces. One section of guns of 10th Battery were even forced to fire over open sights at German troops who had arrived only 300 metres away.[67]

Counterattacks later that evening by the 10th and 16th Canadian Infantry Battalions were coordinated with the French forces to their left. They initially managed to clear the enemy out of Kitchener's Wood, but at the terrible cost of 75 per cent casualties among the assaulting battalions.[68] The French attack in support of this assault was ineffectual, and the Canadians were compelled to withdraw to trenches south of the woods. More Canadian forces were brought up, and by dawn the Canadians had established a tenuous holding line in front of St. Julien. The Canadian batteries, now far too close to the front lines for comfort, moved rearward to establish new battery positions, in some cases in full view of German infantry.[69]

Another German gas release, this time directly in the face of the Canadians, on the morning of April 24 led to further withdrawals by the Canadians, and eventually St. Julien was lost. Over the next few days, with the arrival of fresh Allied battalions, several attempts were made to retake ground lost to the Germans, and each ended in disaster. One assault on St. Julien by the Lahore Division resulted in 1800 casualties in the first attempt, and a second attempt on April 27 produced another 1200 casualties. On April 28, a British and Canadian tactical withdrawal to shore up the defensive lines established a smaller front line with a radius of 2500 yards from Ypres; the salient had been substantially reduced in size but remained intact, while the town of Ypres itself remained in Allied hands. On May 4, the 1st Canadian Division was withdrawn from the line for rest and reinforcement, while elements of 1st Canadian Divisional Artillery remained in action supporting British and French operations. The 3rd Brigade, CFA, was the last to be pulled out of the line on May 14.[70]

In the summer of 1915, imperial authorities in London made the strategic decision to stop distributing British ground forces around the world in diverse theatres of operation, such as the Middle East and Africa. Instead, they would concentrate British divisions in the BEF in France, the theatre of operations that became the British army's focal point for the remainder of the war. To that end, British divisions that were deployed further afield were recalled from the Middle East to bolster

British fighting power on the Western Front. By the summer of 1916 the BEF had increased in size from six to forty-nine infantry divisions.

Shortly after the troops of the 2nd Canadian Division arrived in the United Kingdom in May of 1915, discussions began between military and political authorities in both Ottawa and London about possibly increasing the size of the Canadian contribution. In view of the centralization of British divisions in Europe, the imperial authorities enquired of the Dominion government whether Canada could produce twelve battalions for service in Egypt, either in addition to the 3rd Division or by deferring the creation of a fourth division. The Dominion authorities preferred to keep all the Canadian fighting formations together, and so the Canadian officials made a counter-offer of two more Canadian divisions for service in Northwest Europe. London accepted the Canadian offer, with the caveat that prior to the creation of a fourth division, the necessary Canadian reserve battalions being held in the United Kingdom, which were used as pools from which to draw reinforcements for the three Canadian divisions in action, had to be filled with personnel. Thus, although Ottawa and London agreed in summer 1915 to the creation of the 3rd and 4th Canadian Divisions, the former was not added to the Canadian Army's order of battle until December 1915, while the latter was not created until April 1916.[71]

In the spring of 1916, a year after the heroic stand of the 1st Canadian Division in the face of German chlorine gas, the 1st and 2nd Canadian Divisions were still in the Ypres sector, within British General Sir Herbert Plumer's British Second Army. They were located about five kilometres south of the town of Ypres, near a point in the front line where the trench lines ran, uniquely, east–west rather than north–south.[72] Nearby, the French and Germans were doggedly fighting each other at the Battle of Verdun, while the Canadians found themselves in the first set-piece battle conducted by the 2nd Canadian Division near St. Eloi. Although relatively minor when compared with the enormous engagement going on at Verdun, St. Eloi was nonetheless an important engagement from a Canadian perspective.[73]

St. Eloi

The St. Eloi operation was an imperial one. The British 3rd Division was tasked with conducting the initial phase of the assault, while the 2nd Canadian Division took over the line from the British once they had secured their objectives. Interestingly, this particular assault was unique due to the extensive use of mining operations. In the months preceding the assault, British engineers dug several mines under the German positions in which they emplaced a large amount of explosives. The plan was to detonate these caches at the moment of assault and then consolidate the effects by attacking the line when the defenders were either dead or dumbfounded by the explosion.

At 0415 on the morning of 27 March 1916, the British detonated the explosives. The resultant explosion produced a deafening roar that could be heard as far away as Folkestone in Kent, England.[74] When the dust cleared, seven large craters lay where the German lines had previously stood. The British assault went in and, over the next week, after repulsing German counterattacks, secured their objectives.

The 6th Canadian Brigade moved into the line on the morning of April 4, replacing the British 76th Brigade. The Canadians found a defensive position devoid of proper trenches, many of which had collapsed due to proximity to the detonations of the mines. There was also no barbed wire, and, distressingly, eight of the twelve machine-gun posts lacked an actual machine gun. What trenches did exist were filled with 2–3 feet of water. Perhaps having sensed the arrival of new imperial troops who were unfamiliar with the sector, at daybreak the Germans began a tremendous barrage of the Canadian line. They followed this with several attacks, one of which, carried out on April 6, found a gap in the Canadian line between the 27th "City of Winnipeg" Battalion and the 31st Battalion. The Germans were able to exploit this gap, and, after a brief attack, they secured a large portion of the line.

The situation now became rather desperate; the entire battlefield was a mass of mud and craters, caused by the exploding of the mines, rain, and the churning of the ground by the intense German artillery bombardments. The Canadians could not communicate between battalions on the line, nor could they get information back to their headquarters. Several counterattacks by the Canadians, aimed at retaking the mining craters that had been lost to the Germans, were scuppered because the men, lacking maps and aerial photographs – the latter due to the disagreeable weather and cloud cover that grounded the supporting aircraft – mistakenly attacked outlying craters caused by artillery fire rather than the mining craters now held by the Germans. The Canadians were subsequently bombarded and beaten back.

What followed was a number of days of miscommunication,

confusion, failed raids, and, in the end, a complete victory for the Germans. By April 20, the Canadians in the St. Eloi area had withdrawn to their original positions. The preceding days of intense fighting to exploit the mining craters had cost dozens of killed and wounded, and all of it for naught. The 2nd Canadian Division, and in particular the 6th Canadian Brigade, had been severely bloodied in their first exposure to set-piece attacks on the Western Front.[75]

Mount Sorrel

After the disaster of the St. Eloi craters, the Canadian Corps was joined by 3rd Canadian Division, albeit without the benefit of the 3rd Canadian Divisional Artillery, which stayed behind in England until it received orders to cross the channel to the continent. The Canadian Corps remained in the Ypres Salient throughout the remainder of April and May 1916, where they held the line that formed the southeast corner of the salient. This was the eastern-most protrusion of the line into enemy territory, lying to the south of the Menin Road, which runs eastward out of Ypres. The 3rd Canadian Division was situated on the right and the 1st Canadian Division on the left. Without the support of the 3rd Canadian Divisional Artillery, the soldiers of the Canadian Corps were supported by the batteries of the Lahore Divisional Artillery, a relationship that would remain, off and on, until the 4th Canadian Divisional Artillery was formed in June of 1917. Of particular importance, the area of the salient upon which the Canadians found themselves, in particular the 3rd Canadian Division, included a portion of Ypres Ridge, a small rise of land to the east of the town of Ypres, which afforded the Allies excellent observation of German trenches and defences. The portion of the ridge controlled by the Canadians was only about a thousand yards in length and included several small hills, one of which was referred to as Mount Sorrel.[76]

The Germans hoped to do something about this territorial advantage enjoyed by the Allies. Throughout May 1916, the German forces situated opposite the Canadians, the 26th and 27th Infantry Divisions, prepared themselves for a major offensive to dislodge the Canadians from the ridge. Canadian patrols reported increased digging of trenches forward of the German front line, the arrival of trench mortar batteries, and increased aircraft activities. The blow fell on the morning of June 2, 1916, with the opening of a massive German artillery barrage.

Since the outbreak of the war, both the Allied and German artillery tactics had changed substantially, reinforced by increased industrial production of both cannon and bullets. By the spring of 1916, both sides employed massive preparatory bombardments prior to an attack, designed to destroy wire obstacles and materiel and cause casualties among the defenders. Unfortunately for the Canadian men holding the line in early June of 1916, the German attack toward Mount Sorrel was one of the first opportunities the German army had to employ their newly produced masses of munitions in an attack. The ferocity of the bombardment stunned the Canadians and was indicative of the style of warfare that was to come throughout 1916 and 1917.

The hardest hit were the men of the 8th Canadian Brigade who formed the right shoulder of the 3rd Canadian Division. Within the brigade, it was the 4th Canadian Mounted Rifles who bore the full fury of the German fusillade and suffered, in consequence, a staggering 89 per cent casualties. Of the 702 men of the battalion, only seventy-six were not killed or wounded.[77] Included in the casualty lists was the commander of the 3rd Canadian Division, Lieutenant-General Malcolm Smith Mercer, who had the poor luck to have paid a visit to the front line to review the terrain at the exact moment the German barrage began. Its fury burst his eardrums, and his leg was broken by a bullet when the German infantry assault began. As he lay wounded on the ground, he was killed by shrapnel. Upon learning of the death of the commander, Brigadier-General Hoare Nairne, commander of the Lahore Divisional Artillery, assumed temporary command of the 3rd Canadian Division for the remainder of the battle of Mount Sorrel.[78]

After four hours of massive bombardment, the Germans detonated four mines in front of the Canadian lines, and at one o'clock the German infantry assaulted. Despite attempts by the decimated defenders to resist, the German onslaught was unstoppable. The barrage had killed nearly all of the artillery forward observers, so the weight of Canadian defensive artillery fire never materialized.[79] Deployed well forward, within only 400 yards of the front line, were two 18-pounders of 5th Battery, Canadian Field Artillery, under the command of Lieutenant C.P. Cotton. Most of the gun crews had been killed or wounded, but Cotton, along with the three gunners who were uninjured and two engineers who had joined them, opened fire on the advancing Germans at point-blank range until the guns were overrun and the crews killed. This was the only instance of the Canadian Artillery losing guns to the Germans during the war, and the two 18-pounders were eventually recaptured.[80]

Immediate counterattacks by the Canadians were rebuffed, and a renewed German offensive on June 6, again initiated by the exploding of four mines under Canadian lines, allowed the Germans to advance even further, capturing the town of Hooge.

But the Canadians were not to be denied their revenge. Taking the time necessary to develop a deliberate rather than a hasty counterattack and, in particular, to assemble a superiority in artillery support, which included the allocation of three heavy-artillery groups, a siege battery, and three heavy batteries, they launched a major counterattack on June 12 after a ten-hour bombardment of German defensive works. So intense was the bombardment, the Canadian infantry took only an hour to secure almost all the objectives that had been lost to the Germans on June 2 and 6. The town of Hooge was left in German hands because, although a massive amount of artillery had been assembled for this counterattack, it was ultimately not enough. Consequently, the size of the counterattack had to be scaled down somewhat to reflect the amount of artillery available. Doubtless Byng and his Corps artillery commander, Brigadier-General Harry Burstall, would have preferred to have been allocated more artillery to permit them to include Hooge in their plans, but Field Marshall Haig had issued an order to prioritize the allocation of artillery to an operation he was planning to launch several weeks later, near the Somme River.[81]

The Somme

Normally a placid river that turns through the northern French countryside, the Somme River eventually lent its name to that epic battle that, by dint of the sheer loss of life and lack of success, would come to signify all that was tragic, wrong, and pointless about the Great War. Astride its waters, the better part of a generation of British and German men would expire in a fruitless attempt to dislodge each other from the field of battle.

While the Canadian Corps fought in St. Eloi and Mount Sorrel in the Ypres sector to the southeast, the French army continued to slug it out with the Germans around Verdun. Indeed, the Battle of Verdun was the longest battle of the Great War; it began with a German offensive in February of 1916 and continued for ten months until December of that year. The Germans had hoped that by threatening to take the strategically vital city of Verdun, the French would be forced to draw in reserves to counter the German assault. The Germans hoped this would allow them to inflict massive casualties and prompt the French to negotiate a peace. Locked in this epic struggle with the German army for so long, and suffering horrendous casualties in the process – into the hundreds of thousands – the French naturally looked to the British for some sort of offensive that might draw off some of the German troops from the French front. By the spring of 1916, the number of British forces on the continent had grown substantially, by both the inclusion of colonial divisions and the aforementioned decision to concentrate British forces in the European theatre.[82] As the BEF had become large enough to contemplate a major assault, the Allied military leaders looked for options to relieve pressure on the French armies at Verdun, all the while inflicting losses on the Germans and maintaining pressure on the German Western Front, in order to pre-empt it from transferring troops to the Eastern Front against Russia.[83]

What resulted was the British decision to attack along the Somme River to the northwest of the ongoing fighting around Verdun. The plan was for the French Sixth Army to attack along the Somme River itself, while to the north, the British Fourth Army was to deliver the main effort: an assault of thirteen divisions, with an additional five divisions held in reserve, supported on the left by the British Third Army. Additionally, the French Sixth Army to the right of the British would go on the offensive to add to the pressure being applied to the Germans.[84]

The attack began on July 1, 1916, following a seven-day bombardment in which over 1.5 million artillery shells were fired. Initial successes by the French Sixth Army and the right wing of the British Fourth Army did not compensate for the lack of success in the remainder of the Fourth Army.[85] The massive barrage did not achieve the desired level of destruction of the German trenches, and so, when the British attacked in a slow-moving, extended line, the result was slaughter. On this day alone, over 57,000 British soldiers were killed, among that number almost the whole of the Royal Newfoundland Regiment.[86]

The Battle of the Somme raged on until November 19, 1916, with the Allied forces attempting to maintain pressure on the German line in hopes of eventually wearing them down for a breakthrough that never materialized.[87] The Canadian Expeditionary Force was spared involvement in the initial assault of July 1 but entered into the Somme campaign two months later. On August 30 the Canadian Corps, still consisting of three divisions, relieved the Australia–New Zealand Corps (ANZAC) near the town of Pozières and fell under the command of British General Sir Hubert Gough's 'Reserve' army, which had taken over in the line from the British Fourth Army once that formation commenced the offensive on July 1. The 4th Canadian Division made its way to the front in the fall of 1916, and eventually all Canadian divisions participated in the Battle of the Somme between September and November of 1916.

The Battle of the Somme has become synonymous with the worst aspects of the war. The losses were horrendous, with casualty lists in numbers heretofore unimagined. It is true that it never achieved the success intended by the Allied leadership, but in some cases the front line had been penetrated at least 7000 yards.[88] In retrospect, the cost was far too high for so little gain. The British lost 200,000 men and the French 70,000, while the Germans, who had been ordered not to abandon one foot of ground, lost 200,000 themselves.[89] In the aftermath of the battle, the belligerents stabilized the line over the winter of 1916–17. Offensive operations were paused, but not wholly abandoned. Even as the Allied forces bled themselves white in the Somme and in Verdun, their military leaders were already contemplating the next big offensive, which would come in the spring and which would include, as an objective, Vimy Ridge.

Ends: Why Vimy Ridge?

Why was seizing Vimy Ridge so important? To understand the operational and strategic importance of the ridge, we must go back in time to when it first fell into German hands. It wasn't captured during the initial phases of the conflict, when the German armies fell on France from the north via the Low Countries, but rather once the mobile phase of fighting gave way to the static trench warfare that dominated the Western Front until late 1918. The ridge was first captured by the Germans in October of 1914 during the "race to the sea" and provided the Germans with a dominating feature from which observation over a large swath of terrain to the west of the ridge could be maintained. Initially, it was the French army who sat opposite the Germans, and in a series of operations in the spring of 1915, the French attempted to push the Germans off the ridge, culminating in May of 1915 during the Second Battle of Artois. The French were unsuccessful in pushing the Germans off the eastern slope of the ridge, despite paying a very high price in casualties, and the two sides settled into a static arrangement with the French Tenth Army holding the western slope of the ridge, and the Germans ensconced on the eastern, steeper side.

When the German army fell upon the French defenders around Verdun in February 1916, the French Tenth Army was withdrawn from the Arras sector in order to shore up the French defenders. As the Tenth Army withdrew, its place in the line was taken over by the British First and Third Armies. The British found the French positions rather poorly prepared and even contemplated withdrawing their line a few thousand yards westward in order to establish a more robust defensive position. The idea was, however, politically unpalatable given the steep price paid by the French in blood during the Second Battle of Artois, so the British went about improving their defensive positions as much as possible.

The sector was a hotbed of activity, with constant artillery duelling and repeated instances of mining operations. Due to the nature of the slopes on either side of the ridge, the British generally had an easier task to dig and emplace their mines under the German lines. Faced with rising casualties, the Germans finally resolved to launch a local offensive to push the British off the western slope of the ridge. This attack was carried out between May 21 and 26 behind a thunderous and effective bombardment laid on by the German artillery. Over the course of the operation, the British were forced to fall back, and while some local counterattacks managed to blunt the German offensive, they nonetheless held the majority of their gains. By the end of the engagement, the Germans were masters of the western slope and could make use of the ridge for observation practically unmolested. The British contemplated a large counterattack to regain their lost territory on the western slope of the ridge, but when Haig realized the amount of reinforcing artillery such an operation would require, plus the fact that these same guns had been earmarked for the Somme offensive of July 1916, he ordered the counterattack cancelled; he wasn't ready to risk not having those guns available for his main effort at the Somme. His decision is indicative of how, at this point in the war, having sufficient artillery had become a critical requirement prior to launching any offensive operation. With that, the opposing lines at Vimy Ridge had been redrawn, with the Germans ensconced on the feature. They would remain so until the spring offensive of 1917 and the Canadian Corps' assault on the ridge.

The Entente's military strategy for 1917 was determined in mid-November 1916 during a conference of Allied representatives in Chantilly, France.[90] There it was agreed that, having stabilized the perimeter of Germany and Austria-Hungary, the Entente would maintain pressure on all fronts in order to prevent the enemy from assuming offensive operations.[91] The representatives understood, however, that due to the manpower available to the various member nations, victory would have to come in Flanders, where the combined might of the BEF and the French army possessed sufficient combat power to deliver a successful blow. Consequently, in Chantilly the Entente agreed to give primacy of operations to the Western Front.[92]

The concept of operations for the British spring offensive of 1917 emerged early in the New Year. On January 2, 1917, Lieutenant-General L.E. Kiggell, chief of the general staff at British General Headquarters

(GHQ), issued *General Headquarters Letter OAD 258* to the five British field armies and the cavalry corps that comprised the BEF.[93] In it, Kiggell informed the British commanders of the overall scheme of manoeuvre for the British spring offensive and allocated to the three assaulting armies their objectives: the British Fifth Army was to attack the Ancre Valley in the direction of Achiet-le-Grand, and the Third Army was tasked to attack the Scarpe Valley between Beaurains and Roclincourt, focusing on the high ground near Monchy le Preux with the intent of turning the German defences south of Arras by advancing southeast toward Croiselles and Bullecourt. The First Army, consisting of ten divisions in three corps, the Canadian, I, and XI Corps, would attack Vimy Ridge to secure the northern flank of the Third Army attack and gain observation over the Douai Plain. The operational goal of the three Army-level attacks was to destroy or capture the German forces in a salient near Bapaume, France, which lay to the southwest of Vimy Ridge. Consequently, the main effort of the Battle of Arras, as the action was to become known, was the Third Army's assault, with the First Army serving as a defensive flank to cover the Third Army's advance.[94] The intent of these attacks was to pin the enemy to his position and force him to commit his reserves, thus facilitating a much larger French assault further to the south.[95]

Further refinement of the operational plan occurred during a conference between the recently promoted Field-Marshal Douglas Haig, commander of British armies in France; General W.R. Robertson, chief of the imperial general staff; and General R. Nivelle, commander of the French army. During this conference, the participants agreed that the combined Anglo–French force would aim to take the offensive by April 1, 1917, with the intent that the three planned attacks would establish the conditions from which the Anglo–French armies could exploit their success, and thus provide a decisive result against the German armies opposite them.[96] These plans were further refined in subsequent communications between the British and the French, and on January 26, 1917, Kiggell sent another circular to the army commanders in which he provided more concrete direction on the upcoming operations, including the reallocation of divisions between armies and, of particular interest for this study, the initial allotment of artillery.[97]

After receiving strategic direction, the British First Army, under the command of General Sir Henry Horne, developed the Army-level plan and assigned tasks to the subordinate Corps shortly thereafter. The Canadian Corps formed the right-hand corps of the First Army, bounded on its left by I Corps and on its right by the XVII Corps of the Third Army. In order to ensure the success of the Third Army's operation, it became critical to deny the Germans the ability to use the high ground to observe the Third Army's anticipated operations; therefore, the Canadian Corps' assault on Vimy Ridge became the First Army's main effort.[98] Before considering the details of the First Army's assault plan, which, of course, would influence the fire support plan, it is first necessary to understand the infantry doctrine in use at the time of the operation. To do so we will begin with a brief analysis of the *operational art* as it pertained to imperial armies in general and the Canadian Corps in particular.

Operational art is an odd concept to nail down. Dr. Allan English of Queen's University has defined it as "the skill of translating strategic direction into operation and tactical action." He adds, "It is not dependent on the size of the committed forces, but is the vital link between the setting of military strategic objectives and the tactical employment of forces on the battlefield."[99] In brief, this provides us with the concept: how military leaders analyze the strategic direction they have received and, from that analysis, develop a tactical and operational plan to achieve the strategic objectives.

There was a style to the way the Canadian Corps went about its planning for Vimy Ridge. By the spring of 1917, the Corps had developed a doctrine, although it might also be called an operational culture, that directed their efforts and guided them in the execution of their operation. The Canadian Corps' operational art at that time was profoundly influenced by their commander, British Lieutenant-General Julian Hedworth George Byng.

Byng was a British aristocrat with a long line of ancestors who had served with the British military. He was a regular military officer in the British Army, and prior to assuming command of the Canadian Corps in May of 1916, he had commanded British elements in Egypt, France, and Gallipoli. Despite being a blue-blooded member of the British aristocracy, Byng was laid back, approachable, and far from aloof. Consequently, he was well-loved by the Canadian soldiers, the majority of whom were not professional military men and who were thus not only unfamiliar with the nuances of the more class-based British Army but in many ways downright resentful of them.

This more casual approach to command served Byng well during his time at the head of the Canadian Corps. Ian McCulloch best articulated the profound influence that Byng exerted on the culture of the Canadian

Corps when he wrote the following in *The Changing Face of War*: "[T]he Canadian Corps developed its attack doctrine and its concepts of campaign planning, which became fundamental to its practice of the operational level of war and the key to its subsequent tactical successes... [T]he development was not uniquely Canadian and occurred largely through the influence and direction of Byng, the unorthodox British general, and assisted by a very able and predominantly British professional staff."[100]

Byng's influence on the Canadian Corps' operational doctrine, both at Vimy Ridge and during subsequent operations, cannot be overstated. It was his detailed analysis of the problem, coupled with his decision to undertake a thorough planning process to develop the best possible plan of attack, that were key guarantors of success. McCulloch also wrote that it was Byng's commitment to establishing a rigorous training plan, reorganizing the Corps staff along more efficient and effective lines, and the implementation of a new tactical approach to the problem of trench warfare that gave the Canadian Corps its operational culture and materially contributed to its efficacy. In short, "thorough preparation, attention to detail, and overwhelming fire support ... would become the trademarks that Byng would imprint on the Canadian Corps staff for all future operations."[101]

To develop this operational art, Byng collected lessons from recent operations in an effort to analyze what tactics worked and what didn't. To assist him in this endeavour, Byng was aided by the efforts of Major-General Sir Arthur William Currie. Currie was a Canadian Militia officer from Vancouver, British Columbia. His civilian trade was that of an educator, and at the outbreak of the war in the summer of 1914, Currie was in command of the 50th Regiment, an active militia Highland regiment in Victoria, BC. Upon mobilization, Currie was promoted and was assigned to command a brigade in the first Canadian contingent that sailed for Europe. As brigade commander, he distinguished himself, particularly during his actions at the Second Battle of Ypres in April 1915, where he and his brigade were credited for playing a pivotal role in holding the Allied position in the face of the gruesome German gas attack. Consequently, he was again promoted and given command of 1st Canadian Division in the fall of 1915, a position he held throughout 1916 and during the Battle of Vimy Ridge. Afterwards, he was again promoted, and in June 1917, two months after Vimy Ridge, Currie became the first Canadian commander of the Canadian Corps, a position he held until the end of the war.

In the lead-up to the Battle of Vimy Ridge, the best source of tactical lessons available to Byng and the Canadian Corps was the recently concluded Battle of the Somme. Byng dispatched Currie as his emissary to study the lessons that emerged from the battle in an attempt to distill those observations into a refined doctrine for the Canadian Corps. In addition, Currie was also dispatched to the French army in January 1917 to glean lessons learned by the French during the Battle of Verdun from February to December 1916.

Thus, the lessons of the Somme and Verdun became two sources from which the Canadian Corps developed its operational art and the tactical doctrine that was eventually employed at Vimy Ridge.

When Currie returned to the Canadian Corps headquarters after visiting his British and French colleagues, he recommended to Byng that he do away with the policy of attacking in waves of infantry, and instead employ smaller, less vulnerable columns of men. Thereafter, they would use the principle of infiltration to achieve tactical penetration, and leave follow-on forces to 'mop up' areas of resistance using fire and manoeuvre.[102]

As we saw previously, the orders that eventually defined Lieutenant-General Byng's task at Vimy Ridge emanated from GHQ Letter *OAD 258*. This was produced by Lieutenant-General L.E. Kiggell, chief of the general staff at British General Headquarters, on January 2, 1917, and laid out the general plan for the BEF's operations in 1917. Over the next two months, Byng and his staff developed the plan for the assault on Vimy Ridge; Byng submitted his proposed Scheme of Operations to General Henry Horne, on March 5, 1917.[103]

The First Army scheme made the Canadian Corps responsible for a frontage of 7000 yards opposite Vimy Ridge. Byng arranged the Corps with the four Canadian infantry divisions in the line: from right to left were the 1st through 4th Canadian Divisions.[104] He determined four tactical objectives for the Corps: The Black, Red, Blue, and Brown Lines. The two main objectives were the Black Line and the Red Line. The first and closest to the Canadian Corps' forward positions was the Black Line. It consisted of enemy crater posts, Byng's own observation line, and his front-line defences, all of which were arrayed to an average depth of 700 yards. The next tactical objective, moving east from the Black Line, was the Red Line, which ran about 400–1000 yards beyond the Black Line. Consequently, the Red Line was the final objective of the 3rd and 4th

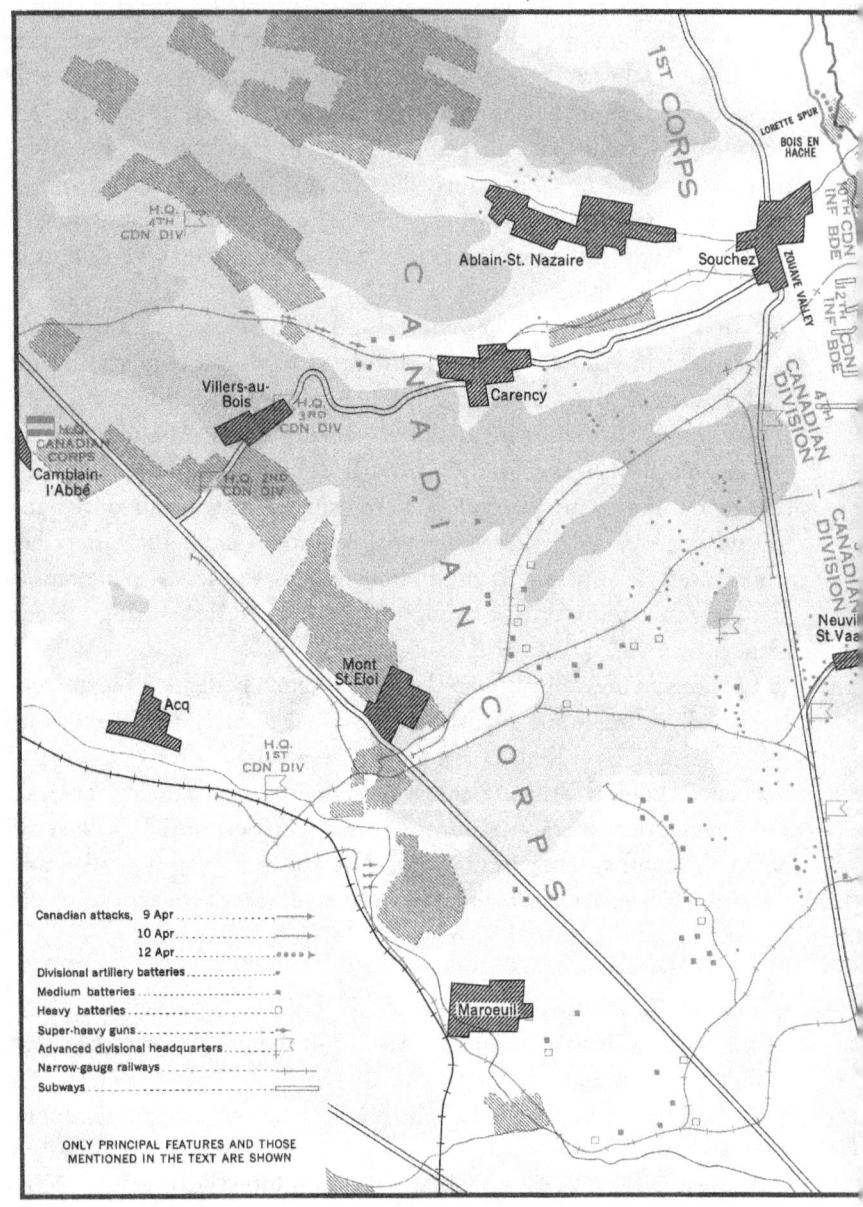

ABOVE: Vimy Ridge, April 9–12, 1917 (Canadian War Museum)

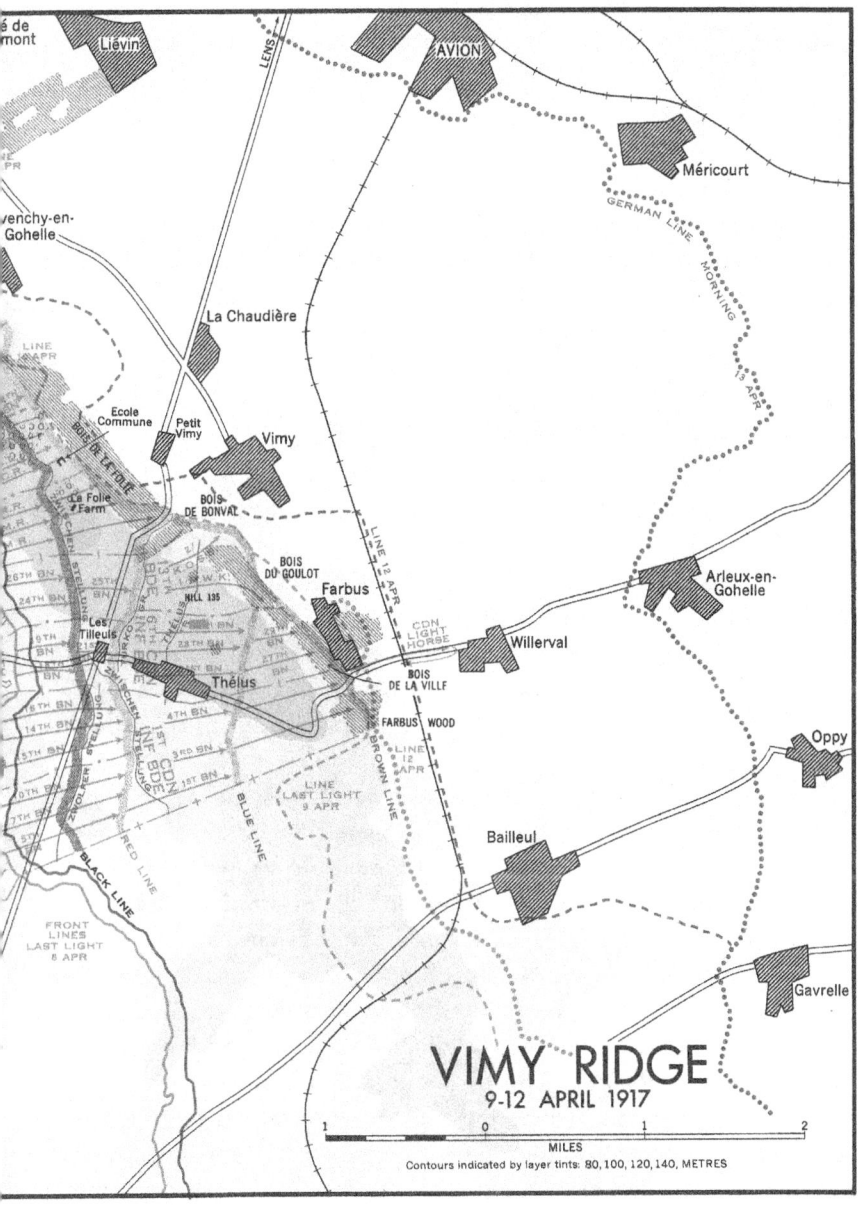

VIMY RIDGE
9-12 APRIL 1917

MILES

Contours indicated by layer tints: 80, 100, 120, 140, METRES

Canadian Divisions. Due to the topographical nature of the ridge, which does not run perfectly north–south but is angled in a more northwest-to-southeasterly fashion the Red Line was well beyond the crest of the ridge in the north, across from the 3rd and 4th Canadian Divisions. In the south, across from the 1st and 2nd Canadian Divisions, the location of the Red Line did not constitute a sufficient penetration of the ridge; consequently, it was only an intermediate objective for the 1st and 2nd Canadian Divisions. Due to the actual contours of the ridge, as the Red Line moved north it actually linked up with the Black Line at the left flank of the Canadian Corps boundaries.

The third objective, the Blue Line, was a subsequent objective that lay 1200 yards beyond the Red Line. The intervening space between the Red and Blue Lines included important tactical objectives, such as the village of Thélus and Hill 140. Thereafter, the Brown Line was the furthest and final objective of the Canadian Corps in general, and the 1st and 2nd Canadian Divisions in particular. It lay beyond the eastern edge of Vimy Ridge and represented a total incursion into German territory of 4000 yards.[105] Each of the four objective lines represented successive stages of the assault, and the attainment of each was synchronized with the infantry advances of the flanking formations, particularly with XVII Corps, which was attacking the Germans to the right of the Canadian Corps.[106]

To seize the ridge, Byng determined that the advance against the Black Line was to occur simultaneously along the whole Corps frontage, with a zero hour, the time of the start of the assault, set for 0530 hours. Having considered the terrain, obstacles, and enemy positions located in the Black Line area, Byng and his staff allocated the Canadian divisions a total of 35 minutes to secure the Black Line objective. Thereafter, a pause of 40 minutes was scheduled to allow the Canadian troops to consolidate on the objective and reform their ranks for the subsequent advance on the Red Line. During this consolidation period, wounded Canadians would be tended to and evacuated to the rear, prisoners would be collected and sent toward Canadian lines, and a resupply of ammunition would be brought forward to the assaulting elements. After this forty-minute pause, the assault would continue toward the Red Line, for which Byng allocated twenty minutes, followed by another, much longer pause of two and a half hours during which the assaulting troops would once again consolidate, resupply, reorganize, and prepare to continue. Thereafter, at 0935 the 1st and 2nd Canadian Divisions would continue the advance toward the Blue Line, where another pause, this one of one hour and thirty-five minutes followed, and at 1226 the final assault would launch, reaching the Brown Line at 1318. The assaulting divisions were instructed to send out patrols to locate or pursue the enemy once they had secured their final objectives.[107]

Although the focus of this work is on the artillery bombardment of Vimy Ridge, it is worthwhile to survey the infantry tactics employed at the time of the assault in order to contextualize the manner in which artillery support was employed. By the time of the assault on Vimy Ridge, a four-wave infantry attack was the doctrinal method with which the imperial armies conducted their assaults. The method was as follows: at the time determined in orders, all four waves of infantry would emerge from the jumping-off point to begin their assault. The second, third, and fourth waves would deliberately move at a slower pace off the start in order to create space between the waves. The first wave followed the barrage as it crept forward, until the barrage arrived on the objective, where it would pause. The first wave would continue to advance until it was within 30–50 yards of the barrage. When they arrived at this distance, the first wave would stop and lie down while the barrage continued to pound at the German forward trench line. When the barrage lifted, the first wave would then charge into the trench, killing any defenders left alive with rifles, pistols, grenades, or bayonets before they could emerge from their dugouts. The first wave would then leave a few guards in the trench and carry on the advance.

As the first wave continued the advance, the second wave would arrive seconds later to 'mop up.' They would complete the destruction of any enemy remaining in the first trench and then carry on the advance; they, too, would leave several men in the first trench line as a guard. The third and fourth waves carried on through the objective without stopping, their primary responsibilities being to carry ammunition, provide stretcher parties for the wounded, and begin the work of digging a communication trench back to the friendly front trench line.[108] In this manner, the infantry advance continued until the final objective was taken.

Once Byng and his staff had determined the manoeuvre plan to seize Vimy Ridge, Morrison then had the information he required to develop, along with his staff, the fire support plan to ensure the assault was a success. Of course, Morrison would have been involved in the planning of the assault phases, and would have provided advice pertaining to fire support matters throughout the process; in other words, no artillery-specific planning occurred before the infantry plan was fully developed. Nonetheless, it was only after the assault plan was finalized that exact details that would shape a detailed fire support plan were available.

The task then fell to E.W.B. Morrison to develop the fire support plan to support Byng's manoeuvre plan. Morrison, now a major-general and the General Officer Commanding Royal Artillery (GOCRA) of the Canadian Corps, had been a an artillery officer in the Canadian Militia and a journalist by profession. Prior to the war he had been editor of the *Ottawa Citizen*, and he was also a veteran of the Boer War, where he won a Distinguished Service Order for his actions serving with "D" Battery of the Canadian Artillery.[109]

Until mid-December 1916, Morrison had been in command of the 2nd Canadian Divisional Artillery. On December 16, Morrison was appointed to the position of GOCRA Canadian Corps, replacing Brigadier-General Henry Edward (Harry) Burstall, who went on to command the 2nd Canadian Infantry Division.[110] Morrison transferred command of the 2nd Canadian Divisional Artillery to Brigadier-General Henri Alexandre Panet, and after spending some time on leave in England, he returned to take the lead of the artillery planning for the assault on Vimy Ridge, arriving at the Corps Artillery Headquarters in Rebreuve-Ranchicourt on January 6, 1917.[111]

As a Canadian, his appointment was somewhat unique in the Canadian Corps where, despite the name, the majority of staff officers in the Corps headquarters, including the commander himself, were British.

Morrison and his corps commander had a tactical objective that had been informed by an operational plan that was in turn influenced by military-, national- and coalition-strategic guidance. Morrison had a number of tools at his disposal to support the Canadian Corps' assault on Vimy Ridge, so we now turn to an in-depth study of the *means* used by the men of the Canadian Corps artillery to support the operation.

OPPOSITE: Brig.-Gen. E.W.B. Morrison, C.B., G.O.C. Cdn. Artillery (LAC 3219263)

MEANS: TOOLS OF THE TRADE

Means are the tools available to achieve an objective. In commerce, these include a broad spectrum of resources, from staff to machines to capital. In war, the means at a commander's disposal are a bit different and definitely unique, but the concept is nonetheless as valid on the battlefield as it is in the boardroom. The fire support system at Vimy Ridge was a vast, intricate network of resources, ranging in type from soldiers to horses to guns, airplanes, and much more, all working harmoniously and synergistically toward a common operational goal. This chapter will lay out the means that Byng and Morrison had at their disposal, allowing them to plan and execute the bombardment of Vimy Ridge, and illustrate the leadership, teamwork, and coordination that were required to make it effective.

The composite elements of the imperial armies' fire support system consisted of both materiel and organizational structures. All of these, to varying degrees, dictated the manner in which the fire support organization was employed against the German defences on Vimy Ridge. While the First World War is arguably known as a conflict in which the artillery achieved a level of technical advancement far beyond that of the other branches, it is important to remember that regardless of the number, size, or calibre of the artillery equipment in use, the critical element of the fire support system – one that is too easily overlooked – is the human element. Before any discussion of the equipment of the artillery, then, we will examine the single most important tool Major-General Morrison had at his disposal: the gunner himself.

Men

Like the Canadian population in general, both then and now, the personnel of the Canadian Corps were not a monolithic cultural block.

Recruiting standards for artillerymen were slightly different than those for their brothers in other trades. Owing to the size of the equipment in use and the requirement for increased manual exertion to load and fire artillery pieces, the minimum height for service in the artillery was initially set at 5'7," as opposed to 5'3" for other trades.[112]

There is a triumvirate of critical requirements for the artillery to function effectively, namely the ability to shoot, move, and communicate. Unsurprisingly, therefore, when a man joined the artillery he had the choice of three roles he could fulfill in a battery: there were the gunners, who worked the guns themselves (*shoot*); drivers, who were responsible for handling the horse teams, or in the case of larger-calibre guns, the tractors that moved the guns about (*move*); and signallers, who operated the phones, semaphore flags, and signal lamps (*communicate*). While the men of each group were collectively known as artillerymen, their expertise and duties generally kept them focused on their respective roles.[113] Hugh R. Kay, who deployed to Europe as part of the 43rd Battery from Guelph, Ontario, recorded in his history of the battery the following description of the three sub-trades of the artillery in the unique tongue of common artilleryman: "the men in the Battery were divided into the sheep [gunners], and the goats [drivers], or the 'fatigue artists' and those who 'followed the ponies.' In addition to these we had the wig-waggers [signallers] or headquarters party."[114]

Gunners were the most numerous of the three sub-trades. They were responsible for the maintenance and operation of the artillery pieces themselves. Hugh Kay referred to them, as noted above, as "fatigue artists"; fatigues were routine administrative duties varying from standing guard, cleaning equipment, digging latrines, and so forth, and those unhappy tasks invariably went to the gunners, as their driver and signaller colleagues were either busy tending to horses or monitoring telephones or wireless sets. Gunner Betram Cox described his duties as a gun detachment member in a letter home thus: "they keep us working all day, improving the gun pit etc., never a moment's rest; the remainder of the time we are hauling ammunition. Usually get to bed about 1 AM. And we nearly always have a call before morning, if not 2 or 3. Each man also has to do a guard of 2 hours every night, so with no sleep in the day, you can quite understand, we need no rocking to sleep when we hit the dugout. I haven't had my pants off for a week."[115]

When they moved about the battlefield, the gunners rode on the gun limbers, battery wagons, and ammunition wagons.[116] They were not, however, responsible for actually conducting the guns and wagons from one position to another; that task fell to the artillery drivers. The duty of the artillery driver, as noted by war correspondent Edgar Wallace, was to "get his gun to the appointed place in the shortest possible time," and thus the driver was dependent, to a great deal, on having a strong relationship with his "two long-faced friends."[117] Indeed, the lives of drivers and horses were intermingled, the former being responsible for the latter's "temper, his cleanliness, his hunger or his thirst [which] were matters to which he was called upon to give his constant attention."[118]

The drivers who handled the teams had a particularly dangerous life. The diarist of the 60th Battery succinctly captured the precariousness of the driver's position when he wrote, "[I]t is, after all, the driver who probably has the hardest task in the artillery. The gunner can always duck; he is generally near some kind of shelter, even if it is not much more than a blade of grass. With the driver, his horses must always come first; when driving he is fully exposed to enemy fire; a moving vehicle is a favourite target, and is far more visible than a camouflaged gun pit. The driver cannot conceal himself, and his only salvation is the darkness during which he does most of his work."[119]

Richard Bennett (R.B.) Talbot Kelly, a captain with the British Field Artillery, made the following astute observation in his memoirs concerning the challenging life of an artillery driver:

> And what of the Artillery drivers? Throughout the war their task was unending, exhausting and cold-blooded. In the long winters they spent their days tending horses, picketed in the open, often kneed-deep in liquid, poisonous mud, six to ten miles behind the guns. At dusk they set out on a nightly journey with food and ammunition, over roads swept by shell-fire, through inky, soaking nights of rain and cold. Often they were wounded; often left with screaming, maimed horses; always they met terror on each night-bound road. After eight to ten hours of inglorious toil they returned, haggard in the dawning to their muddied horse lines, to prepare for the next night. So on, night in and night out, week by week, month by moth for four years. Yet always their horses came first, always in deed and action they were gentle to their 'pair' though rough in speech. The British driver almost alone amongst those fighting in the war, showed this constant, tender, hardiness.[120]

This is an opportune moment to pause our discussion of the men who constituted the artillery and address the characteristics of their "long-faced friends," namely, the horses who supported it. Although some vehicles were used during the Great War, for the most part the imperial artillery was, until the very end of the war, a hippomobile force. Horses were a critical tool in the Canadian Expeditionary Force, and in particular in the artillery. A divisional artillery was extremely dependent on horsepower to move about the battlefield: for example, the three field artillery brigades of the 1st Canadian Division received 2400 horses in total, while the divisional ammunition column received about 600. We will see throughout the rest of the book how the amount of ammunition that was expended by the artillery grew over time, necessitating many more horses to move the bullets around the battlefield. Consequently, by 1917 the official establishment of horses for a divisional ammunition column had climbed to 892.[121]

The main depot for horses in the Canadian Army was Remount Depot at Lachine, near Montreal. It was established in early 1915 in an area of over 300 acres where horses could be trained and maintained. It was certainly a busy site, and when the Canadian forces began heading to Europe, over 38,000 horses were shipped from Lachine to the theatre of operations in seven months of 1915.[122] By 1917, before the United States entered the war, most of the horses for the Canadian Army were purchased from ranchers in St. Louis, Missouri. There were four types of horses, and the Remount Depot was responsible for dividing the acquired horses into the four necessary groupings. There were light draft, heavy draft, pack, and riding horses.

Light draft horses for the artillery weighed 1050–1200 pounds, cost $190 a head, and were used to pull field guns, namely the 18-pounders and 4.5-inch howitzers. An 18-pounder was pulled by a team of six horses, the three left-side horses being those that were ridden by the drivers. Horses that weighed over 1400 pounds were classified as heavy-artillery horses and cost $210 a head. The heavy horses were responsible for the transportation of heavy guns and supplies. Pack animals were used for packing guns parts and ammunition, and theirs was a pitiable existence: "each packing eight shells to the load, in rain and sleet, with mud to their hips and shoulders, over planked, fascine, and unbroken roads, over shelly holes and bog, these animals supplied ammunition to the gun pits, led forward by a solitary man."[123] The final classification of horses, the riding horses, were, as the name implies, used as mounts, mostly but not exclusively by the officers. The ages of horses used in the artillery generally ran from five to nine years, although healthy horses could be employed up to twelve years of age. After they were selected, horses underwent their own sort of basic training at Lachine, being "taught how to behave, to respond to the order of the rein, just as a solider is taught to respect the 'order of command.'" [124]

The fact that horses were so key to the movement of the artillery meant they were to be kept healthy as possible. Unlike motor transports that require a minimum of maintenance from the driver, a horse must be cared for on a daily basis if it is to remain combat effective. Even at rest, the artillery drivers of the artillery had to ensure their horses received the proper attention. The historian of the 6th Battery, 2nd Field Brigade, CFA, included the following satirical observation concerning the constant attention demanded by the horses: "All a fello has to do on a holiday in the Artillery is to feed the horses an' give 'em a drink an' smooth 'em out an take 'em for a walk and then feed 'em an smooth 'em out and feed 'em and give 'em a drink. It makes a fello feel like givin back a dollar out of his pay at the end of the month."[125]

Horses are, of course, finicky animals, each with a personality of its own. Some of the artillery horses were well trained, obedient, and friendly, while others were stubborn or shy. William Ogilvie, an artillery signaller, recounted that he was once tasked, along with some of his colleagues, to take the battery horses to water. He was given charge of a horse named Dynamite. After Dynamite had had his drink, Ogilvie began leading him back to the battery wagon lines and, in the process, began whistling a tune. "Whether or not he took offense to my tuneless whistle I'll never know," Ogilvie reminisced. "Suddenly something hit me a blow on the back, knocking me flat on my face." Dynamite had bitten him on the back with sufficient force to knock him unconscious and send him flying several feet off the track. Ogilvie recalled that he was fortunate to have been of rather spare build, so there was not much muscle for Dynamite to bite into, although a horse-bite sized hole in the middle of his tunic was the result. He also recounted that some of his battery's horses were so bellicose that it took three men to groom them: one to hold a twitch in the horse's mouth to steady him, one to hold a forefoot off the ground to keep the horse off balance, and a third to do the grooming![126]

The grooming of the horse was a rather thorough affair, and one can see by the following description that it was demanding work for a single man, let alone when an insolent horse forced a tripling of the grooming team:

> *You must start brushing your horse at the off-hand right quarter, and progress steadily toward the head, moving your brush in a circular motion with the coat and against it. You must then cross to the near side of the horse (which is his left side) and brush him on top and underneath, brush his legs, and finally add the last finishing touches on mane and tail.*[127]

As the lot of the drivers were to be mounted directly upon the horses they managed, those who were chosen for this employ were preferred to be of lighter build and stature. As Edgar Wallace pointedly observed, the horses had enough of a chore getting the gun from place to place without burdening them with a heavy man atop their back.[128]

We return now to the next class of artillerymen among the ranks, namely those who ensured the batteries could communicate with each other and the supported infantry, the signallers and telephonists. As the artillery is, naturally, dispersed about the battlefield, with forward observers living in among the infantry and the guns being positioned to the rear, communications were critical. Signallers were an important part of the artillery team; their job was to ensure that orders were passed quickly, clearly, and concisely. They were responsible for passing messages and fire orders by telephone wire, semaphore, and even Morse code.[129] Prior to the war, it had been envisaged that the signallers of the artillery batteries and infantry battalions would be soldiers of the Signals Service; however, it was soon discovered that there was inherent benefit in ensuring those soldiers were members of the unit and familiar with the unit's technical and tactical procedures. It was therefore decided that signallers assigned to artillery units would be members of artillery corps.[130]

Signallers were employed throughout the battery, their duties alternating among the command post, the gun line, the observation post, and the wagon line. The signaller was normally more educated than the drivers and gunners, as his tasks were far more technical in nature. Any errors he made could lead to far more unfortunate outcomes than mistakes by a gun detachment member or a horse driver. As F.H. Cooper of the South Africa Artillery recalled of artillery signallers' duties, "A slip of memory or an error in one figure of the range or deflection ordered may start 30 seconds' fiery death toward our own front line, instead of the enemy's before the tragedy can be seen and stopped."[131]

There were definitely some benefits to being an artillery signaller. They were usually not required to do fatigues, as the gunners were, and they were given a horse to themselves to ride as the battery moved from position to position.[132] The downside to their employment was the shift work required of them, as the telephones had to be monitored constantly. Hugh Kay recalls the humorous protestations of signaller Teasdale of the 43rd Battery when woken for his telephone watch in the middle of the night: "Damn telephone! As bad as a baby! Needs somebody to look after it all the time! Ought to have a nurse!"[133]

Telephones were not the only instrument that the artillery signaller employed to pass his messages. Where telephone communication could not be established, lamps would be used to send messages in Morse code to the firing battery. The Lucas Lamp was the means by which these Morse signals were delivered, and the device was in fact invented by an

artillery officer for just such a task. Two variants of the lamp were created, one that employed electric accumulators and was extremely powerful, and another smaller variant that used smaller batteries and was employed in forward positions, such as artillery observation posts, as a backup should the telephone wire be cut by enemy shelling.[134] The Lucas Lamp was first used at the Somme, where it received rave reviews for its performance, and it was adopted thereafter as the main signal lamp of the British and imperial forces. It was so effective that it could even send clear signals in daylight. [135]

Communication was of course critical to ensuring the rounds fired by the guns were both on time and on target. We turn now to a discussion of that most important – perhaps *the* most important – tool in the artillery's arsenal, the true weapon of the artillery: the projectile.

LEFT: 18 pounder artillery shell (Canadian War Museum)

Projectiles

It is a common misperception that the weapon of the artillery is the gun or cannon. Nothing could be further from the truth. The true weapon of the artillery is the projectile, for it is the projectile that produces the desired effect upon the enemy. The gun is only a means of delivery. Brigadier-General A.L. Pemberton, who served in the Royal Artillery during the Second World War and won the Military Cross, articulated this concept beautifully when he wrote in his history of the development of artillery tactics and equipment that "the weapon with which the gunner fights is the shell. Gunnery, reduced to its simplest terms, is the art of delivering the shell at the right place, at the right time, in the right quantity, and of the right quality to achieve the desired object."[136] In using the term "the desired object," Pemberton is referring to the *effect* of the shell, also referred to as the projectile, on the target, a question we addressed in Chapter 1. The gunners who bombarded Vimy Ridge were equipped with a number of different projectiles to choose from; however, to understand how those projectiles produced their effect, a basic understanding of the design of projectiles, as well as the components of fuse, shell, and propellant, is a necessity.

Fuses

In its earliest and most basic form, that of a cannon ball, artillery shells were solid and were designed to smash into fortress walls or enemy personnel and use sheer kinetic energy to do their work. Early shells included arrows and, in medieval times, even biological weapons such as diseased animal carcasses, which were lobbed over city walls by catapult. As time passed and the science of artillery evolved, visionary practitioners of fire support realized that the shell could be modified, filled with explosive, and thus do something other than simply smash into the target when it neared the enemy. Consequently, the *fuse* became a critical element of the artillery projectile. As Belgian army Captain Charles Borman, inventor of the Bormann time fuse, which revolutionized the employment of shrapnel shells, wrote in 1862, "The fuse therefore, is the *soul*, the *groundwork* of any system of explosive projectile [emphasis added]."[137] The eruption of the Great War led to a concomitant eruption of fuses as the scientific and technical effectiveness of the artillery was improved throughout the conflict. In fact, more types of artillery fuses were developed during the four years of the First World War than had been developed in the fifty years leading up to it.[138]

There were three classifications of fuses in use in the British Artillery during the First War: percussion fuses, time fuses, and a combination time and percussion fuse.[139] Percussion fuses were designed to operate once they struck an object, and had several sub-classifications of fuses. Direct action fuses required a heavy blow to the head, or nose, of the fuse at the leading edge of the projectile to cause it to function. Inside the fuse was a copper disk fitted to the very nose of the fuse, and attached to it, facing away from the nose of the fuse, was a steel needle. When the shell struck something, the nose of the fuse would collapse, pushing the steel needle onto a detonator, causing the fuse to function and explode the shell. Direct action impact fuses were similar, but were constructed in such a manner as to require a harder blow for the nose of the fuse to collapse and explode the shell. Graze fuses, however, were very sensitive. Inside the fuse was a small free-floating pellet carrying a detonator. This pellet would be pushed rearward in the fuse due to the shock of firing, but when the fuse grazed something, the shell would slow and the inertia of the pellet and detonator would carry it forward, striking an igniter that caused the detonator to explode the shell. Finally, the direct-action delay fuse was designed to function like the direct action fuse, but instead of the steel needle being forced back onto a detonator that would cause the shell to explode, it lit a column of burning composition, not unlike gunpowder, in a small tube. This powder would burn from the igniting end to the bottom of the tube, which would take a fraction of a second, and then ignite the detonator that would explode the shell. This imparted a slight delay on the shell functioning, allowing it to penetrate ground, earthworks, or wire before functioning.[140]

The percussion fuses in use by the British and Canadian artilleries during the First World War underwent a significant evolution and improvement during the war. Initially, the 101 fuse was employed, but it was found to be unreliable. This was especially the case when it came to using artillery to destroy wire entanglements, as the 101 was not caused to detonate by the wire, but rather by the ground underneath. The resulting delayed explosion of the projectile was normally insufficient to actually cut the wire. This lamentable state of affairs remained in place until the introduction of a much more effective fuse in the spring of 1917.[141]

Known as the No. 106 fuse, it was a marked improvement over its predecessor and was much quicker to detonate. Prior to the introduction of the 106 fuse, artillery percussion fuses still had a slight delay before functioning, and often the striking of barbed wire would be insufficient to cause the fuse to function. As a result, the shell would bury itself into the ground before exploding, causing much of the fragmentation and concussive blast to be absorbed by the ground and leaving the barbed wire intact. The 106 fuse was much more sensitive – striking barbed wire did cause it to function – so the explosion was also far more instantaneous than that of its predecessors. Consequently, the shell of the 106 fuse exploded earlier, without burying itself too deeply into the ground, resulting in more of the concussive blast and fragmentation propagating into the surrounding area rather than being absorbed by the ground. As more fragmentation was expelled into the air by the shell, the efficacy of the round to cut barbed wire and provide anti-personnel effects increased exponentially.

The tactical improvement wrought by the development of the No. 106 fuse warranted special mention in the final dispatch of Field-Marshal Haig. In 1918 he wrote:

> *The invention of a new fuse known as "106," which was first used in the battle of Arras, 1917, enabled wire entanglements to be easily and quickly destroyed and so modified our methods of attacking organized positions. By bursting the shell the instant it touched the ground and before it had become buried, the destructive effect of the explosion was greatly increased. It became possible to cut wire with a far less expenditure of time and ammunition, and the factor of surprise was given a larger part in operations.*[142]

Another benefit of the 106 fuse seems to have been the moral effect of its explosion, which was much louder than that of its predecessors. It was recorded in the *60th Canadian Field Artillery Battery Book* that "the new instantaneous fuse No. 106 was fitted to the H.E. This latter combination formed a shell which was unrivalled in its offensive power; the rending crash of a well-burst '106' has a demoralizing effect which must be felt to be appreciated, as all know who have been near the [mean point of impact] of a battery when it is shooting short."[143]

While instantaneous percussion fuses were an important part of the artillery arsenal, it was equally important to be able to burst shells in the air, a feat accomplished during the First World War by the use of a time fuse. As its name implies, a time fuse is a fuse that can be set to burst a shell at a pre-determined time after firing, making it possible for the shell to function in the air, prior to impact. The fuse accomplishes this through the use of a "bursting charge" ignited by a chemical burning in the fuse. The fuse contains an amount of this chemical composition, and setting the fuse would determine at what point along the burn chain the ignition would start, thereby determining the length of time between the firing of the gun and the functioning of the fuse, which caused the payload of the projectile to function, ideally in the air above the target.[144] As with the naturally occurring errors that produce an elongated beaten zone in the fall of shot, the time fuse also has a certain naturally occurring "zone" in which it may function. All that is to say, one hundred projectiles could be fired with the same time fuse setting, and no two rounds would burst at exactly the same height. Fortunately for the imperial artilleries, the British were able to increase the reliability of their time fuses, and one of the great technological benefits that the imperial artilleries had over their German opponents was an ability to detonate shrapnel shells at an effective height.[145]

Although critically important, a fuse was useless on its own, however, and it was the shell that carried the payload that provided the actual effect on the target.

Shells

There were a number of shells that could be employed against targets, the most abundant of which was the *shrapnel* round, a term that is commonly misused. It is erroneously understood that any chunk of metal emanating from an exploding shell, be it an artillery round or even a hand grenade, is shrapnel. These bits are more precisely known as *fragments* or *splinters*. Shrapnel, conversely, is a very specific artillery round that is intended "not to break up on explosion, but to act as a short gun [sic] and to propel the bullets forward at the maximum attainable velocity."[146]

The shrapnel shell was the product of a prolific eighteenth-century officer of the Royal Artillery, Henry Shrapnel. Shrapnel joined the British Army in 1779 and designed the round that would later carry his name in 1784, although it was not approved for use by the British Army until after 1803. Soon thereafter, it became an indispensable tool in the British arsenal; even the Duke of Wellington, of Waterloo fame, testified to its efficacy and warned his colleagues that the technology for so great a weapon should not fall into the enemy's hands.[147]

Shrapnel designed his round, which was originally officially known as spherical case shot, thus: it was fitted with a time fuse before firing that, when activated, ignited a bursting charge that was sufficient to open up the casing of the shell. Within the shrapnel shell were small balls, resembling musket balls or ball bearings. Upon the opening of the shell, the propagating explosion of the bursting charge and the forward inertia of the shell in flight caused the balls to fly outward in an expanding cone in the direction of the target. The shotgun-like effect was found to be more effective against personnel than the propagating fragments of the cannon ball upon its detonation.

The shrapnel shell constantly evolved over time, commensurate with the overall evolution of artillery pieces and ammunition. By the mid-1850s improvements to the time fuse had made them more reliable, and the addition of a wrought-iron diaphragm helped to prevent the premature activation of the internal powder that was meant to open the casing. By 1858, rifled cannon began entering service in European armies, and consequently in 1864 an elongated shrapnel shell for use in rifled guns was developed.[148]

The use of shrapnel shells in rifled guns provided further tactical improvements. The rotation of the shell in flight, created by the rifling in the gun barrel, caused these balls to fly further outwards when the body of the shell was opened by the bursting charge. Whereas the original spherical case shot produced a conical zone of shrapnel balls that was relatively narrow, the elongated shrapnel projectile for rifled guns produced a larger cone of very deadly and very fast-moving bullets. Thanks to its efficacy, eventually the shrapnel shell became the most abundant shell in use in imperial armies at the start of the Great War. For example, even though the 4.5-inch howitzers were incorporated into artillery brigades specifically for their heavier weight of fire and ability to destroy earthworks, a task for which shrapnel is ill-suited, 70 per cent of the ammunition stores for 4.5-inch howitzers during the war were shrapnel shells.[149]

In addition to the shrapnel shells, the imperial artilleryman had recourse to use HE projectiles. These shells were made of forged steel with thin walls and carried a heavy bursting charge that was detonated upon ignition by the attached fuse, causing the body of the shell to break open and produce splinters or fragments that propagated outward.[150] Unlike shrapnel shells, which had a projectile body filled with shrapnel balls, the HE round contained only the explosive composition. HE rounds were used primarily for the destruction of earthworks and wire, leaving shrapnel shells to be used in anti-personnel roles. Any anti-personnel effect was caused either by the discharge of splinters of the shell body – sharp, jagged chunks of deformed metal hurtling outward at great speed – or by its concussive blast. Although the splinters produced by the round were considered to be the primary means by which destruction of material or injury to enemy personnel were produced, one cannot fully discount the concussive effects of the blast. In July of 1915, Professor Vivian B. Lewis articulated these rather grisly effects thus:

> *The effect of the concussion frequently shows itself by the loss of memory, by nervous breakdown, and by heart trouble, many cases occurring in which men have been disabled without being killed, and have afterwards been found to be suffering from serious displacement of the heart.*[151]

R.B. Talbot Kelly recounted the concussive effects of HE shells landing near him. During the opening phases of the Battle of Passchendaele, he found himself standing near the lip of a crater chatting with a captain from a flanking battery when a German shell landed right next to them. The round burst after penetrating deep into the mud that pervaded the battlefield and thus created a large crater, at the bottom of which Talbot found himself. The colleague with whom he had been chatting was alive but had received thirty-six splinters in his body; one of his arms had nearly been severed and was held in place only by his tunic sleeve. Talbot initially thought he himself was unharmed and attributed his survival to very good fortune. However, several hours later he began to experience pain and realized his 'insides' had been concussed by the force of the explosion and were starting to swell. The next day he was evacuated to hospital "in the greatest agony and for five days and nights [he] got no sleep unless filled with morphia." His wounds eventually resulted in him missing the remainder of the war, and he recalled that "I was, from the first time in my life, an interesting medical case, and because no piece of shell had cut my skin and drawn blood [I] was officially unwounded. Yet I was on the danger list for some ten days before they dared to ship me to England."[152]

As the field artillery ordnance, namely the 18-pounders, would be used almost exclusively for anti-personnel firing during the opening phases of the war, the artilleries of the imperial armies restricted field artillery ammunition to shrapnel only, and were alone among the belligerent powers in not having HE shells in their field artillery organizations.[153] Initially, the construction of the HE shell and the nature of the explosive composition meant that it was not a very effective anti-personnel round. Technological advances that occurred shortly after the start of the war increased its efficacy in that regard, and as the war progressed through 1914, the War Office thought some HE shells for the field artillery might be useful. Although there was initially some reticence from General Headquarters about diversifying the nature of ammunition available for the guns, after receiving 1000 rounds of the new experimental HE rounds, they deemed the results so positive that a request was made for more. Initially General Headquarters requested the War Office to increase HE ammunition production to 25 per cent, and later increased the request to 50 per cent.[154]

Of course, for a gun to deliver a shell to a target where the fuse will cause it to function, it is necessary to have some manner of propelling that shell. By 1914 there were two ways in which shells housed the propellant that produced the requisite propelling force within the bore of the gun. Imperial artilleries used *fixed* and *separate* propelling charges with their guns, each having unique characteristics. Fixed ammunition projectiles were those rounds in which the casing that housed the propelling charge and the shell itself were mated, forming a single enclosed projectile, much like rifle bullets.[155] Separate ammunition projectiles were those in which the shell and the propelling charge were not permanently mated, which allowed the amount of propelling charge to be adjusted by the removal or addition of charge bags. This resulted in the ability to vary the muzzle velocity of the gun, which in turn allowed for the use of variable trajectories and therefore increased the flexibility of the range of the gun as compared to the more rigid trajectories produced by fixed ammunition.

The importance of consistency in the manufacture and storing of propellant charges should not be understated. In order to eliminate naturally occurring errors and provide for a consistent fall of shot, propellant must be manufactured in a consistent manner and a uniformity of the type and nature of propellant must be maintained on the gun lines.

Safety was also a goal of consistent manufacturing. Reginald Grant describes the horrific scene that befell his gun detachment when a defective cartridge detonated upon firing. He recalled ordering his team to fire the gun, and:

the next instant I felt my feet giving way from under me. The gun had blown off at the shield, the muzzle being blown to pieces, gas and fumes filled the air, the spokes were blown out of the wheels, splinters striking me on the feet and legs...there were several pieces of tube lying about...Graham yelled to know what had happened...he was then seized with shell shock and became uncontrollable. Park, who was leaning against the ammunition, was blown up, the shell having driven clean through his spine; the man loading shell had fragment driven clear through his stomach. The man leaning against the gun wheel was beheaded as cleanly as any king's executioner with his axe could do it, his head lying in the fireplace [a pit where the crew cooked meals and sought warmth]! The cartridge had exploded but the shell had not.[156]

Ammunition was obviously a critical element of the battle; the offensive doctrine in use at the time of the Battle of Vimy Ridge included a massive fire support system with a voracious appetite for ammunition. This ammunition had to be dumped on gun positions, and artillery organizations were instructed to ensure that prior to any large offensive, sufficient ammunition for preliminary bombardments and at least the first two days of the attack should be available at all firing positions.[157]

This seems a good point to discuss the strategic resupply of ammunition. This was a truly impressive network that began at the factory where it was made and ended at the battery that needed it to fire. The ammunition was shipped from the factory over land to a port, then by ship over the channel, then forwarded to a railhead, which was a point along a rail line in the rear area of a Corps. From this point, it was brought forward to the divisional ammunition park, which was an artillery dump in the divisional area. From that point, the divisional ammunition column, using horsed four-wheel wagons, brought the ammunition forward to an artillery dump in the divisional area, where the brigade ammunition columns, or in the case of heavy or siege batteries, the battery ammunition column, claimed their ammunition allotments and brought them forward to the respective brigades.[158]

Guns, Howitzers, Cannons, and Mortars

Having considered the projectile in detail, we now turn our attention to the method of delivering that projectile – the gun.

By the start of the First World War, most guns and howitzers were known as *quick-firing* (QF) or *breech-loaded* (BL), although both were actually loaded at the breech, the portion of the gun at the rear of the barrel. What distinguished a gun as quick firing was simply that their rate of fire was much greater than the BL variant. This was accomplished via special types of breech and firing mechanisms, including a recoil brake that allowed for quicker loading and firing. Additionally, QF guns used the previously mentioned fixed charge, in which the propelling charge was enclosed in a metallic cartridge case that sealed the propelling gases within the bore, not unlike an oversized rifle cartridge. Breech-loaded guns, by contrast, were those in which the charge was not enclosed in a metal case, but rather in cloth bags. The sealing of the breech was accomplished by a device in the breech mechanism that made the breech open more slowly than was the case with quick-firing guns. Finally, in breech-loaded guns, the charge bags were placed directly into the bore behind the projectile. When the gun was fired, the bore and the face of the breech would seal the propelling gases inside.[159]

The majority of artillery equipment that served the imperial artilleries of the Great War were the progeny of a complete re-equipment of the Royal Artillery in the decade leading up to the war, based on what can best be described as failures of the artillery during the Boer War and the appreciation of the effects of new artillery weapons in the Russo-Japanese War.[160] In the sections that follow, we shall see how many of the guns in the Great War imperial arsenal had their origins in the technical

ABOVE: 18 pounder field gun. (Canadian War Museum)

evolution of the artillery after the Franco-Prussian War of 1871, as well as the lessons learned by the British in the Boer War, and their observations gleaned from the Russo-Japanese War of 1905.

Field Artillery: 18-pounders

The most numerous of the guns in imperial artillery parks was the 18-pounder gun, which was the backbone of the divisional artilleries of the imperial armies. The story of the conception, design, adoption, and deployment of the 18-pounder goes well beyond the decisions made by British military leaders; in reality, the 18-pounder was conceived based on lessons learned in the Franco-Prussian War of 1870–71, as well as the Boer War of 1899–1902. Its creation was part of a European revolution in military affairs known as the quick-fire revolution, which resulted in an arms race among the future belligerents of the Great War. Consequently, to understand how the 18-pounder came to be the gun of imperial divisional artilleries, one must begin the narrative with an analysis of the French and German reactions to the results of the Franco-Prussian War[161]

The Franco-Prussian War was fought between France and a confederation of Germanic states led by the Kingdom of Prussia between July 1870 and January 1871. It is beyond the scope of this book to go into detail concerning the geo-strategic machinations that brought the two entities to war, but suffice to say it was rooted in the impending power imbalance as the Germanic states coalesced into a single confederation and threatened to unseat France as the dominant continental power. Despite having enjoyed military supremacy in Europe for an extended period, upon the outbreak of the conflict the French army found itself outgunned by its Prussian adversaries who, in their field artillery organizations, employed the Krupp-manufactured, steel-barrelled, breech-loading 90mm C/61 cannon. The French were soundly beaten by the Prussians and embarrassed by their performance. The particularly lacklustre performance of the French artillery in comparison to its Germanic adversary prompted the French to undertake a major improvement of their artillery park. Conversely, the Germans were inclined to bask in the success of the Krupp C/61 and were less motivated to investigate technological advances. Nonetheless the C/61s were getting old, so in 1873 the Prussians introduced a slightly improved C/73, which kept the same calibre as the older 61 variant but included some upgrades, including a rifled barrel.

The first French effort to rearm their artillery resulted in the breech-loading 90mm de Bange 1877 field gun, named after its inventor, Colonel Charles Ragnon de Bange of the French army. The de Bange lacked a recoil system, however, and consequently upon firing, it rolled back 1–2 metres from the shock of discharge, after which the gun crew had to push it back into firing position, reload, and fire again. Because of this cumbersome and laborious process, the French gunners manning the de Bange could maintain a rate of fire of only one round every five minutes.[162] This slow rate of fire, combined with the relative lack of range compared to the German C73, led the French to redouble their efforts to find a way to increase their artillery's effectiveness vis-à-vis their German nemeses, and the answer came, ironically, from a German engineer.

Konrad Haussner was an engineer from Ingolstadt, Germany, who initially worked for the Prussian state arsenal and then later for Krupp, Germanys' biggest private arms firm. He posited that a recoil system could be created, using a sort of hydraulic piston, that would allow the gun barrel to recoil upon firing, but then force the barrel back into firing position automatically, obviating the need for the gunners to physically push the whole gun back into position and thus drastically increasing the rate of fire. He presented his ideas to his Prussian superiors, who, uncomfortable with such a radical departure from centuries of artillery practice, were not smitten with the concept, thinking the shock of firing would damage the recoil system. Nonetheless, he patented his invention in Germany and France but forgot, in January of 1892, to pay the fees to extend the patent in France. Consequently, his design came to the attention of General Charles Mathieu, the director of artillery for the French army, who recognized not only the potential in the design but also the possible threat it represented to France should the Germans develop such a weapon system first.[163]

Mathieu quickly consulted with the French army's Artillery Technical Committee, who eventually brought the War Ministry's artillery workshop into discussions, and by May 1894, the French army had ordered six prototypes of a 75mm recoil-absorbing, quick-fire gun. Although by no means perfect, these first prototypes were able to fire twenty-two rounds per minute. Further refinements followed, and in 1896 the Superior War Committee endorsed the weapon, which went into mass production under immense secrecy shortly thereafter. The new gun was finally disclosed to the general public on Bastille Day 1899 as the famed *soixante-quinze*.[164]

Having enjoyed artillery supremacy during the Franco-Prussian War, the Germans were surprisingly uninterested in adopting revolutionary technical approaches to fire support. The Germans clung to their tried-and-true Krupp C73 as their primary field piece. By 1892, when the French were beginning to develop their recoil-absorbing quick-firer, the Germans found that their venerable C73s were aging: barrels were wearing, and carriages were starting to strain. The Germans therefore asked Krupp to design them a quick-firing field gun of their own. The company produced several options, but the Germans were still leery about the effectiveness of the new-fangled recoil-absorbing system. In the end, they spurned the quick-firer and instead adopted the 77mm Feldkanone (FK) 96, which, due to the lack of recoil-absorbing system, was a much lighter and thus more mobile gun. The Germans viewed this greater degree of mobility as an advantageous characteristic during a war of movement and manoeuvre, which they assumed would be the defining characteristic of any future conflict on the European continent. But while the FK 96 could certainly move from firing position to firing position with speed and alacrity, it could muster a rate of fire of only 5–9 rounds per minute, admittedly much faster than the Krupp C/73 but woefully slower than the soixante-quinze.[165]

The German decision to adopt the FK 96 gave the French the initial lead in the quick-firing arms race in the years leading up to the Great War, leaving the Germans caught on the back foot when the soixante-quinze burst on the scene on Bastille Day 1899. Horrified at the disparity in the rate of fire between the French 75 and the FK 96, the Germans quickly revisited the idea of developing a recoil-absorbing quick-firer. The result was the FK 96 n/A, an upgraded variant of the FK 96 that incorporated a recoil-absorbing-system. Although this was an improvement, it still had a rate of fire only half that of the French 75. Nonetheless, the piece was approved for use in 1904, and was distributed to the German divisions in 1908.[166]

These developments in recoil-absorbing field pieces were watched closely by the military leaders in Great Britain. As early as 1893, the future commander-in-chief of the British army, Lord Roberts, was advocating for the adoption of quick-firing guns by the Royal Artillery, and the War Office did, in the waning years of the nineteenth century, conduct a few technical experiments with converted 12- and 15-pounder breech-loaded guns.[167] But, inasmuch as the British were influenced by the technological developments on the continent, they were, perhaps, even more influenced by the shocking disparity experienced by British gunners during the Boer War. On the South African veldt, the British discovered that their 12-pounders were embarrassingly outgunned by the German Krupp and Schneider field pieces used by the Boers. At Stormberg, Magersfontein, and Colenso, British fire support had been found to be severely wanting.[168] In response, in 1900 the director general of ordnance, General Sir Henry Brackenbury, was tasked to procure a new field piece with greater range for the British Field and Horse Artillery. As an interim solution, Brackenbury purchased eighteen batteries' worth of Erhardt 15-pounder guns from, ironically, a German manufacturer. This was merely a temporary solution, however. In 1901, Lord Roberts, who was now the chief of the imperial general staff, was ordered to recall certain technically and tactically astute commanders of artillery brigades and batteries who were actively engaged in operations in South Africa in order to form an equipment committee with a mandate to determine the technical requirements for a new field gun.[169] In 1901, the Special Committee on Horse and Field Artillery Equipment was established with cabinet approval, under the direction of Major-General George Marshall.[170]

After extensive consultations, the committee produced the *Précis of Conditions to be Fulfilled by Proposed New Equipments*, through which it solicited industrial submissions for a quick-firing gun. This was to be fitted with a shield and capable of delivering effective shrapnel fire up to 6000 yards. It would have a total weight of 28 hundred-weight (cwt) for the 13-pounder horse variant and 38 cwt for the 18-pounder field variant.[171] It is interesting to note that an 18-pound projectile was selected, although it was two pounds heavier than the French 75-mm projectile, which was the standard by which Western quick-fire guns of the early nineteenth century were measured. The decision to use a heavier projectile was taken because, due to their experience in the Boer War, where lighter shells had less effect against dug-in infantry, the British wanted a heavier round that would have a more significant effect against entrenched riflemen.[172] The most promising designs were selected, and in 1902 several specimen guns were built and tested. Ultimately, however, no British manufacturer was able to produce a single piece that met all the stated technical requirements, the most important being increased range. Consequently, Brackenbury chose the best parts from multiple pieces: from Armstrong he selected new barrels, from Vickers the recoil

ABOVE: Canadian gunners conducting artillery training. (LAC 3405482)

system, and from the Royal Arsenal at Woolwich, a carriage – the part of the gun upon which the barrel and recoil system are mounted. The Frankensteinian progeny of this alchemic amalgamation was the Ordnance QF 13-pounder, designed for use with horse artillery batteries supporting cavalry divisions, and its heavier relative, the Ordnance QF 18-pounder for use in field batteries.[173] Production orders for 18-pounders were placed in late 1904, and the new guns began arriving in British and Canadian artillery brigades in 1906.[174] When the new guns first arrived in Canada they received a warm welcome from the Canadian Militia gunners, who found them to be a significant improvement over their predecessor, the 12-pounder: the gun drill was simpler, and the handling of the battery when manoeuvring was easier.[175]

The gun itself weighed 2800 lbs, and the limber, a box-like trailer fitted to the gun, weighed roughly 1700 lbs when filled with its allotment of twenty-four rounds, all of which were pulled, as we saw previously, by a team of six light draft horses.[176] The 18-pounder barrel could be elevated 16 degrees and traversed 4 degrees left and right before manhandling –which is to say physically pivoting the gun – by the detachment was required. [177] At the start of the war, the 18-pounder was able to achieve a maximum range of 6200 yards with its shrapnel shells; however, over the course of the conflict improvements to the carriage allowed the barrel to be elevated beyond the initial 16 degrees, and by the time the war had ended, the 18-pounder's range with shrapnel had increased to 9000 yards.[178] Ten personnel were required to operate the gun: six who manned the gun itself, and four who formed a reserve to draw upon in the case of casualties and to spell off fatigued members.[179]

Field Artillery: 4.5-inch Howitzer

In addition to the 18-pounder, the British divisional artilleries also featured a QF 4.5-inch howitzer within each brigade. Another pre-war piece, the 4.5-inch howitzer, like the 18-pounder, was also a product of the British experience of the Boer War. In fact, the equipment committee that convened to determine the requirements for a new field gun was also tasked to find a replacement for the aging 5-inch breech-loading howitzer used in South Africa. The conditions for the new gun were inspired by the unpleasant experience that many of the committee members had shared when facing the German-made Krupp field howitzers employed by the Boers.

It wasn't simply the performance of the Krupp howitzers that prodded the British to pursue a field howitzer replacement. The decision also stemmed from their observation of the effects of fire in South Africa, as well as their analysis of the effect of artillery fire in Manchuria during the Russo-Japanese War of 1904–1905. In both cases the British remarked that the effect of shrapnel fired from a light gun with fixed ammunition against dug-in infantry was insufficient. The flat trajectory of a gun and the nature of the shrapnel burst meant defending infantry could take cover in trenches, or behind hills or knolls, and remain relatively safe. The plunging fire of a howitzer, which is to say the steeper angle of fall of the projectile accomplished by the higher elevations attainable, coupled with an HE round, was far more effective in these cases.[180]

British attempts to replicate the Krupp fell short, but by 1905 the committee were happy enough with the designs that had been submitted to them by industry to warrant a trial. It wasn't until 1908, however, that the trials proved successful enough for the committee to recommend the adoption of the 4.5-inch QF howitzer designed by Coventry Ordnance Works, although these didn't start arriving in British artillery brigades until 1910.[181]

In 1911 the Canadian government placed an order for twenty-seven 4.5-inch QF howitzers for service with the Canadian Artillery, but unfortunately, by the time the war broke out only seven of the pieces had been delivered.[182] The howitzer fired a 35-pound shell and, in a departure from the breech-loading process of the 5-inch howitzer it was meant to replace, it used separate ammunition. The new howitzer had several important new features: the barrel could be elevated to 45 degrees, and its projectiles could be fired at different muzzle velocities thanks to the employment of separate ammunition, wherein the propellant charge and casing, if used, and the actual projectile were 'mated' before loading, allowing the amount of propellant to be altered. This meant the 4.5-inch howitzer could employ "plunging" fire and drop rounds behind intervening crests up to a range of 7,200 yards, which the 18-pounder, with the flatter trajectory of its fixed ammunition, could not do.[183]

Siege and Heavy Guns: 6-inch Howitzer, the 60-Pounder and the 9.2-inch Howitzer

While 18-pounders and 4.5-inch howitzers were sufficient to suppress and neutralize the enemy, due to their high rate of fire, the siege-like nature of the war demanded a certain weight of shell to accomplish destruction tasks for targets such as dugouts, pillboxes, enemy batteries, and the like. This task was entrusted to the large-bore guns of the heavy and siege batteries. Slow to deploy and slow to fire due to the weight of the piece and the weight of the shell, these large-calibre bruisers were nonetheless powerful in terms of the amount of raw explosive they delivered to their targets.

Prior to the war, the siege and medium artillery of the Entente powers were, at best, neglected. Focused as they were on the forecasted war of speed and movement, the ponderous heavy artillery was considered an outlier. In field exercises conducted by the British in the years before the war, siege howitzers were often left out of the training altogether, and they were rarely even included in the orders of battle.[184] When the BEF arrived on the continent in August 1914, upon the outbreak of hostilities, there were just four heavy batteries, each of four guns, in the entire force.[185] The situation was no better in the French army, who were irretrievably wedded to closing with the enemy and dousing him with 75mm shells at close range. In such circumstances, they thought, why would anyone want to bring a heavy, slow, long-range gun? No less than General Joffre said, in 1914, "A mobile artillery, knowing how to use the terrain, will rarely have need of a long-range cannon to place itself a good distance from the enemy."[186] Of course, as we've seen, this assumption, like so many pertaining to fire support, was proved false when the battles of August 1914 demonstrated that firepower had become more important than mobility.[187]

The siege gun used by the imperial artilleries was the 6-inch 30-cwt breech-loaded howitzer. As with much of the equipment in the imperial artillery park, at the outbreak of the war the in-service 6-inch howitzer was old and obsolete, having been introduced into service in 1896. Moreover, it was cumbersome, weighing in at over 3100 lbs and thus slow to deploy.[188] It could achieve a range of only 5200 metres with its 118-lb shell and was seriously outgunned by the German 4.5-inch howitzer, which could fire out to 7000 metres.[189] As noted previously, in order to be technically a howitzer, the barrel must be capable of elevating beyond 45 degrees. The 6-inch howitzer, while mounted on its carriage, could elevate to only 35 degrees. An elevation of 70 degrees could be achieved, but it was possible only through a laborious process whereby the gun had to be placed on a mounting platform.[190] A replacement, the 6-inch 26-cwt howitzer, was designed by Vickers and began to arrive in France in 1915, although it wasn't fully deployed to all formations until late 1916.[191] The "new" 6-inch howitzer was much more effective and easier to deploy and fire than its predecessor, and it could achieve an elevation of 45 degrees without the need for a mounting platform. Like its smaller British cousin, the 4.5-inch howitzer, it used separate

ABOVE: Moving a howitzer into position, October 1916. (LAC 3395190)

ammunition and could thus provide excellent fire support to almost any range out to 11,000 yards with an 86-lb shell, or 9500 yards with a 100-lb shell.[192]

The breech-loading 60-pounder gun was the principal heavy-artillery piece of the Canadian Artillery. It fired its 60-pound projectile 10,000 yards, although it had the same limitations as its lighter cousin, the 18-pounder, in that its fixed ammunition did not allow for a great deal of variability in the ranges it was able to achieve. Like the 18-pounder and the 4.5-inch howitzer, the 60-pounder was also a child of the British experience in the Boer War. In October of 1902, a Heavy Battery Committee was formed to find a replacement for the British 4.7-inch gun, based on guidance from Lord Roberts that it have a range of 10,000 yards and weigh no more than 4 tonnes with a weight of shell as large as could be constructed. The committee dismissed both a new 4.7-inch and a 30-pounder gun in favour of a 60-pounder experimental gun made by Armstrong. Despite it being the best initial option, the Armstrong 60-pounder still required significant trials and improvements, particularly concerning its ability to travel over long distances. Consequently, it was not until 1905 that the committee recommended the adoption of the Armstrong breech-loading 60-pounder Mark I for employment in heavy batteries.[193]

We've seen that when the war started there was very little interest in using siege or heavy artillery, a philosophy that changed when the British realized the value of their weights of fire during siege warfare. Consequently, the number of 60-pounders in the imperial artillery grew substantially. Over time, certain minor technical changes to the guns' construction were made, producing two new variants. The first was known as the Mark I+ and the second as the Mark I++. These began arriving in imperial heavy batteries in February of 1915. While initially the pieces were pulled by teams of horses, eventually their weight required the use of Holt tractors instead of horse teams to move them around the battlefield, albeit very slowly.[194]

The largest gun in the Canadian arsenal was the monstrous 9.2-inch BL Siege Howitzer. The idea for the massive gun was first floated around 1910 when Coventry Ordnance Works was approached by the British military to construct an experimental heavy howitzer. Coventry undertook the development and produced the 9.2-inch howitzer, which was introduced into service in the summer of 1914. Like most other heavy artillery, it was initially not considered a necessary weapon for a war of movement, but its value became readily apparent when the ability to manoeuvre came to an end in the autumn of 1914. The first use of the 9.2-inch in a major action was at Neuve-Chappelle in November 1914, where it was promptly christened "Mother" by the gunners serving them.[195] The gun was so large that it had to be moved in three sections, each weighing approximately four and a half tons.[196] In order to reduce the overall weight of the piece, Coventry designed it to have a short barrel, which in turn led to concerns that the gun might rear up when fired at lower elevations. To compensate for this risk, the design incorporated a box fitted to the front of the gun. This was meant to be filled with sand so that when the gun fired at a low elevation, the weight of the box would keep the gun from rearing up. Unfortunately for the gunners manning the piece, this meant that upon coming into action, they were required to shovel 9 tonnes of earth into the earth-box before the gun could fire![197] Eventually, twelve of these guns were acquired by the Canadian Artillery and placed in two siege batteries.[198]

Working the heavies was a laborious task. The enormous guns were dug into gun pits to protect the gun and the crew from being seen by hostile observers and from the fragmentation of incoming hostile artillery rounds. For further protection, sandbags and earth were piled on the sides, and the pit was covered by camouflage netting. George Kempling happened to observe a crew digging in a 60-pounder gun pit near his position and recorded the events in his diary, noting:

These emplacements are built by digging about 2 feet into the ground then building a rough strong framework of timbers, railway rails, iron girders, corrugated sheet iron, and mesh wire about 10 ft. high by 8 ft. wide by 20 ft. long. All this structure is heavily built around and over with sandbags and the whole mounded over with loose earth and (looking from an aeroplane like a mound) sodded. This is nearly always done in or behind a small clump or line of low trees, such as willows. The floor of the emplacement is made of layers of broken bricks, then broken stone, then concrete. The timbers and iron come up already cut and fitted together, taken apart and packed up behind the lines somewheres. The building of a casement is about the only work done in broad daylight so the quicker it is done the better for

Fritzies aeroplanes are everywhere spying and if the job is found out a few shells put it nowhere.[199]

Daily routine for the gunners manning the heavy and siege guns was tiresome. One veteran described it thus:

Each gun crew first sets about putting the gun and pit in order in case of a sudden call for action. There are the shells, each two hundred pounds, to lug from dump piles on to shell platforms convenient for loading the guns. Cartridge cans and fuse boxes are to be made ready and convenient for handling. The gun and platform has to be carefully looked over for position and backing so that there may be the least possible chance of necessary delay when in action.... When the gun is not set in line of fire the scotches, or large wedge-shaped blocks for the gun to recoil against, must be evenly placed behind the wheels.[200]

An anonymous author, writing a letter home to his father that was included in a collection of parishioners' letters published by Trinity Methodist Church in Toronto, described his first experience observing the execution of a fire mission from the gun line of a heavy battery:

A row of great shells is ready laid out, fuses are adjusted and charges ready at hand. The order to load is given. Two men lift a shell and place it on the carrier. They carry it to the gun. Another places in the cordite cartridge and closes the breach [sic], the officer calls out a number of figures, the gun layer turns a number of small wheels, the gunner inserts the lanyard and all stand back. The officer looks at his watch and waits. After an interval a caution is given, when everyone holds his ears. The command 'fire' is given. The gunner pulls the lanyard then ensues a terrific ear-splitting, heart-stopping, earth-shaking crash, a ten-foot spurt of flame, the gun recoils on its springs and slowly rises to position again, a quickly diminishing scream and the great shell is on its way.[201]

While the use of siege and heavy guns was initially disparaged, by the end of the war their number had grown exponentially. Having crossed the channel in August 1914 with only four batteries of four 60-pounder guns each, at the armistice the BEF had in its order of battle eighty-seven heavy and 430 siege batteries.[202]

Trench Mortars

The development of mortars in the British Army was very much a response to the superiority the Germans had established with that weapon, along with the mortar's usefulness during static trench warfare.

Mortars have existed since the sixteenth century, but prior to the Great War, they never figured largely in any major conflict.[203] That was to change markedly during the First World War, and it was the Germans who held the lead in elevating the mortar to a key element in the modern fire support network. The mortar came to prominence in the German army alongside the German penchant for howitzers, which will be discussed later, based on the perceived tactical role of these two unique pieces of equipment. While the French 75mm and the British 18-pounder were designed with a view to providing rapid fire over direct sights in support of a mobile infantry engagement, the Germans appreciated early on that if they were required to advance through the Low Countries or even against the French in the Lorraine region, they would encounter a series of fixed defensive positions that would need to be overcome. Rapid shrapnel fire from light field pieces would have no effect on these defences, so the Germans concluded that howitzers and mortars, which could fire a heavier shell at a higher trajectory, would be required to reduce the anticipated defensive works. Thus, alongside field and heavy howitzers, the Germans looked to increase their stocks of mortars and produced, the Minenwerfer.[204]

The Minenwerfer, which is translated literally as mine-thrower, was introduced into the German arsenal in 1910. Boasting a large calibre of 250mm, it could fire a 213-pound projectile up to 400 metres. Later, a smaller and more mobile version with a calibre of 170mm, capable of firing a 112-pound projectile out to 750 metres, was introduced.[205] To these were added, several months after the war began, the 76mm light Minenwerfer, which sported a range of over a kilometre. By the summer of 1916, these became the most numerous of the mortars in the German arsenal.[206]

Faced with German superiority in mortars, the British and French immediately undertook to close the gap. As early as October 20, 1914, Sir John French wrote to the War Office that the BEF required an updated form of artillery to address the static nature of trench warfare. He proposed a piece that was easily mobile and that could fire a shell up to 200 lbs to a range of at least 400 metres using high elevation.[207]

The French, for their part, introduced the Mortier de 58mm type 2, also known as the 58T or, more affectionately, the *crapouillot*, which translates as "little toad," due to its appearance. The 58T was first trialled in combat in January 1915 then deployed within formed mortar units of the French army in February 1915.[208] As the name implied, the mortar had a steel barrel of 58.3mm calibre capable of firing three different shells, one of 40 lbs, one of 44 lbs, and one of 77 lbs.[209]

The British response was the Stokes Mortar. It was designed by its namesake, engineer Sir Wilfrid Stokes, who recalled his motivations, coming mere months after General French's appeal to the War Office, in a lecture to the Junior Institution of Engineers in June of 1918. "The beginning of the present war found us quite unprepared, more particularly in weapons suitable for trench warfare," he intoned. "There were four service trench howitzer designs in use, all more or less slow, heavy, and difficult to manufacture and use. It was suggested to me that we were badly off for 'frightfulness' at the front, and that our men were not having a fair chance. Could I think of anything?"[210] Think of something he did.

Stokes rolled up his sleeves and went to work. His concept was a 3-inch (81mm) mortar, and using trial and error he produced several prototypes, improving the mortar incrementally to make it more effective both in firing and in portability for the soldiers who would carry it into battle. Eventually, he produced a 3-inch, a 2-inch, and a 4-inch variant. In December of 1914 he shared his concept with the War Office, and was aided a month later by H.A. Gwynne, who was the editor of *The Morning Post*. Gwynne become aware of Stokes' invention and wrote to Colonel Fitzgerald, the military secretary to Lord Kitchener, informing him of the progress of Stokes' mortar development. The concept piqued the interest of the military authorities, particularly those in GHQ in France, and the weapon was put to several tests. Although it had several failures, it was nonetheless wholeheartedly embraced by military leadership deployed on the continent, and soon the British placed an order for 800 3-inch mortars and 200 rifled 4-inch mortars. Eventually the 4-inch was abandoned, as was a 2-inch variant that, although of smaller calibre, fired a larger 50-pound projectile.

The 2-inch variant was called, colloquially, a "toffee apple" bomb due to resembling the carnival treat: it consisted of a long stick with the large 50-lb bomb atop it. The stick was slid down the barrel like a normal mortar projectile, and while the bomb itself was too big to slide down the barrel, the igniter was on the base of the stick, so the round fired without the bomb actually going down the barrel. In 1917, the toffee apple mortar was replaced by the 6-inch Newton mortar, as GHQ in France reported that it was "a source of danger, owing to its tendencies to blow back into our trenches."[211]

By the summer of 1916, the imperial armies had standardized their mortar parks. All the variants of the light mortar were removed with the exception of the 3-inch variant, which became the standard light mortar for imperial armies. It fired a 10.45-pound mortar bomb to a range of 450 metres, where it produced an explosive danger radius roughly equalling that of a 75mm shell.[212] The light mortars were assigned to brigades and organized into batteries of eight mortars; these were further subdivided into two half-batteries of four. They were manned by infantrymen and were organizationally an element of an infantry battalion, to be deployed by the battalion commander within his boundaries and used to support the battalion commander's tactical mission.[213] The 6-inch Newton medium mortars were divided into batteries of four, manned by artillerymen, and were part of the divisional artillery. All of this was overseen by an artillery captain at the Divisional Artillery Headquarters, whose duty it was to supervise and control the heavy and medium trench mortar batteries on behalf of the Commander, Royal Artillery (CRA).[214]

Artillery Organization

We turn now to the question of how these different pieces were organized for use. During the Great War, artillery was organized along hierarchical lines; very little has changed since then. At the very bottom level was the gun, which was manned by a collection of artillerymen, referred to as a *detachment* or *sub-section*.[215] Each gun was given a letter to designate it, so each was thus known affectionately by its crew as A-Sub or B-Sub and so on, depending on the number of guns in the battery.[216] Each type of gun had a different size of detachment, depending on its calibre and role, but in general terms the overall detachment structure was consistent. It was commanded by a non-commissioned officer, usually a sergeant, and consisted of a number of artillerymen whose job it was to lay (that is, to elevate and traverse the barrel to the proper elevation and bearing), load, and maintain the artillery piece. The most abundant guns in the imperial arsenal, the 18-pounder and the 4.5-inch howitzer, were manned by detachments of ten personnel. Individual guns were organized into *sections* of two guns, which were commanded by a junior officer, which is why the guns themselves were referred to as *sub-sections* or simply a *sub*.

Gun detachments were uniquely organized. Every gunner had his job to do, and was thus allocated a certain title that denoted his position. What follows here is a description of how the tasks and responsibilities of a gun detachment operating an 18-pounder gun were organized. Of course, different equipment might have slightly different responsibilities dependent on the unique nature of the gun, but the division of labour among the crew of an 18-pounder, the most numerous variant of field gun in the imperial arsenal, provides an excellent illustration of how Great War gun detachments were organized.

The sergeant in command of the gun detachment was also known as Number 1. It was he who exercised overall control of the gun, supervised its deployment and its firing, and commanded its detachment of men. The second most senior man in the gun detachment was the Number 2, who was detailed to operate the breech of the gun and the brake, which kept the gun from rolling out of position. When the gun was brought into action in its new gun position, he, along with the Number 3, would *unlimber* the gun, which is to say unhook it from the limber to which it was attached. The Number 3, when the gun was in action, operated the telescope, which was used to view the gun's aiming point, and the dial sights, which set the elevation and bearing of fire of the gun. The Number 4 was responsible for loading the gun, while the Number 5 issued the ammunition and set the fuses with the assistance of Number 6. Numbers 7, 8, 9, and 10, normally the most junior men of the team, remained in the wagon lines and assisted in bringing ammunition forward, spelling off fatigued members of the gun detachment, and replacing casualties.[217] Cecil Longley of the RFA described the allocation of tasks in his memoir writing that after the order to load and fire was given: "[T]he breech is closed by No. 2 with a clang, No. 3 pulls the firing lever and – bang – followed by a long shrieking swish, getting fainter till – phut! … then you, or rather Nos. 4, 5 and 6, set fuses."[218]

By the time of Vimy Ridge, two or three sections comprised a battery commanded by an officer with the rank of major who was styled the battery commander, although in the first years of the war, the number of sections that constituted a battery fluctuated. The battery commander exercised overall command of the battery and was responsible for the technical and tactical deployment of the battery and the deployment of the observation post (OP) from which he, or an observing officer he so delegated, would observe the battery's zone of fire.[219]

The battery commander was assisted in his duties by several key personnel. The section leaders also acted as *reconnaissance officers*, who assisted with the technical occupation of a battery position, including the selection of the actual gun platforms. Although the battery commander was ultimately responsible for the reconnaissance of new gun positions, the duty was normally assigned to a subaltern who became known as the reconnaissance officer upon receipt of the task.[220]

Given his scope of responsibility, the battery commander's duties often demanded that he move about the battlefield between the wagon lines (more on these later), gun line, and OP. Consequently, junior officers were often tasked to act as *battery leaders* and were in voice or signal command of the guns, either in action or on the march, when the battery commander was absent.[221] Additionally, the battery had a *battery captain*, who acted as the second-in-command and was referred to as simply the "captain." The battery captain was responsible for all the administrative and support functions that a battery required in order to shoot, move, and communicate. He was in command of the wagon lines wherein ammunition and other stores were maintained, and where the limbers and teams of horses were held once the battery was in action. He was also in charge of organizing ammunition resupply and casualty replacement, and, most importantly, he was understudy to the battery commander and would take over command of the battery should the battery commander become a casualty.[222]

Life as a subaltern in an artillery battery was described by Alexander Thornton of the Royal Artillery thus: "[T]he routine of duties for an officer on duty with his battery, in the line, was, generally speaking, two days as a battery officer, two days at the battery OP (all day observation duty), and three days FOO [forward observation officer – officers tasked to observe and adjust the fall of artillery fire from forward positions] with the infantry."[223]

The backbone of the army is the non-commissioned officer corps, who provide experienced, tactical-level leadership to the enlisted personnel. Then, as now, it is essential for a battery commander to have a senior non-commissioned member to enforce discipline and to provide the commander with advice based on years of experience serving the guns. During the Great War, the senior non-commissioned member of the battery was the *battery-sergeant major*, who provided this assistance and advice to the battery commander and who was responsible for controlling the battery headquarters.[224]

In addition to the sections of guns, the battery also included the *wagon lines*, which were a collection of ammunition and supply wagons that were used to keep the battery firing. The wagon lines were situated away from the guns in order to ensure that any counter-battery fire aimed at the gun line would not also threaten the wagon lines and the stockpiles of ammunition they carried. Normally they would be sited far enough away to ensure their safety, but close enough to ensure communication and rapid resupply of ammunition. The local terrain and the availability of cover, as well the location of other units, dictated how far the wagon lines were removed from the guns, and from time to time they could be situated quite a distance from the guns, in some cases up to seven miles.[225] Harry Butters, an American citizen who joined the RFA, gives a description of the preparation of the wagon lines that shows the scope of the administrative and support elements of the battery that were to be found there.

> *Next day I spent very busily in installing the wagon lines on permanent basis – solid, well set up, picket lines for the horses – harness racks, properly lined in rear – wagons parked in column of route [a line facing in the same direction] under a hedge ready to hook in and move off at a moment's notice – men's bivouacs line along another hedge – Quartermaster's stores covered over – two kitchens for officers and men – officers' bivouac, etc., etc.*[226]

Removed as they were from the firing line, the wagon lines were used as a locale to send men for a rest, particularly the officers returning from duty at the OP where they had spent their time dodging bullets and shelling the enemy.

Oftentimes a rest was not to be had, however, for it was from the wagon lines that ammunition resupply to the gun line originated. Only so many rounds could be kept at the gun position, and when the action was hot and firing intense, resupply was critically important and all hands were required to assist in delivering the rounds to the guns. Of course, this was no mean task, particularly when the wagon lines were some distance from the firing pits. Reginald Grant, who served in the 1st Battery, CFA, recalled one instance when he volunteered to be the ammunition orderly after the original orderly had been felled by a shell splinter while delivering ammunition to the guns. He was dispatched to the wagon lines to deliver the order to bring the rounds forward to

ABOVE: Canadian artillery loading their limbers from a dump by the roadside. May, 1918 (LAC 3395370)

resupply the guns, so he duly mounted the limping horse, who had been injured in the strike, only minutes after his colleague had slumped out of the saddle dead. He galloped as fast as the lame horse could manage back to the wagon lines. Arriving at the quartermaster, he delivered his message: "Ten loads of ammunition wanted at once, sir; ammunition pretty nearly exhausted at the guns." At this,

> *[t]he Quartermaster blew his whistle – 'Stand to! Ammunition up!' he yelled. The sergeant then carried on; the men were standing easy by their horses waiting for the word… 'Prepare to mount! Mount! Walk—march! Trot!' yelled the Sergeant in quick succession, each command being executed with clock-like exactness, and they trotted from under cover of the trees where they were concealed from the airplanes and proceeded rapidly up the road under shell fire, bumping and stumbling along.[227]*

If the ammunition column made it to the gun line without grievous misadventure, it would deliver its precious cargo to the guns. Grant is once again an excellent witness to the way the men of the wagon lines, the drivers, and the gunners at rest worked with their colleagues in the gun pits to dump the ammunition, in this case in the middle of an active barrage when the ammunition was running low: "Chains of men were formed from the ammunition wagons into the gun pit," Grant recalled. "Shells were passed from hand to hand to the guns where the men were waiting [for] them, and I thought I saw tears of joy in the eyes of the Tommy as he caressed the first shell handed him… the gunners exploded [fired] them as fast as they were handed them."[228]

Despite their distance from the front lines, wagon lines were not completely immune from enemy action. Butters recalled a time when he was deployed to the wagon lines for four days of rest after spending a stressful period in action at the OP. As he relaxed, a German balloon flew overhead and mistook the wagon lines for a battery of heavy artillery. Butters and his colleagues were then subjected to an intensive bombardment of German six-inch guns. "I lost one man with his foot blown off," Butters recalled in a letter home, "but managed to get the horses away, and all clear with no further casualties. This, of course, added to the strain, and before the end of the week, through lack of sleep and the trouble preying on my mind – I had to take myself to the doctor."[229]

The sheer amount of ammunition, not to mention the various classes of resupply equipment and personnel in the wagon lines, meant its loss or damage would have wide-ranging ramifications for the battery. John McCartney-Filgate of the RFA remarked as such in his history of the 33rd Divisional Artillery with the simple observation that "the shelling of wagon lines is at all times most unsettling and likely to do great damage."[230]

A complete battery thus was composed of three functional elements: the resupply wagons in the wagon lines, several sections of guns, and the OP from which the fire of the battery was directed and coordination with the infantry was carried out.

Moving the battery about the battlefield was a challenge in its own right. Movement was initiated by receipt of orders from the artillery brigade headquarters indicating the time of movement and the location of the new position. At the prescribed time, the battery commander ordered "Prepare to advance" and issued the delegated battery leader with his instructions. The gun limbers and wagons were then brought forward to the firing line, and as they neared the guns the battery commander would order "Cease firing," which was the order for the gun crews to prepare to depart the position, followed by "Prepare to limber up." Upon this order the battery captain would dispatch the wagon lines to a rendezvous point where they would meet the guns and limbers, and the guns would be pulled out of action and attached to the gun limber. Once limbered, the guns moved independently to the position of assembly, the location of which was detailed by the battery captain.[231] From here the battery began their movement to the new position.

An artillery battery being a large organization, obviously it occupied a large swath of terrain when in action, and due to the weight of the guns and equipment, the route of march was necessarily along roads. However, in order to find a battery firing position large enough to accommodate the whole battery, often the gunners found themselves deployed in positions some distance from a road. Consequently, upon receiving their orders to move, the gunners would sometimes have to cover rough, shell-pocked ground from the battery position to the road they were to move along. In such cases, the gunners would be ordered to dismount from the limbers and wagons and walk along beside the guns to alleviate the strain on the horses – and the gunners' backsides.

Colin Hutchison recalled one such experience of his battery moving out of a position while under fire after a German battery had been spotted coming into action nearby:

> We got the order 'prepare to advance.' The horses came up and we had just hooked in when over came four ranging rounds from the German battery. We got the order 'Column of sections, from the centre, dismount the gunners! Walk, march!' We had about ½ a mile of absolutely open ground to cover to reach the road, and proceeded to do it at the walk. The next four rounds from the German battery (7.7 cm) got our line and was also pretty fair for range. We continued to walk out of action and did so under fire, getting about 20 rounds in all into us. Two men were hit, one poor devil had to be left behind.[232]

The battery commander and his reconnoitring team would depart on horseback to find the new position and select the appropriate gun positions for the battery to occupy. This was the *technical reconnaissance* of the new position, which focused on establishing the battery firing line and carrying out all the technical drills required to ensure the battery was able to fire. Batteries deployed their guns in gun pits at intervals, when possible, of at least 20 yards.[233] When ordered to adopt a new battery position, each battery would reconnoitre alternative gun positions so that should they be forced to abandon the primary position, for example due to enemy fire, they could readily move to the alternative position and promptly return to action.[234] The reconnaissance officer commanded the team tasked to prepare the new position; this included signallers, who accompanied the team and were responsible for laying wire for the battery to use upon its arrival. Once the wire had been laid from the wagon lines to the gun position, the reconnaissance officer ordered the guns to move into their new positions.[235] The guns would then move into their new firing locations, establish themselves, and start developing the individual gun platforms – the terrain assigned for a gun and its crew to occupy, sometimes also known as 'gun pits' if dug in for protection.

The gunners, when not firing, were constantly improving their gun pits to ensure survivability. The diarist of the 55th Battery, CFA, records that when the battery was deployed in the Lieven sector in February 1917, the gun crews worked incessantly on the pits in order to make them "5.9 proof," referring to the German 5.9-inch howitzer. To do so, they built them up with bricks, sandbags, rails, and logs until they all began to resemble small hills rising out of the terrain, earning them unique nicknames such as "Mountain Range," "Pike's Peak," and "Cave of the Winds." Perhaps in a spirit of patriotism, the men of one gun detachment of the 55th Battery, CFA, painted the inside of their gun pit red and white.[236]

Horses were held in horse lines sometimes as far as three miles away from the guns, the distance being dictated by the tactical situation and of course the local terrain.[237] It was critical to maintain this distance in order to preserve the mobility of the guns, since the loss of horses would render the guns immobile and consequently useless in the event of an advance or withdrawal. It is important to stress that "horse lines" were usually separate from "wagon lines," where the sustainment elements of the battery were held. The anonymous diarist of the 60th Battery, CFA, captured the concern that accompanied a battery when deploying into a new position, recording that in one position, "the guns were pulled in close to the [gun] pits, un-limbered, ammunition and rations unloaded, and the vehicles returned to the wagon lines. When the teams were clear, everyone heaved a sigh of relief, for it is always an anxious time when the horses accompany the guns into action."[238]

As opposed to the *technical* reconnaissance of the battery position, its *tactical* reconnaissance involved liaising with the supported infantry brigade to determine the infantry's zone of operations and devising the best way to support their operations therein.[239] The two were equally important, indeed synergistic: one could not be considered without the other. The former consisted of all the scientific and technical requirements to deliver fire support, including the various survey calculations that allowed for indirect engagement of targets; the latter provided the guidance pertaining to where that fire support was required.

Upon arrival in the new battery deployment area, the battery commander's first duty was to select and occupy the observation post. It was to be established as close to the battery as possible and have a good view of the field of fire in which the battery was expected to engage the enemy, and was derived from the battery commander's orders or his discussions with the supported infantry commander. *Field Artillery Training 1914* stipulated that it was the battery commander who observed fire from this position, and any other officer who was sent to assist at the OP was known as the *observing officer*.[240] Eventually, as the war adopted its siege-like characteristics and the observing stations were not, as initially intended, very close to the guns but much farther forward, the observing officer became the forward observing officer, or FOO.

It is wise to pause here and discuss the role of the FOO. As mentioned previously, each artillery officer was required to fulfill the position of FOO on a regular basis, and it cannot be overstressed how important a position that was. The FOOs provided invaluable liaison with the supported infantry and were critical to the successful application of fire support. FOOs would move forward toward the trench line in order to find advantageous positions to establish OPs from which to observe the enemy and direct fire. Often this was in a trench with the infantry, but the prime requirement was an ability to observe. Colin Hutchinson described one such OP he established during operations near Givenchy in 1915:

> We have a beautiful observation post we call Artillery House. It is what remains of a house, you have to get up two very shaky ladders, crawl along on your stomach and get through a shell hole through a dividing wall, worm your way across the floor of a room with practically no walls standing to half of what was once a window built up with sandbags. You have to look through a slit of a sandbag loophole on our trenches which are 200 yards away. The German trenches are some 80 yards beyond.[241]

Naturally, camouflage and concealment were immensely important in the establishment of an OP. Hutchinson relates one story of carefully establishing an OP in a tree over the course of three weeks, slowly tying down branches to clear fields of observation so as not to alert the enemy to their presence, while also assiduously avoiding leaving tracks leading to the OP that might be observed by enemy aircraft thus exposing its location. One night, a work party was sent out to lay a wire through the area of Hutchison's OP and left an obvious track to the tree while also breaking all the branches off it, rendering it useless. Needless to say, Hutchinson was quite put out and vented his anger at the divisional staff offer responsible. Of his angry outburst toward the staff officer, he reported that "I have seldom had such an enjoyable half hour."[242]

Protection was of course of premium importance for a good OP, as they were high-priority targets for Germany artillery fire, should they be discovered. When in the line near Lieven in February 1917, the 55th Battery, CFA, established an OP in an empty cellar that provided them with both excellent observation and protection. It was nicknamed 'Aurora,' and it was established four hundred yards behind the front lines. Its "upper part was covered with cement, with a slit on the level of the ground which overlooked Cite St. August, and the Carvin Road… below was a forty-foot dugout with bunks for three signallers and an officer."[243]

In another example, one enterprising young engineering officer devised a unique and extremely effective OP near Vimy Ridge. In his memoir of the war, *A Surgeon in Arms*, Canadian medical officer Captain R.J. Minion recalled that,

> *A large tree which stood upon this spot had been shattered by a shell, the shattering having taken place when the Germans held Vimy Ridge. This shattered tree was only four hundred yards from the enemy front line. Months before the Battle of Vimy Ridge some quick-minded engineer noticed this tree, and the idea occurred that it could be utilized to good advantage. [A] steel frame was made and covered in exact imitation of the tree trunk, all other arrangements made, and one night the tree was removed and this counterfeit of it was put up. When day broke an observer was sitting comfortably in this strange observation post looking out upon the enemy trenches, watching the movements of the Germans, at the same time being safe from any danger except the straight hit of a shell.[244]*

As important as the reconnaissance, selection, and occupation of an OP was, even more important was the establishment of communication with the firing batteries. Wireless communication was in its infancy during the Great War, so communication between FOO and battery relied on the use of telephones connected by wire. The FOO and his signallers were required to ensure wire was laid out to the OP, connecting it with the battery, and to repair the wire when it was inevitably cut by enemy shelling. To avoid such an occurrence, the wire was usually buried, in some cases up to three feet underground. One can imagine this was hot work – digging wire to an OP that was near to the enemy lines was bound to draw the attention and fire of the enemy.

A well-established OP with an excellent view of the zones of fire and clear lines of communication to the battery was a deadly combination. While FOOs had important roles to play in programmed, which is to say pre-planned and scheduled, bombardments, they were lethally effective at engaging targets of opportunity. As Brigadier-General McNaughton observed: "It is the business of the FOO, who is forward and in touch with the situation, to shoot first and report afterwards."[245] Jeffrey E. Marston, who served in the RFA, recalled that engaging targets while employed as a FOO was one of the best ways to pass the time. He wrote:

> *[T]here are diversions of course, which help to pass the long hours. One is 'shooting the battery.' The F.O.O....is allowed, within fairly wide limits, to shoot when and at what he likes provided always that he has a reasonable objective. The principles laid down are simple enough: while never wasting a round if he can help it, he must also never miss an opportunity. That is to say he must keep a ceaseless watch for signs of movement or of new work being carried out by the enemy, for the flashes of hostile batteries, for suspected O.P.s, for machine gun emplacements and snipers' posts – for almost everything in fact. And when he sees, he must shoot – at a rapid rate and for a few moments only. For it is useless to 'plaster' the same spot for any length of time: the enemy will not be there – he must be caught unawares or not at all."[246]*

Duke Hutchinson gives an excellent account of the effectiveness of the artillery in this regard:

> *I saw a large working party of 40 or 50 men... perhaps repairing some damage we had done. I sent up through the phone "Battery action. Target 30 degrees [right] of zero line. Concentrate 15' on no. 2. Correlates 15b 4750, Salvo!" I have to admit to a curious feeling when I gave that order to destroy human life, the first time, of course but I hope it will not be the last.[247]*

A CFA officer, Lieutenant Coningsby Dawson, writing a letter to his father in February 1917, described FOO work thus:

> *All to-day I've been having a cold but amusing time at the O.P.*
> *... It seems brutal to say it, but taking pot-shots at the enemy when they present themselves is rather fun. When you watch them scattering like ants before the shell whose direction you have ordered, you somehow forget to think of them as individuals, any more than the bear-hunter thinks of the cubs that will be left motherless. You watch your victims through your glasses as God might watch his mad universe. Your skill in directing fire makes you what in peace time would be called a murderer.*[248]

From time to time the FOO would be required to accompany the assaulting infantry in order to provide them with intimate fire support advice and coordination. Cecil Rose, an officer of the RFA, described such an operation, conducted in the Ypres Salient in 1916, in this way:

> *The party consisted of two officers and fourteen signallers and linesmen from the Brigade, who, during the past fortnight had received full instructions as to their duties. Every detail had been carefully worked out beforehand: the men had been divided into several groups, each armed with telephones, reels of wire, flags, and Lucas lamps, all these things being necessary from the provision of each relay station. One of the officers was to accompany the attacking waves of infantry with this staff, consisting of a telephonist, linesman, and signaller, while the duty of the other was to work in conjunction with him and to maintain, as far as possible, uninterrupted communication with the Brigade after laying down the wire.*[249]

Rose describes the FOO party advancing behind the second wave of infantry, detailing how the signallers were working to repair the wire being played out when it was damaged by enemy counter-bombardment. In this particular case, the FOO party was fortunate as the wire broke in only three places. Owing to the additional weight of equipment required of the FOO party, they advanced at a rate slower than the assaulting soldiers and were subsequently overcome by the third wave of infantry. Upon reaching the crest of the hill that was the objective, the FOO party established a relay station in a pillbox recently abandoned by its former occupants, and linked it by telephone wire with the infantry headquarters occupying another nearby pillbox. Some of the party remained here, while the remainder of the FOO party carried on behind the assaulting infantry, during which time the FOO reported on the progress of the infantry's advance to his battery. Meanwhile, the Lucas Lamp was established on the top of the relay station in order to provide backup communications lest the wire be cut.

Eventually the infantry would arrive at their final objective, and the FOO selected and occupied an advantageous OP. Based on the FOO's reports, batteries limbered up and moved forward to ensure sufficient range was available to the infantry in order to repulse any counterattacks. The BC would order the FOO to register the guns, which means to fire them at potential targets in order to determine the proper firing data – range, deflection, fuse setting, and the like – through ranging in order to ensure the targets were recorded for rapid re-engagement. Counterattacks would be launched and repulsed. Meanwhile, the linesmen would be busily running up and down the line repairing wire and passing written reports to the relay station for onward passage to the battery and brigade headquarters. In the evening, the FOO party, exhausted, would be replaced by a fresh group of officers and signallers.[250]

Returning now to the deployment of the guns, having selected the OP location suitable to support the infantry, the battery commander determined the best place to deploy the gun line, ensuring that the new gun position would allow the guns' trajectory to clear any intervening crests and achieve the desired fields of fire to support the infantry.

There were three types of gun positions that a battery could occupy: *open*, *semi-covered* or *covered*. These terms were used in relation to how exposed the battery was to observation and, in turn, how open the battery was to observe its targets from the gun. An open position was one in which the field of fire and targets could be seen over the sights of the gun and in which direct laying, or aiming, was possible. A semi-covered position was one in which indirect laying was required and the gun position had some cover between itself and the area it meant to engage, but not sufficient cover to provide any flash cover or obscure the observation of smoke and dust caused by its firing. A covered position was one in which the guns could not see the area they intend to engage and could not be seen from it, and in which the flashes, smoke, and dust produced by the firing of the guns was fully obscured from observation by the enemy due to tree lines or hills. Each type of position had its benefits and drawbacks. The greater degree of cover provided protection from enemy fire, but also increased the difficulty of command and control of the direction of fire due to the need to use what *Field Artillery Training 1914* called "artificial means of communication," such as telephones, semaphore, or lanterns, as well as the requirement to conduct trigonometric calculations to find the proper elevation and bearing to strike the target, rather than simply laying the gun on the target by use of the gun's sights.[251]

While the technical and tactical reconnaissance of the new position was occurring, the battery continued to move toward the new position under the guidance of the battery leader. When orders came for a battery to move forward or to retire toward the rear, it was of immense importance that the battery be there at the prescribed time and, perhaps even more importantly, be as "complete" as possible. This alludes to the equipment of the battery not being lost along the way, which was rather a challenge given that the battery would move first along rough tracks out of the gun position to the nearest road, and then along roadways that were probably well-cratered by artillery rounds or reduced to a quagmire of mud and wheel ruts. Consequently, every single piece of equipment had its prescribed place of storage on the wagons, limbers, and caissons.[252] Despite the team's best efforts, however, the rough terrain and the hasty atmosphere of moving a gun out of one position and into a new one, particularly if under fire, meant that invariably all sorts of equipment would be found strewn about the route of march. As one artillery veteran recalled, "[I]f you ever have the luck to march behind a badly disciplined battery, you will find many useful things on the ground, canvass water buckets, nosebags, mess tins, almost anything; even knapsacks containing perhaps a bible, a few letters and spare underclothing. With difficulty the knapsacks will be returned to their owners, but you won't return the other things as they are fair spoil."[253]

As the battery neared the new gun position, the battery leader would order the guns into a nearby area, preferably off the route of march, and order the guns to prepare for action. This order resulted in the guns carrying out a series of drills and administrative tasks designed to ensure each gun was ready to move into the new position and thus expedite its deployment when the battery came into action on the actual gun position.

The battery was the principal fire unit of the Great War, and as we have seen there were a multitude of tasks and responsibilities that the battery members had to fulfill in order to provide the critical fire support to the infantry. Batteries were aided to a certain degree by the addition of superior command-and-control elements at the next hierarchical level. Multiple batteries comprised a brigade, commanded by a lieutenant-colonel. Understandably, the use of the term *brigade* produces some confusion, particularly for the historian, considering that in the infantry a brigade was a brigadier-general's command and comprised several battalions. Nonetheless, for several historical and cultural reasons the term *brigade* was maintained at the unit level in the artillery throughout the Great War. It was not changed to the current term of *regiment* until 1938.[254]

At the artillery brigade level, the batteries were joined in the organization by another sub-unit, an "ammunition column," which was commanded by a major and was responsible for ammunition resupply for the entire brigade. Several brigades – the exact number varied throughout the war – formed a divisional artillery, referred to simply as a divisional artillery in the British Army, and a Canadian divisional artillery in the Canadian Army. The divisional artilleries were commanded by a brigadier-general who held the title of CRA and was responsible for coordinating the fire support to an infantry division.

In the years prior to the war, on providing intimate direct fire to the infantry, the role of the CRA in the coordination of fire support was minimal. Although he was, nominally, in command of all the guns in a division, he had none of the resources, either human or technological, through which he could execute that authority. Although a brigade major was added to the roster in 1913 to assist in planning and execution, the CRA still lacked the communications required to control the fire of the guns.[255] Shelford Bidwell and Dominick Graham noted that the artillery mindset before the war focused on simplicity and worried that increasing artillery staffs would only result in delaying the pace of operations. They wrote that in the pre-war British Army it was thought "there was no need to improve artillery communications nor to increase artillery staffs. Those who advocated a complex system of fire support were windbags who complicated what was a simple matter."[256] The necessity of a more deliberate execution of fire support, enabled by an appropriately staffed planning organization, came to be understood, slowly, during the course of the war.

During the first two years of the war, the exact organization of the divisional artilleries and their subordinate artillery brigades was in a constant state of flux. At the beginning of the conflict, the war establishment of a divisional artillery consisted of three brigades of field artillery, each with three batteries of six 18-pounder guns, one brigade of field artillery consisting of three batteries of six 4.5-inch howitzers, and one battery of four 60-pounder guns from the RGA. Although this was the doctrinal structure of a divisional artillery, the exact composition of divisional artilleries varied from formation to formation. Divisional artilleries were often structured on equipment holdings or even the personal whims of the divisional commanders, a kind of "come-as-you-are" approach to warfare.[257] By the close of 1915, in order to eliminate the variations in divisions and develop a common composition throughout the army, a single organizational structure was adopted for all British and imperial artillery organizations. Thereafter, a divisional artillery consisted of four brigades of three four-gun 18-pounder batteries and one four-gun 4.5-inch howitzer battery.[258]

This organizational structure did not survive the horrific casualties of the Somme, which resulted in a serious lack of experienced artillery officers, specifically in positions of command. For example, Duke Hutchison reported to his sister in a letter after the Somme that "both our brigade and the divisional artillery have been very much knocked about. One brigade has lost all its commanding officers and many lost 50%."[259] His nephew, Colin, serving in a different brigade, reported that toward the end of the battle, four senior officers in the brigade were incapacitated in less than three weeks.[260] In response, in 1917 divisional artilleries were reorganized to consist of three brigades each of three six-gun 18-pounder batteries and one six-gun 4.5-inch howitzer battery each. This organizational structure grouped guns into larger individual fire units but did not change the total number of guns available to an infantry division.[261] This was the structure of British and imperial divisional artilleries at the time of the attack on Vimy Ridge; the new structure was adopted in mid-March 1917, mere weeks before the assault took place.[262]

In addition to the brigades that comprised a divisional artillery, ammunition resupply was provided by divisional artillery columns. These organizations, commanded by a lieutenant-colonel, were responsible to provide the link between the divisional artillery and the Corps ammunition supply. They were rather large organizations. For example, upon mobilization, the 2nd Canadian Divisional Artillery Column consisted of a headquarters and four sections comprising 825 personnel, all ranks, and 902 horses.[263]

While the divisional artilleries formed the backbone of the artillery arm of imperial armies, they were joined by heavy and siege batteries and brigades as well. The organization of heavy and siege batteries evolved over the course of the war as the role these weapon systems played became far more important. We have seen that at the outbreak of the war, very little attention was paid to the big guns, and during training exercises they were often left out of the scheme and outright forgotten. Consequently, when they deployed to the continent, all heavy and siege batteries remained under the control of General Headquarters. As the war became more violent, and the need for heavier fire support increased, so did the number of larger calibre guns. The Canadian Expeditionary Force eventually included thirteen siege and two heavy batteries that were formed into three garrison brigades and two heavy brigades.

Bringing it all together, the divisional artilleries fell under the authority of the GOCRA, who commanded all the artillery assigned to a Corps. As we shall see in later chapters, the GOCRA had several staff officers supporting him. His organization was normally divided into the divisional artilleries, which provided fire support to the infantry divisions, and heavy-artillery and counter-battery groups, which were responsible for providing the heavy fire support needed and winning the artillery duel before and during the execution of an operation. The level of command exercised by the GOCRA varied over time from that of simply an advisor to the corps commander to the outright commander of all the artillery of a corps, a topic to which we shall return in the next chapter.

WAYS: TACTICS, TECHNIQUES
AND PROCEDURES

How were the tools at the disposal of the leadership of the Canadian Corps' artillery employed? In this chapter, we will examine the doctrine, tactics, techniques, and procedures that defined how the tools available to the Corps were used to accomplish its tactical aims. As one can imagine, the large and very powerful artillery organization at Vimy Ridge required some degree of guidance and control to direct its efforts. Doctrine and tactics ensured that all the members of the fire support team that had assembled for the assault on Vimy Ridge were playing from the same song sheet.

In the two and one-half years that preceded the Canadian Corps' attack on Vimy Ridge, artillery doctrine and organization evolved considerably, arguably to the point that the fire support hierarchy at Vimy Ridge would be unrecognizable to its predecessor of autumn 1914. Although the changes were profound, they were more evolutionary than revolutionary, and reflective of a broader change in tactical doctrine writ large.

When war erupted in August 1914, British military leaders expected, and had trained for, a style of combat that was characterized by fluid movement, manoeuvre, and penetration. British doctrine focused unwaveringly on achieving the Edwardian holy grail of war – the breakthrough. Allied generals intended to end the war quickly by smashing through a weak point in the German line and then pouring cavalry through the breach to pursue the withdrawing enemy. This all changed when manoeuvre became impracticable, and the war adopted the siege-like characteristics of trench warfare.

Doctrine: From Dispersed to Centralized Operations

Artillery doctrine had evolved with manoeuvre doctrine in a complementary fashion. A hippophile artillery, whose leadership spurned technical precision, followed a simple doctrine: aggressively gallop guns well forward and deploy them to engage the German defences over open sites, win the artillery duel in a direct-fire contest with the opposing artillery, and then, after having won the duel, assist the infantry in creating the breach by firing into the enemy ranks.[264] The proper place, it was thought, for the artillery in support of infantry was in the open, where the gunners could see the target.[265] Eminent historian of artillery Major-General J.B.A. Bailey (retired) has defined this initial evolutionary phase of Great War artillery doctrine as one of *artillery manoeuvre*, which he described thus:

> *Warfare in 1914 was a linear affair, with prevailing doctrines emphasizing flanks, envelopments, and annihilations. Its essence was the contact battle of physical encounter, with masses of infantry and cavalry manoeuvring, supported by artillery firing directly, generally at short range, with guns deployed in the open.*[266]

This is not to say that firing indirectly from concealed positions was completely unknown. Colonel H.A. Bethell of the RFA wrote in 1911 that prior to the development of the quick-fire gun and the addition of gun shields to protect the gun crew, concealed positions were favoured in order to protect the guns from enemy infantry and artillery fire. But, he continued, "it was soon realized that when opposing troops come into contact, and the combat assumes a complicated form, mechanical fire direction cannot replace direct vision over the sights."[267] The fluid battlefield that personified the opening stages of the war, according to this doctrine, demanded gun deployments that facilitated direct engagement of enemy artillery and infantry by the supporting guns. The use of concealed positions and indirect fire was to be reserved for engaging static targets, such as enemy batteries out of contact and lines of trenches.[268] The centralization of artillery was anathema to artillery doctrine at the outbreak of the war, when the prevailing doctrine emphasized the deployment of batteries scattered about the battlefield and operating independently. In 1911 Bethell observed,

> *If it were attempted to introduce complete centralization of fire-direction as the normal method, this would have a prejudicial effect upon the initiative of the artillery brigade commanders and the Divisional Artillery would become a slow, inactive force, incapable of doing anything without an order and unfit for the close co-operation with the infantry which is the object of its existence.*[269]

The doctrine of manoeuvre and penetration was unsuccessful. British attempts to force a breach of the German line could not overcome the robust German defences, reinforced as they were with interlocking machine guns and wire obstacles. Hopes for a war-winning breakthrough, like so many unfortunate soldiers, became fatally entangled on German barbed wire. In the opening phases of the war, the command and control of fire units was decentralized and thus hodgepodge; indeed, when the war erupted in the summer of 1914, the organizational establishment of the BEF called for no higher artillery control than the CRA, who nominally commanded all artillery in a division. Despite being in command of the artillery of a division, however, practically speaking he exercised this command only in exceptional circumstances. This may have been a function of the relative novelty of the post of divisional artillery commander; the position had been created just a few years before, in early 1908.[270] Moreover, the staff manual of 1912 made no reference to the duties of the divisional artillery staff. The situation in 1914 worsened as one climbed the hierarchical ladder. In the original BEF order of battle, there was no Corps artillery whatsoever, and the only guns that fell under the army commander's authority among the six initial divisions of the Expeditionary Force were the aged 60-pounder guns of the RGA.[271] It is true that there existed an artillery advisor at Corps headquarters; however, his role was strictly advisory, and he had no actual command authority over any artillery units whatsoever. Even if the Corps artillery advisor had wanted to exercise some degree of command and control over any artillery that nominally fell to him, he had no mechanism to do it effectively: he had no artillery staff through which to exercise that authority, and in fact he did not even have his own clerk!

The poor command and control that characterized the imperial artillery during the opening months of the war was exacerbated by operational and tactical-level weaknesses; adjustment of fire was primitive, communications were unreliable, ammunition was limited, and counter-battery fire was ineffectual. Additionally, the British artillery was frighteningly outgunned by the Germans in the number of guns available, the achievable range of the artillery pieces, and the effectiveness of shells.[272] We find therefore that in the opening months of the war, the imperial artillery was woefully unprepared for a war of manoeuvre.

Any pretense to manoeuvre evaporated as the size of the forces committed to battle by both sides swelled with the infusion of reserves, recruits, and conscripts. The burgeoning armies produced extended frontages that all but removed the ability of the opposing armies to attempt any clever manoeuvring around flanks. Avoiding frontal assaults became impossible, and in response the war adopted a style of immobile trench warfare that became the defining characteristic of the conflict, one that endures in popular understanding of the war.[273] Unable to manoeuvre and restore the initial fluidity of the battlefield, both sides settled into a system of protracted siege warfare, a phase that was described defined by Bailey as one of *artillery destruction*, in which massive artillery barrages were employed to facilitate frontal assaults. No longer would the artillery presume to gallop into the open and engage the enemy over open sights. For the remainder of the war, the artillery would mass behind intervening terrain and pound away at enemy defences for days at a time in an attempt to batter his defences to the point where friendly infantry could close with and seize the objective.

The transformation was not immediate, however. While imperial leadership was willing to use artillery to pulverize the enemy line and create a gap, there was a significant lack of materiel in the form of the number of guns and, most importantly, shells to actually accomplish this. The commander-in-chief of the BEF in 1914, General Sir John French, neatly summed up the need for ammunition in February 1915 thus: "The problem set is a comparatively simple one – munitions, more munitions, always more munitions."[274] Major-General Andrew George Latta (A.G.L.) McNaughton, a Canadian Permanent Force artilleryman and future commander of the Canadian Army during the Second World War, recalled in 1926 that in the early stages of the war the ammunition situation was so dire that Canadian field pieces were limited to only three rounds per gun per day![275] Indeed, in 1915 ammunition was scarcer than guns.[276] The cause of this disparity came from the short-sightedness of military leaders in all of the belligerent nations, who thought that the war would be over in a matter of months and never envisioned the type of prolonged bombardments that would come to characterize the war. When the BEF arrived in France in August of 1914, the scale of issue for artillery rounds allowed a total of 1500 rounds per gun and 1200 rounds per howitzer. After six months, an additional 500 rounds per gun/400 rounds per howitzer would be available from industry.[277] Based on these scales, British artillery doctrine allocated 100 rounds per gun for an offensive operation. By 1915, that number had tripled, and of course by 1917 it was exponentially larger.[278]

Eventually, British industry was expanded sufficiently to provide the scores of ammunition required for destructive artillery bombardments, but it was not able to achieve this until the spring of 1917.[279] Some idea of the herculean efforts of the British munitions industry during the war can be found in comparisons of the numbers of guns and shells available at the start of the war compared to the end. In the fall of 1914, the entire BEF was supported by 504 guns. By November 11, 1918, that number had increased to 6,406.[280] The provision of shells for imperial armies grew substantially, from the three rounds per gun per day at the start of the war, to an average expenditure of forty-two rounds per gun per day in the Canadian Corps during the last hundred days of the conflict.[281] Only when the numbers of guns and shells grew to the point that long, destructive barrages were logistically feasible did the doctrine of artillery destruction emerge.

The mode of command and control employed by the artillery during the *artillery manoeuvre* phase, in which batteries were dispersed and fire was diluted, was incompatible with the *artillery destruction* phase. With no command-and-control hierarchy in the upper echelons of command, namely division and higher, it was impossible to achieve the level of centralized concentration of fire that was required in order to achieve the desired level of destruction of enemy defences. In fact, the British Artillery made a virtue of necessity and resolved to adjust the command-and-control structure of the fire support hierarchy to accommodate the new doctrine of artillery destruction.

The nature of siege warfare demanded a more centralized, controlled, and programmed approach to fire support. The organizational changes in artillery doctrine that characterized the system of artillery destruction first emerged, albeit embryonically, in 1915. In the summer of that year, recognizing that the swelling ranks of the BEF and exponential growth in its artillery arm demanded far more centralized control, the British

GHQ instituted the practice of appointing temporary commanders to coordinate the fire of all the artillery, with the exception of heavy artillery, assigned to support a corps.[282] After the Battle of Loos, in September 1915, this policy was amended somewhat, and the British War Office approved the appointment in each corps of a GOCRA (see earlier discussion in Chapter 6). Going forward, each GOCRA would be furnished with a small staff that included a brigade major, responsible for planning and executing operations, and an aide-de-camp.[283]

As more and more heavy and siege artillery were mobilized, the position of corps heavy artillery commander was created with the rank of brigadier general. Like the field artillery, siege and heavy artillery also experienced an organizational evolution as the war progressed. Although divisional artilleries were allocated a battery of 60-pounder guns at the outbreak of the war, due to a shortage of pieces, ammunition, and a general lack of interest among the division commanders to employ the cumbersome brutes, the 60-pounders, along with the 6-inch howitzers, were withdrawn and held by no less than the commander-in-chief at General Headquarters.[284] This bit of over-centralization was eventually relaxed when commanders realized how vital the destructive effects that were produced by these guns were to destroying German defences.

To exercise command and control of the medium and heavy guns, the British Army created heavy artillery organizations at the army level, which allowed the artillery commander in a field army headquarters to augment the firepower of subordinate corps artillery as required by temporarily detaching heavy artillery to the corps artillery commander. Thus, by July of 1916 the oft-changing organizational structure of imperial artilleries had stabilized into one in which divisional artilleries held 18-pounder and 4.5-inch guns, corps artilleries held medium guns, and army artillery held heavy guns. As the heavy guns were often detached to corps to augment their fire, the corps' artillery headquarters were augmented by a permanent heavy artillery headquarters whose duty it was to coordinate the medium- and heavy-artillery fire that had been allocated to it.[285]

The role of the heavy artillery in the overall fire support team was twofold: the destruction of defences and communication trenches as part of the normal barrage work, and counter-battery fire.[286] As mentioned above, heavy-artillery batteries belonged to army headquarters, who detached them to Corps Artillery Headquarters based on the army's scheme of manoeuvre for operations and the requirement to augment fire at the point of main effort. Once detached, and because the heavy-artillery batteries were independent and not organized into brigades for command and control, they were folded into heavy-artillery groups, which fell under the command of the aforementioned heavy artillery headquarters in the Corps Artillery.[287] To exercise command and control of the heavy artillery attached to a corps, the position of general officer commanding – heavy artillery was created. This officer, a brigadier-general, was responsible to issue daily orders for counter-battery work, allot tasks to the actual batteries, and arrange all details for heavy artillery.[288]

The existence of two artillery brigadier-generals in a single corps naturally led to some ambiguity regarding who was the corps commander's principal artillery advisor. The result in the British Corps was for the GOCRA to revert to the role of advisor instead of commander. The same cannot be said of the Canadian Corps, where the leadership recognized the importance of having a single artillery commander in the corps; thus, the authority of the GOCRA as a legitimate commander, rather than simply a coordinator or advisor, was maintained. In a uniquely Canadian approach to corps-level fire support, a command and control policy was instituted consisting of three elements. The first was known as Corps Control, and was it was a command relationship that, when instituted by the GOCRA, stipulated that all artillery assigned to the Canadian Corps came under the direct authority of the GOCRA. This method of command and control was usually put in force during large, set-piece operations, such as the assault on Vimy Ridge. The second method was called Divisional Control, which automatically came into effect at the end of a set-piece barrage; the fire support assets assigned to support divisions were directly responsive to that divisional commander through the CRA. The final method was called Normal Control, a command relationship that existed during routine operations.[289]

By the end of 1916, a year renowned for violent clashes, not the least of which was the calamitous Battle of the Somme, the British realized that their split approach to corps-level fire support was ineffective. The style of warfare that emerged in 1916 demanded the centralization of artillery, and thus, in 1916, imperial artillery doctrine adopted a far more centralized hierarchy. To achieve this centralization, the CRA, who had previously exercised only nominal authority over the guns in support of the division, began to exercise a far greater degree of command and control over his subordinate artillery brigades. Moreover, the GOCRA now assumed the Canadian Corps model of full command of all the artillery brigades in the Corps' divisional artilleries, as well as all reinforcing artillery that was assigned to support a corps during its operations.[290] Additionally, an actual Corps Artillery staff emerged to assist in this regard, and by early 1917 the establishment of the Corps Artillery Headquarters included the commander, a staff captain, a staff officer, and a reconnaissance officer.[291] These seemingly bureaucratic additions were vitally necessary in order to exercise effective command over a large artillery organization.

Once *command* was centralized at the Corps Artillery Headquarters, *control* followed suit. Under the doctrine of artillery destruction, the Corps Artillery Headquarters was responsible to set the timings for the fire support program, deduce the artillery objectives, prepare barrage maps, and even allocate forward observation officers. Divisional Artillery Headquarters received these instructions from the Corps Artillery Headquarters and executed the plan on behalf of the GOCRA.[292] This system, wherein command and control was centralized at higher echelons, was a far cry from the scattered, independent batteries firing over open sites that characterized the opening stages of the war.

Centralizing the command and control of fire support at the corps level is considered one of the great strengths displayed by the imperial armies during the war. The Germans preferred to centralize the command and control of their artillery at the divisional level, with no similar organization at the corps level as the imperial armies had done. This short-sightedness limited the Germans' ability to switch fire from one division to another, or bring to bear higher-echelon fire units across a wide frontage.[293] As Nicholson notes in his history of the Canadian Artillery, "in the Canadian Corps the whole force of the artillery within range was immediately available to support any sector, and the Corps' entire system of artillery intelligence was centred on those who had the means at their disposal to take immediate and effective action."[294]

This is not to say that the situation was perfect – in fact, notwithstanding the very beneficial developments in the centralization of artillery command and control at the division and corps levels, there was still a latent lack of cooperation between the general staff and the artillery staff officers of formation headquarters. Writing in the Royal United Services Institute's *Journal* in 1919, an author using the nom de plume F.W., who had spent the war as an artillery staff officer and as a regimental artillery officer, observed that

> *often there is no artilleryman on the staff of a formation of*
> *all arms; the influence of the formation staff, shy of artillery*

> *technique, is exercised largely in saying 'Don't' like an anxious*
> *nurse, and not always giving the maximum assistance to the*
> *Artillery Staff Captain, part of whose work is the comfort of*
> *the artillery, but whose position is too junior to get all that is*
> *necessary, and whose hands are already full of priority work*
> *dealing with ammunition.*[295]

Fortunately, these hiccups were not sufficiently restrictive to materially disadvantage what had become a very effective, centralized fire support network.

By the spring of 1917, the evolving nature of imperial artillery organization and doctrine required official doctrine to be issued in order to ensure all the guns in the imperial arsenal conducted their operations in a similar manner. This was particularly important because the units of the various imperial artilleries that fought together on the Western Front – British, Canadian, South African, Australian, Indian, etc. – were far more likely than any other element to be used in support of other imperial armies. Indeed, we shall see that the fire support organization in support of the Canadian Corps was a multinational one. This demand for doctrinal uniformity among the imperial artillery after a period of robust change, in not only organization but also doctrine and tactics, resulted in the release of a doctrinal pamphlet entitled *Artillery in Offensive Operations* by British General Headquarters only a month prior to Vimy Ridge. *Artillery in Offensive Operations* defined the role of the artillery in the new doctrine thus:

> *The rupture of the enemy's front, generally strongly defended and*
> *organised in depth, is the first phase of an offensive battle. This*
> *entails the destruction of the obstacles to the infantry's advance*
> *and of the means of defence that support those obstacles; the*
> *moral and physical reduction of the defenders; and lastly a rapid*
> *and combined advance of all arms acting in close cooperation.*[296]

Although the number of guns and batteries had grown exponentially since the beginning of the war, the robustness of the German defences meant there were as yet insufficient guns to achieve the required level of destruction in a short period. This drove the requirement for prolonged, meticulous, sustained bombardments designed to cut wire, destroy trenches and fortifications, and demoralize the enemy defenders. In order to facilitate this system of artillery destruction, a two-stage doctrinal fire plan emerged: a preliminary bombardment, followed by direct support to the assault.[297]

Artillery in the Offence: The Preliminary Bombardment

As its name implies, the preliminary bombardment was the fire delivered prior to an attack. As the overture to the symphony of fires, the goals of the preliminary bombardment were threefold: first, to overpower hostile artillery, a stage in the artillery preparation known as the counter-battery fight; second, to effect the physical and moral reduction of the enemy's infantry; and finally, to complete the destruction of the enemy's defensive obstacles, particularly wire entanglements.[298]

The Counter-Battery Fight

By the spring of 1917, the silencing of hostile batteries was a critical part of Great War imperial artillery doctrine, although the verve with which the British pursued the counter-battery fight fluctuated in the years both before and during the war. The *artillery duel* was an element of the doctrine of mobile warfare that emerged in the early nineteenth century, particularly with Napoleon's creation of the *grande batterie* of massed guns, which were used to smash his opponent's artillery early in the battle.[299] As we have seen, the importance of the artillery duel continued during the opening phases of the war, when the role of the artillery battery commander was to gallop into an open position and first defeat the enemy artillery over open sights before concentrating on reducing the enemy infantry. But while this was definitely a concern, in the years leading up to the outbreak of the war British artillery doctrine was less concerned with winning the counter-battery fight than it was with supporting the infantry during the assault.[300]

Once the freedom to manoeuvre faltered with the adoption of trench warfare, the artillery were forced to adopt covered positions and employ indirect fire methods; naturally, galloping forward and engaging the enemy's guns over open sights was impossible when guns were concealed behind hills and tree lines. In the opening stages of the war, the distance between the belligerents' artillery was normally only about 2000 metres, but once the guns of both sides moved rearward to more protected positions, that distance increased dramatically to approximately 4000–

6000 metres.[301] Interest in the counter-battery fight waned as the tools necessary to accurately locate the enemy's artillery, now hidden and farther away, had not yet been introduced into the British arsenal.

By the fall of 1915, however, these tools and processes, which would eventually include aerial observation, sound ranging, and flash spotting, were slowly becoming available to British gunners, and interest in the counter-battery fight began anew. Eventually the *artillery duel* came into vogue once again, albeit in a modernized fashion. Soon, the belligerents of the Western Front began dedicating large portions of their artillery parks specifically to the counter-battery fight. The number of guns so dedicated grew substantially between the summer of 1916 and the spring of 1917. As a result, the greatest difference between the battles of the Somme and Arras was that in the latter, a much greater proportion of the guns were allocated to counter-battery duties than to support the infantry, whereas in the former the opposite was the case.[302]

The importance of having an effective counter-battery system in place was reinforced by the fact that, despite the many technological advances of the British artillery throughout the war, the German artillery had likewise improved. From the very outset of the conflict, the German artillery enjoyed a technological lead over the British in terms of achievable range, which it never relinquished.[303] Consequently, the importance of counter-battery work, whose primary object was to protect friendly infantry from hostile artillery, increased exponentially for imperial armies.[304] So important was the counter-battery fight that when General Headquarters issued *Artillery Lessons Drawn from the Battle of the Somme* in December 1916, it warned:

> Nothing must permit us to be deflected from the pursuit of our object [of the destruction of hostile artillery.] This is easy to say, but there are two tempters ever on the prowl to lead us away from our quarry. The first is the employment of the counter-battery heavy howitzers for other tasks, and the second is the employment of counter-battery aeroplanes for bombing enterprises.[305]

In short, when it came to counter-battery work, concentration of force and maintenance of the aim was key. Commanders were to scrupulously avoid frittering away counter-battery resources on other tasks.

From a procedural perspective, the imperial artillery developed an effective counter-battery system that was in place by the time of Vimy

Ridge. McNaughton, a pioneer of counter-battery work, stressed the importance of the counter-battery fight when he wrote, "During the period preceding a deliberate attack, while the infantry are in their forming up positions, every gun which can be fired must be available to assist in the neutralization of the hostile artillery should they open a destructive bombardment on our forward system."[306]

The control of the counter-battery fight fell to the counter-battery staff officer, who was responsible for collecting artillery intelligence and directing the engagement of hostile batteries based on that intelligence.[307] Doctrinally, the counter-battery staff officer worked at the heavy artillery headquarters, located in the Corps Artillery Headquarters and, while nominally only a staff officer, nonetheless exercised executive command of the batteries allocated to him for counter-battery work.[308] Of course, the actual command of the heavy artillery that was allocated to the counter-battery fight was still retained by the general officer commanding heavy artillery. In order to ensure a proper and harmonious division of responsibility between that officer and the counter-battery staff officer, the former was responsible for the technical efficiency of the heavy artillery, while the latter was responsible for their tactical employment, which is to say the direction of their fire.[309]

The object of the positional-warfare artillery duel was to "destroy as many [hostile batteries] as possible, and to obtain full value for every round of ammunition expended."[310] Counter-battery fire was no mean task; the number of rounds required to destroy a hostile battery was substantial. *Artillery Notes No. 3 – Counter-Battery Work* stipulated that, under favourable conditions, the following expenditures-by-calibre were required to destroy an enemy battery: 6-inch howitzers – 200 rounds; 8-inch howitzers – 150 rounds; 9.2-inch howitzers – 100 rounds; and 12-inch howitzers – 50 rounds. Of course, a critical element of the counter-battery fight was finding the enemy's artillery, and there were a number of resources available to the counter-battery staff officer to achieve this.

Locating hostile batteries was an integrated effort that improved throughout the war. First, the counter-battery staff officer received reports from liaison officers in infantry brigade headquarters. When friendly infantry received fire from German artillery, the artillery liaison officer at the supported infantry brigade was required to provide information concerning the area shelled, the time and intensity of fire, the nature and size of projectiles, the direction from which shells came, and the time when fire ceased.[311] In addition to these liaison officers, the forward observation officers deployed by artillery brigade commanders to observe a zone of fire and report back to artillery headquarters also provided valuable artillery intelligence to the counter-battery officer. As the war progressed, these integral elements of the artillery organization were augmented by three new methods of locating hostile artillery, which evolved over time and were in use at Vimy Ridge, namely air reconnaissance, flash spotting, and sound ranging.

Aeroplanes were a significant force multiplier during the counter-battery fight, despite the fact that before the outbreak of the war, the use of the aeroplane in support of the artillery fight was not at all contemplated. Indeed, initially the prime, and in some respects only, role of the aeroplane in support of a BEF was in the capacity of aerial reconnaissance. Despite these inauspicious beginnings, the use of aeroplanes to direct artillery fire became one of the primary roles of the Royal Flying Corps as the war progressed.[312] Their importance to the artillery was not limited only to the counter-battery fight, however. McNaughton wrote that "from the advantageous position of the aeroplane, the observer is able to locate the position of conspicuous things, like a flash or a body of troops or transport, with a considerable degree of accuracy."[313] The aeroplane thus became an indispensable element in the imperial fire support system on the Western Front.

The realization that the aeroplane could be a valuable tool in the location of targets emerged quite early in the war. As early as November 1914, General Sir John French asked the War Office to ensure that all artillery officers received instruction on directing fire by aeroplane observation.[314] Perhaps indicative of the simpatico between the two arms, in the British Army many of the pilots who eventually conducted aeroplane observation in the Royal Flying Corps came originally from the Royal Artillery.[315]

The technological ability to adjust artillery fire from an aircraft was, initially, quite wanting. Before the outbreak of the war, in 1913, the British first used aircraft to find targets for the artillery. Finding targets was easy, but transmitting the target location and correcting the fall of shot was far more difficult, as wireless technology was not yet available. They conducted several experiments to solve this dilemma, with solutions that ranged from the novel, such as dropping a smoke signal indicating where the target was or flapping wings in a prescribed fashion indicating the type of correction to make, to the effective yet time-consuming practice of simply landing the plane next to the battery and handing a note to a runner indicating the adjustment in fire to be made.[316] The versatility of the aeroplane as an artillery observation platform developed substantially throughout the war, however, particularly when wireless sets were installed in the aircraft. Some aircraft had been equipped with wireless as early as the retreat from Mons in August of 1914, but in that case the fluid nature of the battlefield made it difficult to control fire by aircraft. Nonetheless, technology advanced and by February 1915, at least one flight outfitted with wireless sets was included in every squadron of the Royal Flying Corps.[317] As with so many other elements of the imperial fire support system in 1917, the importance of the aeroplane to artillery observation grew exponentially with the adoption of trench warfare on the Western Front, as it was only then that airborne artillery observation became practical.

Initially, those aircraft equipped with a wireless set had radio transmitters but no receivers, as they were too heavy for the aircraft to carry. Even so, the weight of the transmitter alone meant that the aircraft was reduced to a crew of one rather than the normal two in order to compensate for the added weight. Consequently, the air observer became a master of multi-tasking: he had to fly his craft, observe the target, and then send wireless telegraphy messages to the guns indicating the correction.[318] Certainly, the versatility of the aeroplane to range about the battlefield and, most importantly, to see over ridges into the dead ground behind, which was concealed from the earthbound artillery observers, made it a valuable resource, but the limitations of the technology nonetheless meant the transmission of artillery adjustment orders by an airborne observer was a laborious process. Below is a transcript of a wireless artillery adjustment sent on September 24, 1914; note that the total time to engage the target was forty minutes. The length of time required to adjust the target demonstrates how, in the fluid environment of the opening phases of the war, artillery adjustment by aircraft was impractical. The situation was quite different in the static environment of early 1917.

4.02 p.m. A very little short. Fire. Fire.
4.04 p.m. Fire again. Fire again.
4.12 p.m. A little short; line O.K.
4.15 p.m. Short. Over, over and a little left.
4.20 p.m. You were just between two batteries. Search [meaning to sweep with fire] two hundred yards each side of your last shot. Range O.K.

4.22 p.m. You have them.
4.26 p.m. Hit. Hit. Hit.
4.32 p.m. About 50 yards short and to the right.
4.37 p.m. You last shot in the middle of 3 batteries in action; search all round within 300 yards of your last shot and you have them.
4.42 p.m. I am coming home now.[319]

Over the years, as the technology and the tactics progressed, the manner of adjusting fire became more accurate and expeditious. In 1915 the clock code was put into use and remained in force for the remainder of the war. In using the clock code, both the pilot and the artillery command post imagined the face of a clock superimposed over the target with the centre of the clock correlating to the target location and 12 o'clock oriented to true north. Concentric circles were imagined emanating from the centre/target at distances of 10, 25, 50, 100, 200, 300, 400, and 500 yards, labelled Y, Z, A, B, C, D, E, and F, respectively. The aerial artillery observer would indicate the fall of shot of the ranging round to the artillery command post, such as Y4, meaning the round impacted 10 yards southeast (or 4 o'clock) from the target. Thus, the artillery command post knew to adjust the fire of the gun to the northwest by 10 yards.[320] As the aeroplane itself evolved throughout the conflict, their facility for locating hostile batteries increased. Eventually, on average at least 30 per cent of hostile batteries engaged during operations of Canadian Corps were located by aeroplanes of the Royal Flying Corps.[321]

In addition to the versatility of the aeroplane, as the war progressed the science of sound ranging was developed to help locate enemy guns. Sound ranging was relatively new technology during the Great War; its technical foundation is based on the propagation of sound waves created by the fire of artillery batteries. Although the science of sound ranging originated before World War I, it was in the static conditions of trench warfare that the tactical and technical efficacy of the practice really came into its own.[322] In fact, the scientific principles that were developed in sound ranging during the Great War remained unchanged well into the future.[323] The first sound-ranging section was formed under the command of a British officer from Cambridge University, Lieutenant W. L. Bragg, who was also a Nobel-laureate scientist.[324]

A sound-ranging team consisted of a headquarters section, three or four microphone posts that were deployed several kilometres apart parallel to the front line and about a mile and a half behind the forward trenches, and a centralized listening post well forward of the microphone line. When the listener in the listening post heard the report of a gun, he would press a button that would initiate the operation of an oscillograph in the headquarters; this device would record the sound waves at each microphone onto a film. The operator in the headquarters could then measure the difference in time for the sound to reach each microphone. Knowing the speed of sound, it was thus possible to determine the location where the sound originated through trigonometric calculation. Over time, this process was improved to produce a bearing from the microphone to the point of origin of the sound. The intersection of the bearings of multiple microphones provided the location of the enemy battery.[325] By the end of the war, when conditions were favourable, "a sound ranging section [could] locate a hostile battery to within 50 yards and give the position of the shell burst and the calibre of the gun. It [could] then range a battery successfully on to the hostile and correct its fire."[326]

In addition to sound ranging, flash spotting became another tool with which the imperial gunners could divine the location of the enemy batteries. Flash-spotting batteries were deployed on the battlefield and would install two or, ideally, three observation posts on prominent ground. Each was equipped with survey instruments, a telephone connection to the counter-battery staff office, and a buzzer system that, when pressed by the operator, would illuminate a light in the headquarters. When one post observed the flash of a hostile battery, the operator would lay the survey instrument on the location of the flash and report his bearing and the estimated range to it. This would be conveyed to the other posts, who would then lay their own survey instruments on the calculated bearing to the estimated location. The posts would observe through the instrument, and when a flash was observed, they would press the buzzer and correct the bearing on the survey instrument, which had been laid on the bearing to the estimated location, onto the observed sight of the flash. Back at the counter-battery staff office, when the operator observed the lights of all the deployed posts flashing at the same time or quite near to it, he could reasonably assume they were laid on the same enemy battery. He then directed the posts to report the bearing on their instruments, and through triangulation based on the known location of the observation posts, the counter-battery staff office operator could determine a very precise location of the enemy guns – indeed, as close as five yards.[327]

With these assets in hand, the counter-battery staff officer had a robust system in place that allowed him to sense, locate, and engage hostile batteries in order to ensure firepower dominance. Every piece of intelligence that came into the office was analyzed, sorted, and catalogued. Once a hostile battery was confirmed, it was assigned an identifying number that was then shared with the fire support team through the distribution of the Daily Artillery Intelligence Report. Through collection, analysis, interpretation, and recording, the preponderance or even the whole of the enemy's artillery network could be divined and thereafter scheduled for engagement through counter-battery resources. Once this new version of the classic artillery duel had been won, or at least when the enemy artillery had been reduced sufficiently in capability in order to ensure they could deliver only minimal interference on imperial infantry operations, the focus of the artillery preparatory effort turned to the physical and moral reduction of the enemy's infantry.

Physical and Moral Reduction of the Enemy's Infantry

The main goal of the preparatory fire, as it pertained to the enemy infantry, was to reduce the enemy's power of resistance. The enemy soldier was attacked on two fronts – the physical and the moral. Physically, artillery fire was used to kill or injure the enemy soldier and thus eliminate him as a source of resistance during the eventual assault. This is intuitively easy to understand, and the anti-personnel effects of shrapnel, splinters, and blast have been covered at length earlier in this study. The psychological effects, however, require some deeper analysis.

Artillery was used during the preliminary bombardment to attack the psychological fitness of the enemy by sapping his will to resist. This was accomplished through constant, incessant shelling over a prolonged period, which had the effect of developing a sense of hopelessness and impotence among the enemy infantry. Such harassment kept the enemy in a constant state of fear and hyper-apprehension by presenting an enduring threat to his personal safety and by exposing him to the death, dismemberment, and mutilation of his colleagues. This isolation was enhanced by the enemy soldier's lack of a tangible element against which to direct his frustration and vengeance. In a 1918 study entitled *War Neuroses*, Dr. John MacCurdy of Cambridge University observed:

> [T]he soldier must remain for days, weeks, even months, in a narrow trench or a stuffy dugout, exposed to a constant danger of

the most fearful kind; namely, bombardment with high explosive
shells, which come from some unseen source, and against which
no personal agility or wit is of any avail…a man may be exposed
for months to the appalling effects of bombardment and never
once have a chance to retaliate in a personal way.[328]

This effect was enhanced by reinforcing the enemy's sense of physical isolation. When not directed specifically against the enemy soldier holding ground, artillery was used to interdict reinforcements, ammunition resupply, and communications. It was also employed in harassing fires that consisted of short, sharp bursts, repeated at irregular intervals, aimed at denying the enemy respite and keeping him in a state of nervous agitation and concern over when the next intense bombardment would arrive. Fire was to be increased at night to magnify the feelings of isolation and to ensure there was no lull in action that would allow the defender a chance to rest. Gas shells were also used at night to force the defenders to wear gas masks and thus limit or reduce the quality of sleep.[329]

One should not discount the adverse effect this activity also had on the gunners firing. To them lay the daunting task of maintaining the all-night drumbeat of harassing fire. In addition, the Germans were by no means defeated, and night-time harassing fire always carried the risk of drawing retaliatory rounds from them. Regardless of the threat of personal harm, the gunners found themselves forced to man the guns, aiming, loading, firing, and repeating for hours at a time. While detachment commanders would spell off their soldiers and rotate troops for periods of rest, even those who managed to catch some sleep had to do so with the staccato firing of their comrades only yards away.

Destruction of Material Obstacles to the Advance of the Infantry

Wire was the principal enemy defensive structure that the artillery was tasked to eliminate.[330] Despite wire having been used to augment defensive preparations for a number of years, at the start of the war the British Army was completely inept at addressing the problem.[331] The amount of ammunition required to destroy wire obstacles was immense, and as this book has demonstrated previously, the initial British artillery ammunition stores were woefully inadequate. *Artillery Notes No. 5 – Wire Cutting* advised artillery commanders to calculate the requisite number of rounds by determining one-third of the hundreds of yards in range to the target for each yard of front.[332] For example, a gun firing at wire emplaced 3000 yards away would require ten rounds *per yard* to cut the wire.

Even if sufficient rounds had been available during the opening phases of the war, the requisite technical knowledge in wire destruction was absent in the imperial armies, and British leaders were myopically focused on trench destruction.[333] By the time of the assault on Vimy Ridge, the British military leaders had come to learn, through horrific loss of life, that the destruction of wire was critical to the success of any infantry attack. Consequently, the field guns and howitzers of the divisional artilleries and their supporting trench mortar batteries were assigned the task of wire cutting along their respective infantry division's front.[334] It was not until the introduction of the No. 106 fuse in 1917, however, that the artillery achieved the ability to adequately cut wire (see Chapter 5).

Notwithstanding the increased technological capacity to affect the destruction of wire obstacles, the process was nonetheless painstaking. Colin Hutchinson described the laborious nature of wire cutting in the early days of the war:

> *Wire cutting cannot be done efficiently at a quicker rate than four rounds a minute. Due to the care we have to take of our guns, it impossible to fire more than 40 rounds on end at this rate without some slight adjustments taking place. So the hours of firing are divided into 40 rounds per gun, 5 guns only taking part, the 6th gun resting, then half an hour so-called rest, during which time the men have to do a hundred and one odd things, and the guns had time to cool.[335]*

Artillery in Offensive Operations stipulated that commanders of assaulting battalions should visit the OPs established by their supporting artillery commander in order to confirm that the wire they were expected to breach during the assault was indeed clear. Uniquely, British artillery doctrine concerning the destruction of obstacles by artillery stressed that the infantry commander held overall responsibility, while the role of the artillery was to "give advice and provide a service." This is understandable given that it was the infantry commanders' men who would pay the price in blood for uncut wire and unmolested trenches.[336] Artillery commanders, for their part, were determined not to be blamed for ineffective wire cutting should the attack not succeed. Brigadier-General Henry Burstall, who preceded Morrison as the GOCRA for the Canadian Corps between September 1915 and December 1916, went so far as to demand of his artillery brigade commanders that when they determined the wire to be sufficiently cut, they were to secure written certification from the infantry battalion commander attesting to the fact.[337]

Once gaps in the wire were achieved, it fell to the infantry division commander to ensure that the enemy was not able to repair the gap. To achieve this, a symphony of weapons including artillery, mortars, and machine guns were employed, principally at night when German wire repair parties preferred to operate, in order to ensure any repair patrol approaching the gap was beaten back before the wire could be replaced.[338]

Wire was not the only defensive work against which the artillery was used. Machine-gun emplacements, strong points, trench junctions, dugouts, command posts, signal communication sites, observing stations, and even water-pipe systems were all subject to artillery bombardments in an attempt to disrupt the enemy's defence. As mentioned previously, achieving this level of destruction required a sustained bombardment that was extremely costly in time and ammunition, so artillery commanders were directed to focus on the most dangerous enemy defences and use the suppressive effect of the barrage during the actual assault to deal with defences that were not destroyed during the preliminary bombardment.[339]

By winning the artillery duel, by reducing the enemy infantry's physical and psychological powers of resistance, and by eliminating as much of the defensive obstacles as possible, the artillery preliminary bombardment shaped the tactical battlefield conditions in order to lay the ground for a successful infantry assault. In addition to the incredible amount of artillery fire that went into this opening phase of an attack, there was still plenty of work for the artillery to do.

Artillery in the Offence: Support to the Assault

Supporting the assault of the infantry after they went "over the top" was the second doctrinal phase of the artillery battle. The direct artillery support provided to the assaulting infantry battalions had two objectives: first, beating down all resistance to the advance from either their front or their flanks, and second, preventing the assembly of enemy infantry for a counterattack, or blocking any counterattack that might manifest during the friendly assault. The primary means of accomplishing these goals was the use of a *barrage.*

Barrage

We touched on the barrage earlier, but here we'll go into more detail. Like the term *shrapnel*, the term *barrage* has likewise been co-opted in daily usage to mean something quite distant from its original definition. The term can be heard in near daily usage, usually referring to some flurry of activity: politicians are subject to a barrage of questions in the House of Commons, goaltenders are subjected to a barrage of shots during hockey games, and the like. Artillery historian Ian V. Hogg bemoaned this cursory usage of what was, originally, a very technically specific term, writing that "nothing annoys a professional more than the misuse of his private jargon by outsiders or amateurs...the word [barrage] has come to be loosely used for any heavy concentration of gunfire, when, in fact, it has a precise and exact meaning."[340]

In the British War Office publication *Barrages*, a barrage was defined as a moving curtain of fire that was "used for covering the infantry when attacking by preventing the enemy from manning his position and installing his machine guns in time to arrest their advance."[341] More to the point, A.G.L. McNaughton described the intent of a barrage as being to "tie the enemy to the ground, to inflict casualties and to demoralize him and prevent his using his rifles, machine guns, trench mortars, etc., and to screen the advance of our infantry by a wall of bursting shell, and smoke and dust."[342]

Although barrages were attempted, mostly ineffectually, during the South African War, their use became widespread during the First World War. Barrages were not born or invented, per se; rather, they evolved into existence once the conditions necessary for their use, both technical in regard to the ability to calculate the gun firing data, and logistical in regards to the artillery ammunition available, were attained.[343] The necessary conditions for the successful application of barrages were twofold. First, a barrage is utterly dependent on the use of a large number of shells in order to achieve its aim. As we've seen, in the opening stages of the war, the imperial artillery lacked sufficient stocks of artillery ammunition. Therefore, until British industry were able to mass-produce the large volumes of artillery rounds required for the doctrine of artillery destruction, the employment of an effective barrage was logistically unattainable. Second, the detailed scheduling of a fire plan coordinated with the movement of the infantry required significant time to develop and implement; the highly fluid nature of the opening stages of the war did not provide the necessary time required to develop the very detailed timetables required of a barrage. Consequently, it was not until March 1915, during the Battle of Neuve-Chappelle, when sufficient ammunition supplies were available and the war had adopted its siege-like character, that a barrage was first employed, albeit in embryonic form, (see Chapter 4). Interestingly, the British attack at Neuve-Chappelle was carried out over a relatively narrow front, so, despite the fact that this attack occurred in the earlier stages of the war, the number of guns per yard of frontage was unsurpassed; in fact, it was even larger than the number used during the massive bombardments of spring 1917.[344]

The barrage continued to evolve both technically and tactically until it reached its most efficacious form during the Battle of Arras in 1917. Consequently, as artillery historian Major-General J.B.A. Bailey observed in his seminal work *Field Artillery and Firepower*, the fire plan employed at Arras became the standard upon which imperial artillery doctrine was modelled for the remainder of the war.[345] By the time of the assault on Vimy Ridge, imperial artillery doctrine identified four classes of barrage: creeping, standing, protective, and back. Curiously, even the latter was included in the doctrinal publication, only to be termed "obsolescent."[346]

According to Lieutenant-Colonel Weber of the RFA, the creeping barrage was, in his opinion, the biggest artillery technical development arising from the Battle of the Somme in the summer of 1916. In those muddy killing fields, the tactic of the creeping barrage, which would become de rigueur for the remainder of the war, first came into being in response to evolving defensive tactics on the part of the Germans.[347] Having lost too many machine guns to Allied bombardment of the trench lines in previous battles, the Germans adjusted their defensive doctrine and instead decided to deploy their machine guns between the trench lines. This had the effect of locating them outside of the fall of shot of the artillery bombardment, which, until the Battle of the Somme, would lift from trench line to trench line, leaving the terrain between the trenches unmolested. General Sir Henry Horne, a former Royal Horse Artillery officer and Inspector of Artillery who was in command of XV Corps at the Somme, addressed this by directing his guns to fire just in front of the infantry and to creep forward as they advanced.[348] The resultant *creeping barrage* was a line of fire dropped in front of the attacking infantry that crept forward in incremental *lifts* instead of merely dwelling on trench lines.[349]

Ideally, for safety reasons, the mean point of impact of shrapnel bullets was calculated to be 200 yards in front advancing infantry.[350] Consequently, the initial line of fire was planned to open 200 yards in front of the jumping-off line, also known as the *start line* or the *line of departure*, and lifted forward at the pace at which the infantry advanced, generally 100 yards every 3 or 4 minutes, depending on ground conditions.[351] The depth of zone – that is, the beaten zone – of an 18-pounder brigade was 200 yards, so lifts were planned to be 100 yards at a minimum.[352] Doctrinally, this pace of a barrage was based on the principle articulated in *Artillery Notes No. 4* of March 1917, which stated that the timing of the lifts should be such that "the slowest man can easily keep close up under the barrage. 100 yards in 3 minutes is a good average pace over dry ground pitted with shell holes."[353] Moreover, this conclusion was based on lived experience in the killing fields of the Somme, where the lifts were planned much more quickly and the barrage subsequently outpaced the advancing infantry.[354] As the technical aspects of artillery progressed, and the gunners themselves developed more experience over the course of the war, the speed of the barrage also changed from being simplistic – i.e., the same speed throughout the assault – to being more reflective of the tendency of the infantry to slow down over time due to fatigue. Major-General Archibald Montgomery noted in his history of the Fourth Army that:

> *for the first 200–300 yards the barrage should be timed to advance at the rate of 100 yards every two, or three, minutes, while the men were fresh, their nerves highly strung after a long night's waiting, and while the enemy was still stunned by the initial shock of our artillery fire. Then the rate of advance should be reduced to 100 yards every four minutes over good ground; to be further reduced to six, or even eight minutes if there were any obstacles or the ground was much cut up.*[355]

As the creeping barrage moved forward with infantry behind it, it eventually joined *standing barrages*, which were fired concurrently on interim or final objectives. *Standing barrages* differed from creeping barrages in that they remained stationary on targets in order to suppress or neutralize them. They were employed primarily on trenches that were about to be assaulted in order to prevent the enemy manning his parapets in time to arrest the advance, and to keep defenders of neighbouring trenches that were not to be assaulted in their dugouts during the attack.[356] Doctrinally, the creeping and standing barrages were to be used together.

The creeping barrage preceded the infantry, who were following it as close behind as was safe – this was referred to as *leaning in to the barrage*. While the creeping barrage moved forward, the standing barrage suppressed the known enemy locations. The advancing fire of the creeping barrage then joined the stationary fire of the standing barrage, after which both barrages lifted off together in a more voluminous creeping barrage toward the subsequent objective.[357] This didn't occur all at once, however; as the infantry neared the objective, the guns were successively lifted off the objective by calibre, in accordance with safety considerations: the heavier the gun, the larger the blast and thus the larger the safety area that was required around the point of impact to avoid fratricide. Consequently, heavy guns were lifted off first, followed by medium guns and finally field guns, in order to ensure that fire was kept on the objective until the infantry was as close as possible.[358] Once all the guns lifted off the objective, if the infantry paused to consolidate, as we will see was the case at Vimy Ridge, the guns thereafter fired protective barrages.

Protective barrages, as the name implies, were employed during pauses in the attack in order to keep enemy to the front and on the immediate flanks of the assaulting infantry from engaging them while they consolidated on the objective and prepared to continue the advance. As noted above, a barrage crept forward a safe distance beyond the objective once the infantry arrived on it, where it formed a protective barrage. The protective barrage did not remain stationary, however. Part of the fire was used to *sweep* forward and backward with small lifts across a zone with a depth of 2000 yards in order to prevent any assembly of a counterattack force.[359]

The calculation and planning of a barrage began at the highest possible point in the artillery hierarchy, dependent on the size of the organization involved in the operation. For a Corps-sized operation, such as the assault on Vimy Ridge, the commander of the Corps Artillery initiated the artillery planning. For smaller operations, such as battalion raids, the commander of the supporting artillery brigade or battery was responsible to initiate the planning. Regardless of the hierarchical level of the operation, the key initiating document that framed the artillery *problem*, for which the artillery commander needed to provide a *solution*, was the assaulting infantry commander's plan. As L.C.L. Oldfield, the colonel-commandant of the Royal Artillery, reminded his audience at the Royal United Services Institute in 1922, "the barrage is a good servant but a bad master, and must be made to conform to the plans of the commander."[360]

We turn now to the process by which a barrage was planned and distributed. When planning a barrage supporting a Corps-sized attack, the divisional artilleries involved were allocated a *lane* by the Corps artillery commander. This was a section of the front, normally corresponding to the supported infantry division's share of the front line, for which each divisional artillery was responsible. Doctrinally, the frontage that could be covered by a divisional artillery was 1,200 yards; however, infantry division frontages could be broader than this, and so mitigating measures were employed to compensate for such situations. From an artillery perspective, the allocation of reinforcing artillery brigades to the divisional artillery allowed the supporting CRA to *thicken* the fire in his lane. Failing that, the deployment of tanks in support of the infantry could also provide intimate, direct-fire support.[361]

Having received the lane that they were responsible for, the CRA in turn divided that lane among his allocated artillery brigades. The brigade commanders then divided their assigned lanes among their constituent batteries. During prolonged barrages, two guns from every battery dropped out of the barrage every 5–10 minutes to allow the crew to rest and carry out routine maintenance of the gun. In order to ensure that this did not create a gap in the fire of the battery, barrages were designed to ensure that each brigade's lane was narrow enough to accommodate the temporary loss of two guns per battery; the fire of other batteries was also superimposed. The superimposition of artillery batteries could be accomplished in two ways: in the first option, the brigade lane was divided in half, creating two battery lanes with a battery assigned to each, while the third battery fired across the whole of the artillery brigade frontage. The second option forwent the creation of battery lanes; instead, all three batteries were tasked to fire across the entire width of the artillery brigade lane. This superimposition of battery fire ensured that, even if guns were spelled off to rest, or if a battery were tasked to engage targets of opportunity, there was still fire landing across the whole of the brigade front.[362]

The batteries of 18-pounders were the busiest fire units during a barrage, but guns of all natures had a role to play in what was a layered, coordinated fire plan that incorporated every firing element available. The United States Army's *Field Artillery Notes No. 2*, issued in May 1917, was essentially a reprint of British artillery lessons. It included a list of principles that contributed to an effective 18-pounder barrage, indicative of the intensive work that occurred in the batteries and artillery brigades during a barrage. These principles included smart and accurate drill, rehearsals, timekeeping, simplicity, the sorting of ammunition by propellants, the adjustment of sights (on the gun), and calibration and consequent gun corrections.[363] In the fall of 1918, Brigadier-General Morrison provided a snapshot of what a common barrage looked like to the representatives of the Canadian Press:

> *A normal barrage consists of an 18-pounder shrapnel gun to every 20 yards of front, lifts 100 yards every three minutes; rate of fire, three rounds per minute from zero. 4.5 Howitzer firing 35-pound shell H.E. with jumping barrage 300 yards in front of shrapnel barrage. 6-inch How., shell 100 pounds, about 400 yards in front, taking on strong points, machine guns and C.Ts. 8-inch and 9.2-inch howitzers firing 200 pound and 286 pound shells respectively, 500 to 700 yards in front taking on road and trench junctions, tramways, Headquarters, O.P's and strong points. 60-pounders shrapnel sweeping road and approaches in rear. Concluding with protective barrage by 18-pounders and general strafing of Hinterland by heavier calibres.[364]*

Naturally, planning such a barrage was an intensive affair – it couldn't just be knitted together in the space of several minutes. At the battery, three hours of warning were required for a barrage to be properly organized: the coordinates had to be plotted, the ranges calculated, the fuse lengths determined, and the timings for each 'lift' of the barrage synchronized. After all this, the detachment commanders and officers had to be briefed on the barrage and then left to coordinate the requirements of their own particular areas of command.[365] In battery command posts further calculations were made, while on the guns the sergeant laid out his ammunition, set the fuses on the rounds, and briefed his detachment on their duties. Naturally, the challenge of ensuring everything was well prepared so that the barrage began precisely at the time scheduled was exacerbated when fatigue, stress, and enemy shelling were added to the mix.

Having discussed *ways* by which the artillery supported infantry offensive operations in the spring of 1917, let us turn now to a consideration of how the guiding doctrine shaped the development of the artillery plan for the assault on Vimy Ridge.

DEVELOPING THE FIRE PLAN

The fire support plan for attack on Vimy Ridge began at the very top. As it was the British First Army that determined the breadth and depth of the Canadian Corps' operations, it was the artillery commander at First Army that ensured General Byng had sufficient artillery support to accomplish his task. The importance of properly assigning fire support resources to the critical point in the battlefield grew exponentially when trench warfare became the norm. Robbed of the ability to demonstrate cleverness or ingenuity through manoeuvre, the only way that British commanders could demonstrate their grasp of operational art was through their ability to marshal resources and apply the effects of firepower.[366]

The allocation of fire support assets was established by the major-general Royal Artillery of First Army, Major-General H.F. Mercer, who issued orders directly to his two subordinate artillery commanders, the GOCRAs of both the British I Corps and the Canadian Corps, and allocated to them Army-level artillery units to augment their fire. General Headquarters issued OAD 274 on January 10, 1917, which allocated heavy and siege artillery to the three armies of the BEF, and followed that up with the allocation of field artillery in OAD 286 on January 26, 1917.[367] The First Army fire plan was issued to the subordinate corps on February 8, 1917. As the fire units that were allocated to support the attack came from not only the Canadian Corps but also from flanking Corps and First Army, the major-general Royal Artillery of the First Army held overall command of the Canadian and flanking corps' artillery. The fire plan that supported the Canadian Corps' assault was thus top-down; that is to say, the planning started at the top of the fire support hierarchy and was distributed to subordinate formations and units who executed the plan.

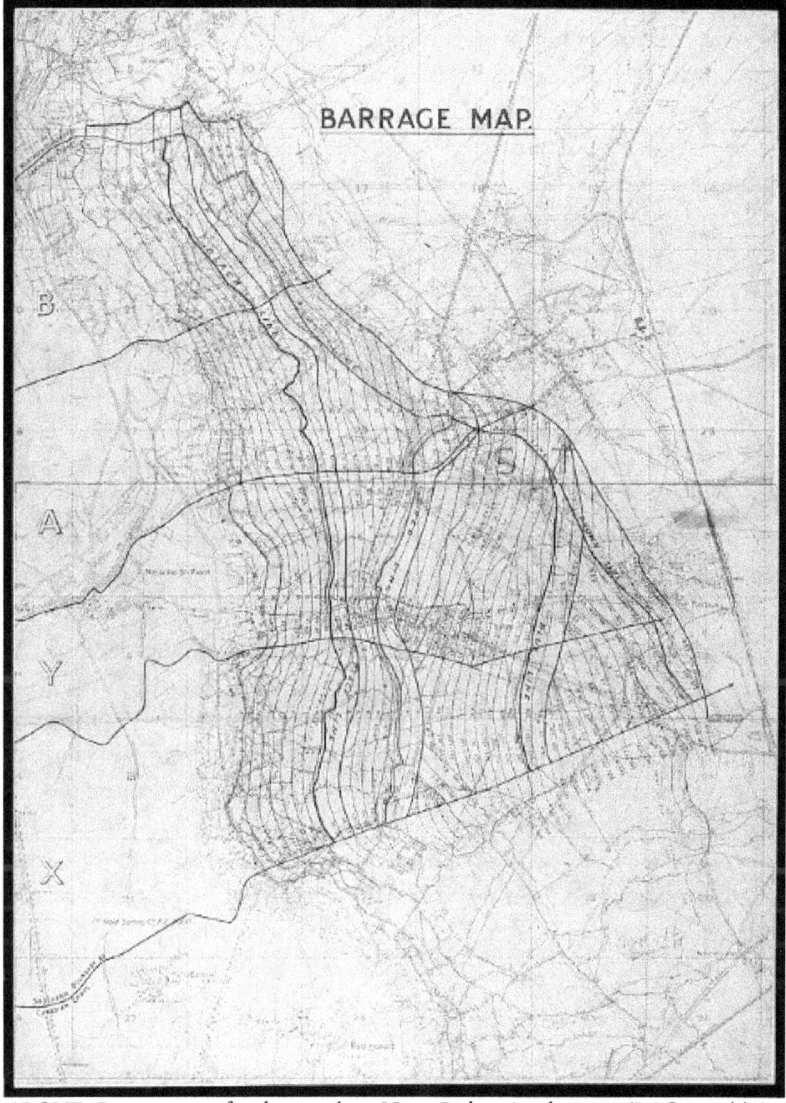

ABOVE: Barrage map for the attack on Vimy Ridge, April 1917. (LAC 178448)

All Brigadier-General Morrison's fire support plans emanated from the singular requirement to support the Canadian Corps infantry assault, and the process continued down throughout the organization hierarchy: the needs of the Canadian infantry division commanders would have to be met, and the overall Corps fire plan would have to accommodate their requirements for immediate intimate support, while also shaping the battlefield before they crossed the line of departure. Morrison recalled that the task before him was daunting, to say the least. He learned early that he had been allocated at least 480 18-pounders, 126 howitzers, and 275 heavy and siege guns, all of which had to be incorporated into the Corps fire plan and thus necessitated the most thorough and detailed planning in order to use them effectively. He recalled that "never before had there been so much artillery massed for one attack."[368]

To accomplish his task, Morrison asked the CRAs supporting each of the four Canadian infantry divisions to draft a fire plan for their own front. These plans were submitted to the Corps Artillery Headquarters, where Major Alan F. Brooke, the artillery staff officer at the Canadian Corps headquarters and the future British Chief of the Imperial General Staff during the Second World War, integrated the division fire plans into a single corps-level fire support plan that met the demands of the four Canadian infantry divisions and the guidance of the Canadian corps commander.[369] Plenty of work went into it, and it showed. Brigadier-General Hussey recalled in his history of the 5th British Division, whose divisional artillery was attached to the 2nd Canadian Division for the assault, that "the barrage map, timing the Artillery tasks for eight hours and dovetailing in with that of the Third Army, was a work of art."[370]

Morrison issued his fire plan to his subordinate CRAs on March 28, 1917, although some initial guidance had been given and, indeed, the bombardment had already started. In it he articulated how the fire support to the Canadian Corps was to be divided into four phases. The first two phases consisted of preparatory fire, which served to set the conditions for the actual assault. Phase 1, denoted as Z-20, was scheduled to begin twenty days before the attack and it would last until one week prior to the attack, denoted as Z-7. Thereafter, phase 2 was scheduled from Z-6 to Z-Day. With the previous twenty days having been devoted to shaping the battlefield, phase 3 consisted of the intimate support to the infantry in the form of the barrage that preceded it during their advance on the four objectives, articulated above. Finally, phase 4 represented the forward movement of the artillery to ensure continuous fire support in depth beyond the final objective.[371] We will now turn to an in-depth review of each of the four phases of artillery support.

Phase 1 – Initial Preparatory Fire

The first thirteen days of the Vimy Ridge fire plan focused on a general increase of artillery fire that intensified over time as the schedule neared the transition to phase 2, all while maintaining some degree of surprise concerning the total amount of fire support available to the Canadian Corps. In order to achieve the latter, no more than 50 per cent of the heavy and siege artillery batteries were allowed to disclose themselves by firing, while the CRAs were ordered to use no more than two brigades of guns.[372]

During this period Morrison had two goals: the destruction of trenches and the cutting of wire obstacles. The fire that was employed to destroy the German trenches leveraged the target acquisition resources of the Royal Flying Corps in order to identify and engage the German trench network, while the fire that was directed toward cutting the wire obstacles was to be provided by the 18-pounders of the divisional artilleries and focused on the German first and second lines of defence. Any wire that could not be adequately cut by the divisional artilleries was to be nominated for engagement by heavy artillery assets by the responsible CRA. To assist in the efforts at wire cutting, the artillery supporting I British Corps on the Canadian Corps' left flank was also tasked to fire in support of wire cutting in the Canadian zone of operations.[373]

Concurrent to the divisional artillery trench destruction and wire cutting, during this phase the counter-battery staff officer was to carry out the systematic destruction of hostile batteries using the counter-battery and heavy-artillery groups. All accurately located hostile batteries, their locations divined by aeroplanes of the Royal Flying Corps flying reconnaissance missions as well as by sound-ranging and flash-spotting resources, were to be engaged during this period. This fire was to focus initially on independent German batteries and subsequently on larger groupings of fire support elements.

It is advisable to pause here to briefly survey the German artillery that opposed the Canadian Corps' gunners. We saw in a previous chapter that, thanks to the development of the soixante-quinze and the 18-pounder in the French and British armies respectively, the Germans were outclassed by the Allied field guns in rate of fire. Such was not the case, however, in the field of howitzers, where the Germans truly excelled; in fact, throughout the war the Germans possessed a significant technical advantage over their adversaries on the Western Front in their large inventory of howitzers. Indeed, at the outbreak of the war, only Germany had established modern howitzers as integral parts of their divisional fire support organizations.[374]

Similar to developments in France and the United Kingdom, the pursuit of howitzers for the German army was born of their appreciation of the nature of conflicts in the latter half of the nineteenth century and the opening years of the twentieth, including, among others, the Boer War and the Russo-Japanese War. The German military leadership noted in their studies that the flat trajectory of the cannon-like guns that were employed during these conflicts proved ineffective against troops who had sought protection in trenches. Consequently, anticipating a war in which they would be on the offensive, in 1898 the Germans produced the 105mm howitzer, which was later upgraded with a recoil brake in 1908 to produce the 10.5cm FH 98/09.[375] Thus, in August 1914 the German artillery had a smattering of both field cannons and field howitzers on which to rely; at the outbreak of war German divisions held one light field howitzer to every five light field guns, 5076 FK 96 n/A and 1230 FH 98/09, deployed in 1069 batteries.[376]

The German artillery was organized into batteries of six guns, and the artillery brigade of each active division was divided into three battalions of 77mm light field guns and one battalion of 105mm light field howitzers. The corps artillery battalion was composed of four batteries of 150mm heavy field howitzers, which the corps commander usually assigned to one of his divisions, where it came under the control of the divisional artillery brigade.[377] Heavy howitzers were prominent in the German army due to the assumption that French or Belgian fortresses would have to be reduced. As a result, whereas French and British gunners were initially uninterested in incorporating heavier artillery in their organizations, the Germans started the war with 148 batteries of heavy artillery.[378]

Like their opponents, the Germans amended the organization of their fire support to reflect lessons learned. As manoeuvre ground to a halt and trench warfare began, the side with the larger howitzer park enjoyed the advantage. Realizing this, in October of 1914 the ratio of light field howitzers to field guns in German divisions was raised from 1:3 to 1:2, and was raised again in December 1914 to 1:1. Also in December of 1914, each division was allocated a battalion of eight 150mm heavy howitzers, and by March 1915 the Germans settled on a divisional artillery consisting of a single field artillery regiment of two field gun battalions and one light howitzer battalion.[379]

These were, of course, the doctrinal organizational arrangements of the German artillery, which naturally varied based on local tactical circumstances. On the eastern slope of Vimy Ridge, Morrison's adversary in the artillery duel was the commander of the artillery assigned to support the German 79th Division – Colonel Rudolf Bleidorn.[380] Bleidorn had at his disposal the 63rd Reserve Field Artillery Regiment of nine batteries, deployed in covered positions on the eastern slope of the ridge, as well as a section of the 69th Field Artillery Regiment. In addition to this firepower, and in order to fire deep into the Canadian lines, Bleidorn deployed three howitzer batteries, four mortar batteries, and two direct-fire batteries near the crest of the ridge.[381] While it might seem that the Germans were well supplied with indirect fire, in reality the 79th Reserve Infantry Division had only eighty-nine guns to support it – well overmatched by the more than 1000 guns serving the Canadian Corps.[382]

Returning now to the overall goal of the Canadian Corps' fire plan's first phase, when the heavy and siege batteries were not engaged in the counter-battery fight, they were to assist the divisional artilleries in their fire support tasks, specifically during night operations. Morrison directed that during periods of darkness, the CRAs were to use available heavy and medium artillery to fire on the *back country*, the term contemporaries used to describe the terrain behind the enemy front lines where sustainment and logistical operations were undertaken. The primary back country targets that were to be engaged during the first phase of the fire plan were reinforcement routes, communications trenches, light railways, refilling points, and ammunition dumps.[383]

Phase 2 – Intensified Preparatory Fire

The second phase of the Vimy Ridge fire plan was scheduled to being on Z-6. During this phase, Morrison directed that the amount of fire was to increase exponentially with the intent, by the end of the phase, of having all the artillery brigades engaging the enemy, with the exception of the silent batteries that were deployed forward in the 1st and 2nd Canadian Divisions' boundaries. The work of trench destruction, wire cutting, and counter-battery fire was scheduled to continue along the same lines as during phase 1, although the number of guns that were allocated to these tasks, and the amount of ammunition that was approved for use, was to be substantially increased. Of note, during this phase of the fire plan, Morrison planned to incorporate the fire of the trench mortars, starting at Z-4. Unique to this phase was the planned destruction of villages that fell within the zone of operations. The villages of Thélus, Tilleuls, Farbus, Givenchy, Vimy Ridge, Petit Vimy Ridge, La Chaudière, and Willerval were all scheduled to be subjected to intense bombardments coordinated by Morrison's staff.[384]

Phase 2 of the fire plan also included the incorporation of feint barrages; two corps-level feint barrages were planned by the Corps Artillery HQ to be carried out along the whole Corps frontage, while each CRA was also tasked to conduct additional minor feints along their respective division frontages during the same time frame. The goal of the feint barrages was twofold: first, they served as a rehearsal of the barrage, and second, they provided an opportunity to observe how the Germans reacted to the barrage. In particular, the Canadian Corps artillery staff hoped the feint barrages would incite the Germans to retaliate with defensive barrages, which would then disclose the locations of the German batteries through sound ranging and flash spotting and thus facilitate their engagement by the counter-battery staff officer. In addition to assisting the counter-battery fight, the feint barrages were also intended to trick the Germans into remaining in their dugouts.

To this end, the feint barrages were designed to follow this procedure: first, batteries were to open their firing on a trench line; then, a creeping barrage would roll forward as if supporting an advancing line of troops and then quickly return to the original opening line of fire on the trench line. The intent of returning fire to the original start line was to catch defenders who had emerged from their dugouts back into their unprotected defensive positions, thinking that the barrage had moved on – which it had not. The Corps leadership hoped the feints would induce the Germans to believe the fire would return once it passed over and thus trick them into remaining in their dugouts until the assaulting infantry was upon them.[385]

Phase 3 – Support to the Assault

Phase 3 of the artillery program was the intimate fire in support of the actual assault. The fire plan consisted of a creeping barrage, the purpose of which was to suppress "any machine guns or riflemen that may still lurk in shell holes" between the line of departure and the four coloured-line objectives.[386] The creeping barrage was planned to "lift" every 100 yards, firing three rounds per gun, per minute. The barrage map issued by the GOCRA provided the specific location and timing for each line of the barrage. This barrage map was then passed to the divisional artilleries, who divided their divisional lanes among their subordinate artillery brigades. The brigades, thereafter, took their assigned lanes and divided them among their subordinate batteries.

The Vimy Ridge barrage plan generally adhered to doctrinal timings. A review of the barrage map indicates that the average lift was about five minutes per line; the extra two minutes were likely added to accommodate the slope of the ridge and the expected heavily pockmarked terrain, which would result from the intense preliminary bombardment scheduled for phases 1 and 2.[387] During this phase the silent batteries, which were deployed well forward and intended for use once the infantry advance went beyond the range of initial supporting guns, were ordered to remain silent and in readiness to respond to what were referred to as "LL Calls" – these were calls for fire from all available guns, used for emergencies and targets of opportunity.[388]

While the majority of 18-pounders were scheduled to execute the rolling barrage, a portion of 18-pounders, 4.5-inch howitzers, and the medium- and heavy-artillery batteries were also tasked to fire standing barrages on known trenches and defensive systems.[389] The heavy-artillery and counter-battery groups were to complete the counter-battery program during phases 1 and 2. Thus, the role of the counter-battery staff officer and his guns during phase 3 shifted to the intense neutralization of any remaining hostile artillery, the timing of which was determined by the observation of the timing of the retaliatory fire during the feint barrages that had been executed in phase 2.[390] The goal of this neutralizing fire was to "paralyze and blind those hostile batteries which [had] not been destroyed [during phases 1 and 2] by a sudden and violent application of all available means."[391] In order to assist with the neutralizing effect of the counter-battery program, for the first fifteen minutes of the assault the Canadian divisional artilleries supporting the 1st, 2nd, and 4th Canadian infantry divisions were tasked to delegate one 4.5-inch howitzer battery apiece to reinforce the counter-battery groups.

A key element of the fire plan at Vimy Ridge, which remains critical during modern operations as well, is the close coordination between the assaulting infantry and their fire support. This close liaison was achieved in a number of ways. First, divisional artilleries, groups, and brigades were ordered to deploy their headquarters as close as possible to their affiliated infantry headquarters.[392] If that was not possible, each headquarters was tasked to dispatch a liaison officer who was to be "as senior an Artillery officer as can be spared without affecting the formation" to coordinate with the supported infantry.[393] Second, the Canadian divisional artilleries in particular were tasked to provide a liaison officer to each of the battalion headquarters attacking on their frontage. These officers were tasked to "gather all possible information from Infantry Reports, and to transmit such information to their Artillery Brigades... [and] investigate and report on cases of short-shooting."[394]

We've seen that by 1917 the aeroplane was a valuable fire support asset. The Corps Artillery Instruction observed that "the necessity of close liaison with the Royal Flying Corps [Royal Flying Corps] is now fully appreciated." To this end, battery commanders were tasked to visit No. 16 Squadron, Royal Flying Corps, "with a view to making the personal acquaintance of observers and pilots working with them."[395] This cooperation was essential, and establishing a good rapport between pilots and gunners became commonplace. It wasn't simply the artillerymen who paid visits to their flying friends, but from time to time pilots would pay visits to the guns to see how they operated. Wilbert Gilroy, a dentist turned pilot from Winnipeg and a member of 4 Squadron, RFC, wrote to his mother with a story of his visit to several batteries, a practice he greatly appreciated, noting that "we are supposed to go up from time to time to call on them [the batteries]. It makes it more interesting when one knows the people on the ground."[396]

Phase 4 – Forward Movement of the Artillery

The final phase of the fire plan involved the forward displacement of the artillery in order to provide continuous fire support to the advancing infantry. On the left, within the boundaries of the 3rd and 4th Canadian Divisions, the problem was not deemed overly dangerous as the distance to the final objectives for these two divisions was substantially shorter than that for their sister divisions farther to the right. Consequently, the plan was to move only a few batteries forward once the 3rd and 4th Divisions had secured their objectives; the trigger to initiate their forward movement was when the distance of the infantry advance rendered their fire ineffective.[397]

The situation on the right flank, where the 1st and 2nd Canadian Divisions were attacking, was much more problematic. Because the objectives assigned to these divisions were much farther away, the fire plan was crafted such that fire support between the objectives Blue Line and Brown Line was provided by the silent forward batteries. Understanding the importance of having artillery well forward to defend against the inevitable counterattacks, Morrison knew that the batteries that had been firing since the beginning of the fire plan would have to move forward as soon as possible in order to ensure that there was sufficient fire support available to the infantry once they attained their final objective. He therefore directed that it was "essential for these batteries to move forward as soon as circumstances will admit, to ensure sufficient defence of the newly gained objectives during consolidation."[398] Of course, such a broad forward displacement would be a logistical and administrative challenge, to say the least. Morrison stressed the importance of planning each detail to the letter. He directed his CRAs to produce the schemes for the forward movement of their batteries, which included

> *the sequence of batteries detailed to move... with estimates of the time required for the completion of the move of each battery, exact roads and tracks to be followed, state of previous preparation of the forward positions, and forward wagon line dispositions...these preparations will include bridging trenches up to the front line, a reserve of artillery bridges (60 at present under construction by [Construction Engineers]) and the organization of fatigue parties from Trench Mortar batteries to assist guns forward.*[399]

In order to expedite the process and maintain some command and control, Morrison also directed that field artillery brigade headquarters would remain in place until the batteries were deployed into their forward positions. In addition, he stipulated that the advancing batteries were to link into the telephone wire previously established by artillery officers advancing with the infantry, in order to maintain communications.[400]

The forward deployment of the heavy-artillery groups was also deemed essential. Morrison knew there was destined to be a determined German counterattack that would require augmented defensive fire and that the advance of the Canadian infantry would prompt the German artillery to move eastward, placing hostile batteries out of range of the Canadian counter-battery fire. This necessitated the hasty forward movement of the medium and heavy artillery. With priority going to the 6-inch howitzers, the GOCRA was tasked with developing a bold plan to get the heavies forward as soon as possible.[401]

A great concern for Morrison was that, due to the location of the final objective, lying as it did on eastern slope of the ridge and hence out of sight of the Canadian Corps prior to Z-Day, it was impossible to register defensive barrages prior to the launch of the attack. To this end, he directed that as soon as observation could be made onto the eastern slope of the ridge, the registration and preparation of defensive barrages should commence as soon as possible. He encouraged the CRAs to work out a system of communication, combining flares, visual signals, telephone communications, and runners, to link the infantry to their supporting guns. In this way fire could be brought to bear quickly and effectively, hopefully avoiding unnecessarily long and ineffectual barrages that would expend the limited ammunition remaining.[402]

The plan developed by Morrison for the support of the Canadian Corps' assault on Vimy Ridge was consistent with the prevailing artillery doctrine of the time. It began at the very top, when the commander-in-chief of the imperial forces allocated artillery priorities to the various armies implicated in the spring 1917 offensive. From there, the British First Army's Major-General Royal Artillery, who was the senior artillery officer in a field army, allocated the resources he received to his subordinate corps, including the Canadian Corps, based on their role in the upcoming operation. Morrison developed a plan to employ these resources, based on the manoeuvre plan devised by Corps Commander Lieutenant-General Byng and his staff. We turn now to the question of how the fire plan devised by Brigadier-General Morrison was executed.

PUTTING IT ALL TOGETHER

The execution phase of the fire plan in support of the Canadian Corps consisted of more than simply firing the preliminary bombardment and supporting barrage. An indispensable element of the execution was the assembly of all the fire support units that were allocated to the Canadian Corps from across the Western Front into the Canadian Corps' area of operations. Thus, the actual execution of the fire plan began, perhaps counter-intuitively, months before Z-Day when the number and nature of artillery brigades and batteries that were to be employed at Vimy Ridge were determined. We saw in the previous chapter that the heavy and siege artillery batteries were allocated to each of the three armies constituting the BEF in an order issued on January 10, 1917, and the allocation of field artillery assets was ordered a little over two weeks later, on January 26, 1917. These two directives set in motion the deployment of artillery brigades and batteries in order to ensure they would be in place in time for the beginning of the preliminary bombardment.

To say that the artillery organization supporting the Canadian Corps' assault was robust would be a gross understatement. Conforming to the doctrine of artillery destruction, an extremely large, centrally controlled fire support organization consisting of 624 field and 224 heavy guns served by 45,760 men was poised to pulverize the German defences over an extended period of time with an intense bombardment designed to destroy trenches, eliminate wire, and kill and demoralize enemy soldiers.[403] Overall command of the artillery was vested in Brigadier-General Morrison, who exercised command and control over the subordinate artillery formations and units through the use of two functional groupings: the four Canadian divisional artilleries that provided close support to the assaulting infantry divisions, and the heavy and counter-battery groups that delivered depth fire and counter-battery work (see Figure 9.1). We shall consider the size and organization of each of the two organizational grouping.

Divisional Artilleries

The four assaulting Canadian infantry divisions were supported by the three like-numbered Canadian divisional artilleries and the British Reserve Divisional Artillery, also referred to at times as the Lahore Divisional Artillery. The 1st Canadian Divisional Artillery, for example, supported the 1st Canadian Infantry Division and so on. As the 4th Canadian Divisional Artillery was not organized until June 1917, the British Reserve Divisional Artillery was tasked to provide direct artillery support to 4th Canadian Infantry Division. Additionally, a further four British divisional artilleries were attached to the Canadian Corps to increase the available fire support resources; each of these was integrated into a Canadian divisional artillery, or the Reserve Divisional Artillery in the case of the 4th Canadian Division. For example, the British 31st Divisional Artillery was integrated into the 1st Canadian Divisional Artillery, so that while the CRA of 31st Divisional Artillery retained command of his three

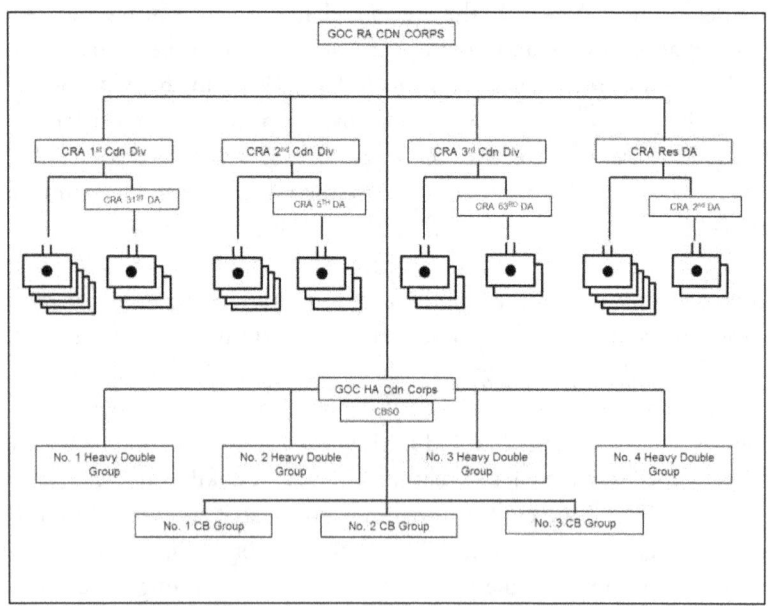

ABOVE: Fire Support Organization of the Canadian Corps (Author's Collection)

artillery brigades, he answered to the CRA of 1ˢᵗ Canadian Divisional Artillery.[404] To add a joint flavour to the organization, one of the British divisional artilleries was the 63ʳᵈ (Royal Navy) Divisional Artillery, comprising surplus Royal Navy and Royal Marines personnel assigned to service on land.[405] Additionally, several independent batteries and army field artillery brigades were attached to the Canadian Corps,

The number of guns that were allocated to each assaulting division was determined based on the frontage that each of the four Canadian infantry divisions was allocated and the depth of those divisions' assigned objectives. Consequently, the wider the assaulting division's frontage was, and the farther it was expected to advance, the more guns were allocated to the corresponding divisional artillery.[406] When finally tallied, the artillery in direct support of the four Canadian divisions assaulting Vimy Ridge consisted of a total of 480 18-pounders, 138 4.5-inch howitzers, ninety-six 2-inch trench mortars, and twenty-four 9.45-inch trench mortars.[407] We will turn now to an investigation of the four reinforced divisional artilleries that supported the Canadian Corps, and the unique ways each was organized.

The 1ˢᵗ Canadian Divisional Artillery

On the right of the Canadian Corps' front was the 1ˢᵗ Canadian Division, which was supported by the 1ˢᵗ Canadian Divisional Artillery. Of the artillery formations in the Canadian Army, the 1ˢᵗ Canadian Divisional Artillery had served the longest during the Great War. It was mobilized in the summer of 1914 when Canada had initially agreed to contribute to the war effort. After the reorganization of the imperial artillery in March 1917, the 1ˢᵗ Canadian Divisional Artillery consisted of the 1ˢᵗ, 2ⁿᵈ, and 3ʳᵈ Brigades, CFA, and it was commanded by Brigadier-General Herbert Cyril Thacker. A Permanent Force soldier who commissioned in the Royal Canadian Artillery in 1891, Thacker had served with the guns in South Africa during the Boer War and had been awarded the Queen's Medal with three clasps for his conduct and performance. At the outbreak of the Great War, he deployed to Europe with the first Canadian contingent, and eventually rose to command the 2ⁿᵈ Canadian Divisional Artillery from 1914 to 1915. He was transferred to command of 1ˢᵗ Canadian Divisional Artillery in September 1915, which he commanded until the end of the war.

At Vimy Ridge, the 1ˢᵗ Canadian Division had a broad frontage, totalling 2000 yards. As the division's objectives were the farthest away from the Canadian start line, Thacker was allocated a substantial amount of firepower. He had under his command his own 1st Canadian Divisional Artillery, which consisted of nine of the original twelve 18-pounder field batteries, as well as the 2nd, 9th, and 48th howitzer batteries. Reinforcing artillery that was allocated to the 1st Canadian Divisional Artillery included the 31st Divisional Artillery, the 72nd Brigade, RFA, the 5th Brigade, Royal Horse Artillery, and the 26th Brigade, RFA. The latter two artillery brigades were grouped into a single formation under the command of Colonel A.T. Butler of the Royal Horse Artillery and adopted the name Butler Group. Butler was relieved by Colonel A.B. Hinton, RFA, on April 3, 1917, after he was injured by shrapnel while returning to the brigade after a visit to one of his batteries; the group was then renamed Hinton Group.[408] The guns of the 1st Brigade, CFA, were placed under the command of the 31st Divisional Artillery along with the 120th and 160th Brigades, RFA. In addition to these brigades, two groups of medium trench mortars were included in the order of battle: the Right Group, which was placed under the command of the CRA of 31st Divisional Artillery, and the Left Group, which was retained by the CRA, 1st Canadian Divisional Artillery.[409] The total number of guns that Thacker had at his disposal were 144 18-pounders, thirty-four 4.5-inch howitzers, eighteen 2-inch trench mortars, and six 9.45-inch trench mortars.[410]

2nd Canadian Divisional Artillery

The 2nd Canadian Division fell to the left of the 1st Canadian Division and was supported in its assault by the 2nd Canadian Divisional Artillery, commanded by Brigadier-General Henri Alexander Panet. A graduate of Royal Military College and a Permanent Force soldier, Panet was a veteran of the Boer War, where he had served in C Battery. Prior to the Great War, he had commanded the Royal Canadian Horse Artillery Brigade as of 1911. He had also supervised the training at the momentous artillery camp held in Petawawa in 1912, mentioned in Chapter 1. As the head of the RCHA Brigade when the war broke out, Panet led his unit to Europe with the first Canadian contingent in the fall of 1914, and crossed with it to Flanders in the summer of 1915. After serving at the Somme, he was promoted to colonel in June 1916, and then to brigadier-general in December of that year, after which he assumed command of the 2nd Canadian Divisional Artillery. He served with great distinction throughout the conflict, and remained at the head of the 2nd Canadian Divisional Artillery until April 1919, when the formation was demobilized. During his service in the war, he was mentioned in dispatches (MID) a total of seven times.[411]

Supporting a frontage of 1400 yards with a rather deep penetration into the objective, Panet received a large allocation of guns. The integral field brigades of the 2nd Canadian Divisional Artillery included the 4th, 5th, and 6th Field Brigades. These were augmented with substantial reinforcing artillery, including the British 5th Divisional Artillery, which itself came to the fight augmented with the 28th Army Field Artillery Brigade and the 93rd Army Field Artillery Brigade.[412] To effect command and control, Panet divided his guns into four groups, which he titled G, H, I, and J, each consisting of a field artillery brigade: G – 93rd Army Field Artillery Brigade; H – 4th Brigade, CFA; I – 6th Brigade, CFA; and J – 5th Brigade, CFA. The 5th Divisional Artillery was deployed forward as silent batteries to remain hidden until zero hour, when they would reveal themselves by firing. Their forward position would allow them greater range to support the 2nd Canadian Division assault beyond the crest of the ridge.[413] Under Panet's command he had a total of 126 18-pounders, thirty-four 4.5-inch howitzers, eighteen 2-inch trench mortars, and five 9.45-inch trench mortars. As the 93rd Army Field Artillery Brigade did not have a 4.5-inch howitzer battery attached, Panet was the only CRA who was not tasked to detach a battery of howitzers to a counter-battery group.[414]

3rd Canadian Divisional Artillery

The 3rd Canadian Divisional Artillery was under the command of Brigadier-General J.H. Mitchell, an active militia officer from Toronto who originally commanded the 3rd Brigade, CFA, when the first contingent deployed overseas. He assumed command of the organization when it arrived in England over the course of several weeks in February and March of 1916. The brigades of the divisional artillery spent several months in England training; eventually, they were reorganized based on the newly adopted standard of imperial divisional artilleries consisting of four mixed brigades of three 18-pounder batteries and one 4.5-inch battery each. The 3rd Canadian Divisional Artillery crossed from England to France in July of 1916 and went immediately into action.[415]

On March 22, 1917, in accordance with the direction to once again alter the imperial artillery organization, Mitchell divided his divisional artillery into three functional groupings: Eaton's group, under the command of Lieutenant-Colonel V. Eaton, consisted of three 18-pounder batteries and a single 4.5-inch battery; Carscallen's group, commanded by Lieutenant-Colonel H.G. Carscallen, consisted of three 18-pounder batteries and two 4.5-inch batteries, one of six guns, and one of four guns. The third and final group in 3rd Canadian Divisional Artillery was Ralston's group, under the command of Lieutenant-Colonel G.H. Ralston, which consisted of two 18-pounder batteries and a single 4.5-inch howitzer battery.[416] Sadly, Lieutenant-Colonel Eaton was wounded the night before Zero Day while visiting forward batteries; Ralston took over command of his group at 11:00 p.m. that night. Eaton succumbed to his wounds on the evening of April 11, 1917.[417]

For the assault on Vimy Ridge, the 3rd Canadian Division was assigned the smallest frontage of the four assaulting Canadian divisions, as well as a relatively narrow penetration of the objective. As a result, Mitchell was allocated the least number of reinforcing guns. The British artillery units that were assigned to support Mitchell included the 63rd (Royal Navy) Divisional Artillery, which joined the Canadian Corps on March 28, 1917.[418] The naval artillery consisted of the 223rd and 317th RFA brigades; the former held four 18-pounder batteries and a 4.5-inch howitzer battery, while the latter held three 18-pounder batteries and a 4.5-inch howitzer battery. Thus, in the two divisional artilleries supporting 3rd Canadian Division under Mitchell's command were a total of eighty-four 18-pounders, thirty-four 4.5-inch howitzers, thirty-six 2.2-inch trench mortars, and eight 9.45-inch trench mortars.[419]

Reserve Divisional Artillery

We've seen that the 4th Canadian Divisional Artillery was not created until June 1917, two months after the Battle of Vimy Ridge. For this reason, the commander-in-chief allocated the Reserve Divisional Artillery, also known as the Lahore Divisional Artillery, to the Canadian Corps to provide direct artillery support to the 4th Canadian Division, thus ensuring each of the assaulting divisions in the Canadian Corps had a divisional artillery available to support it. The Reserve Divisional Artillery was augmented with the fire of the British 2nd Divisional Artillery as well as the 18th, 76th, and 242nd Army Field Artillery Brigades.

The 4th Canadian Division was responsible for a large frontage of 2000 yards, and as such received a large complement of fire support resources, totalling 126 18-pounders, forty-two 4.5-inch howitzers, twenty-four 2.2-inch trench mortars and five 9.5-inch trench mortars.[420]

The divisional artilleries were fully stocked with an impressive array of fire support resources to provide direct support to the assaulting infantry. To give you an impression of how much reinforcing artillery was added to the corps, the normal, integral fire support resources of a four-division corps consisted of twelve brigades of artillery sporting thirty-six 18-pounder batteries and four 4.5-inch howitzer batteries. For the Canadian Corps' assault on Vimy, the assaulting divisions had at their disposal a total of eight divisional artilleries and eight army field artillery brigades for a total of 144 18-pounder batteries and sixteen 4.5-inch howitzer batteries.[421]

The Heavies

While the divisional artilleries had the responsibility to provide the direct support to the assaulting infantry divisions, in addition to this intimate support was a robust organization of heavy artillery who stood ready to provide the much-needed superior "punch" to support the Canadian Corps. These elements focused the majority of their fire on enemy artillery batteries and, thanks to their extended range, at targets deep behind the German front line where reinforcement routes, ammunition dumps, and reserves were located.

The heavy artillery supporting the Canadian Corps fell under the command of Brigadier-General Roger Henry (R.H.) Massie, who held the position of general officer commanding heavy artillery.[422] Massie was a British Artillery officer, although he was originally born in France, and the grandson of a Royal Navy admiral, Thomas Leeke Massie. Roger Massie was commissioned into the Royal Artillery in 1896 after completing studies at the Royal Military Academy in Woolwich, and subsequently served in the Sudan Campaign, followed by service in the North-West Frontier in India and the Boer War. After the Boer War, as a major, he was made supernumerary – meaning he remained in the British Army but did not hold a permanent position. That changed in 1911 when he was seconded to the Indian Mountain Artillery and became commandant of the Indian Mountain Batteries. At the outbreak of the war, he was restored to the British Army and recalled to active service.

ABOVE: Loading a heavy howitzer. (LAC 3194239)

In January of 1917 he was assigned to command the Canadian Corps' heavy artillery.[423]

Massie's command consisted, ultimately, of two components: firstly, a number of heavy artillery double groups, and secondly a number of counter battery groups.

Covering the frontage of each assaulting division was a *heavy artillery double group*.[424] Each double group was composed of, as the name implies, two heavy-artillery groups. Although heavy and siege batteries were normally independent, once the number of heavy and siege batteries became as numerous as they did, it became necessary to brigade them for command and control, thus, heavy-artillery brigades were created as a lieutenant-colonel's command. The nomenclature was changed to *heavy-artillery group* in April 1916, but later reverted back to *heavy-artillery brigade* in December of 1917, hence the use of the term *heavy-artillery group* during the Battle of Vimy Ridge.[425] Originally, imperial doctrine stipulated that the general officer commanding heavy artillery in a Corps was allocated two heavy-artillery groups, which was the case at the time of the assault on Vimy Ridge as the Canadian Corps artillery consisted of the 1st and 2nd Canadian Heavy Artillery Groups. However, in order to beef up the Corps' firepower for the assault on Vimy Ridge, the commander of the British First Army allocated a large portion of his heavy artillery to support the Canadian Corps, totalling nine British heavy groups.[426] The additional guns grew the number of double groups supporting the Canadian Corps to four.

The heavy artillery double groups assigned to Massie consisted of a total of fourteen heavy-artillery batteries and twenty-four medium-artillery batteries.[427] Double Group No. 1 was assigned to cover the 1st Canadian Division's front and consisted of Heavy Artillery Groups Nos. 1 and 2; the former was based on the 18th Heavy Artillery Group and consisted of two heavy-howitzer and three medium-howitzer batteries, while the latter was based on the 44th Heavy Artillery Group and consisted of three heavy-howitzer batteries and two medium-howitzer batteries. Double Group No. 2 covered 2nd Canadian Division's frontage and consisted of Heavy Artillery Group 3, based on 64th Heavy Artillery Group, with three heavy- and two medium-howitzer batteries, and Heavy Artillery Group 5, based on 70th Heavy Artillery Group, RGA, with four medium-howitzer batteries. Double Group 3 consisted of Heavy Artillery Groups 4 and 7; the former was based on 13th Heavy Artillery Group, RGA, and held two heavy- and three medium-howitzer batteries, while the latter was based on 53rd Heavy Artillery Group, RGA, and consisted of one heavy- and three medium-howitzer batteries. Finally, Double Group 4, covering 4th Canadian Division, consisted of Heavy Artillery Groups 6 and 8. The former was based on 1st Canadian Heavy Artillery Group and had a single heavy-howitzer battery and four medium-howitzer batteries, while Group 8 was based on 30th Heavy Artillery Group, RGA, and had two heavy- and three medium-howitzer batteries. Heavy Artillery Groups 2, 4, and 8 were also tasked to hold one heavy-howitzer battery each in readiness to reinforce the fire of one of the counter-battery groups.[428]

As mentioned above, in addition to the four heavy-artillery double groups, Massie had three counter-battery groups that were nominally under his command. To facilitate the quick and effective engagement of hostile batteries, the counter-battery groups were actually under the de facto executive command of the counter-battery staff officer, Canadian Lieutenant-Colonel A.G.L. McNaughton.

Andrew McNaughton was destined to become a prominent Canadian soldier and statesman. He was born in the small town of Moosomin, Northwest Territories (now the Province of Saskatchewan), on February

25, 1887. He originally joined the Non-permanent Militia in 1909, and when the war broke out in 1914, he deployed overseas as the battery commander of 4th Canadian Field Battery, in the 1st Brigade, CFA.

An engineer by trade, he studied engineering at McGill University in Montreal. Due to this background, he applied an extremely scientific approach to gunnery, which ensured his rapid advance through the Canadian officer corps, and eventually came to hold the position of counter-battery staff officer in the Canadian Corps for the assault on Vimy Ridge.

As we saw in a previous chapter, the control of the firing of the counter-battery groups fell to the counter-battery staff officer. McNaughton had available to him a significant amount of fire support with which to silence German batteries, namely three organizations known as Counter-Battery Groups 1 through 3. No. 1 Counter-Battery Group, based on the British 50th Heavy Artillery Group, consisted of two heavy-artillery batteries, one medium battery, one 4.5-inch howitzer battery allocated to it from a divisional artillery, two 60-pounder batteries, and one-half of a 6-inch MK VIII howitzer battery. No. 2 Counter-Battery Group, based on the British 76th Heavy Artillery Group, consisted of one heavy battery, one 4.5-inch battery allocated from a divisional artillery, four 60-pounder batteries, and one 6-inch Mark VII battery. Finally, No. 3 Counter-Battery Group, based on the 2nd Canadian Heavy Artillery Group, consisted of a heavy battery, a medium battery, a 4.5-inch howitzer battery allocated from a divisional artillery, three 60-pounder batteries, and the other half of the 6-inch Mk VII battery shared with No. 1 Counter-Battery Group. Consequently, McNaughton had at his call the fire of four heavy, two medium, three 4.5-inch, nine 60-pounder, and two 6-inch Mk VII batteries.

In total, Massie had a massive amount of fire support at his disposal in the heavy double groups and counter-battery groups: a total of eighteen heavy, twenty-six medium, three 4.5-inch, nine 60-pounder, and two 6-inch batteries. The work that these guns were expected to do over the period of several weeks was immense, and required significant logistical support to ensure it went smoothly. To support their efforts, *siege parks* were created at the corps level. These were originally entitled Army Service Corps Motor Transport Companies, but in January 1917 they were renamed siege parks – only to revert to the name Army Service Corps Motor Transport Companies in September of that year.[429] At the time of Vimy Ridge, the Canadian Corps had a siege park assigned to it to assist the heavy artillery in the movement of ammunition. The siege parks were wholly mechanized but did not have many resources, so they routinely had to draw on the horses of the field brigades and the divisional artilleries to assist in the delivery of ammunition. Colonel Puckle of the Army Service Corps described the activity of the Siege Park as follows:

> *The siege park is an interesting organization, the establishment of which concerns only the headquarters [and] some 26 lorries; but it is the nucleus of all the heavy artillery at a corps. When I left the first army the Canadian corps siege park had over a thousand lorries. Now, I must tell you how this occurs. Heavy batteries of whatever calibre, from 6-inch howitzer, 4.7 inches, and 60-pounders upward, have certain mechanical transport attached to them which forms an ammunition column. These batteries come in from all points of the compass to prepare for a general attack on some part of the line, e.g.: Arras, and as they come these lorries are all flung into this rapidly expanding unit entitled the siege park: so when you get many batteries you will have as many as a thousand lorries, as was the case the other day. The heavier batteries have no horse transport attached to them, and when the situation is such that ammunition cannot be got by mechanical transport to the guns, the divisional ammunition columns and the gun teams themselves of field artillery and 60-pounder heavy artillery horse-drawn guns are called upon to take the ammunition from where the mechanical transport is halted to the guns themselves. If that be not possible, the remaining distance to the guns must be done by hand.[430]*

Between the divisional artilleries, with their reinforcing brigades, and the heavy and siege artillery allocated to the Canadian Corps, Morrison, like Massie and McNaughton, had at his disposal a massive array of firepower; he had command and control of a sufficient number of cannons to produce a density of one heavy gun for every 20 yards of frontage, and one field gun for every 10 yards of coverage. For the sake of comparison, at the Somme in 1916, the British artillery density was one heavy gun for every 57 yards of frontage, and one field gun for every 20 yards.[431]

Assembling the Force

From across the British area of operations, artillery batteries concentrated on the front near Arras. The artillery commanders received their orders from all points and plotted their routes to bring them into their assigned deployment areas. The CRA of the 33rd Divisional Artillery, Brigadier-General C.G. Stewart, whose formation was to support the 3rd Army assault south of the Canadian Corps, received his orders to deploy in the fourth week of March and departed on a reconnaissance with his brigade commanders on the 24th of that month. The very next day, his batteries began making their way north. The divisional artillery's diarist gave an impression of the immense number of guns concentrating in the area, recalling:

> *all along the line of that march the direction of the coming battle was clearly indicated. Vast columns filled the road, columns of infantry, guns and transport, columns of motor-lorries and ambulances, all with their faces set toward the north, all forming part of a great moving stream inexorable in its progress... [this] indicated a great concentration in progress, a mighty gathering of the storm clouds.*[432]

Captain James Belton and Lieutenant Ernest Odell, both of the CFA, recalled that:

> *the road was alive with excitement – the very atmosphere reeked of it...it was an awe-inspiring spectacle. To the right of the road the ammunition column men on mules were hauling to the various artillery dumps large and small shells, fodder for hungry guns that were to give us victory...as we passed these men they wished us the best of luck, shouting some friendly remarks such as "We are working like h--- for you boys; see that you give Fritz h--- tomorrow!"*[433]

The assembling of the reinforcing heavy artillery was particularly important for shaping the coming battle. The early days of March, over a month before the actual assault on the ridge, witnessed a constant influx of heavy and siege artillery batteries into the Canadian Corps area. On 1 March 1917 alone, 129th and 136th Heavy Batteries, as well as the 49th and 180th Siege Batteries, and the 4th and 6th Canadian Siege batteries arrived in the Vimy area. The headquarters of the heavy-artillery groups began arriving on March 20. On the same day, the headquarters of the 6th, 18th, 30th, 44th, and 57th Heavy Artillery Groups arrived in the Corps Area and fell under the command of the general officer commanding heavy artillery of the Canadian Corps.

The 1st Canadian Divisional Artillery was relieved by the British 24th Divisional artillery between March 7 and 9, 1917 to allow it to move to the Vimy Ridge sector. Its headquarters were established at Ecoivres, nearer Vimy Ridge, on March 9.[434] On March 11, the general officer commanding 1st Canadian Divisional Artillery assumed command of all artillery along the 1st Canadian Division's sector.[435] For most of March, the 1st Canadian Divisional Artillery was divided into two groups, at least until the arrival of their reinforcing artillery. The first of the reinforcements arrived on March 21, with the arrival of the 26th Army Field Artillery Brigade, followed by the 31st Divisional Artillery and the 170th Brigade on March 25. The latter relieved the 26th Army Field Artillery Brigade, RFA, who moved into forward positions as one of the silent brigades to be used to fire in depth.[436] The last bit of the puzzle for Thacker and the 1st Canadian Divisional Artillery fell into place on March 29 with the arrival of the 5th Brigade, RHA, and the 71st Army Field Artillery Brigade.

The 2nd Canadian Divisional Artillery received their first word about the proposed attack on Vimy Ridge as early as December 21, 1916.[437] They were pulled out of the line for rest and training at the end of January and settled into the area of Fontaine-lès-Hermans to the northwest of the Vimy sector. There, the time out of the line was interrupted, for several elements including the 6th Brigade, for inspection by no less than Haig himself, along with a constellation of accompanying VIPs including the commanders of the First British Army, the Canadian Corps, and the 2nd Canadian Division.[438]

Panet had been ordered to replace the 3rd Canadian Divisional Artillery and take over their area of operations in the Vimy sector. He issued his orders for the movement of his brigades on February 6, 1917, which was scheduled to commence on February 15 and complete on February 17. The order issued to the divisional artillery remains in the war diary and is a fascinating snapshot of how an organization such as this would move. Panet and his staff divided his force into three groups, named Right, Centre, and Left, each under the command of one of the artillery brigade commanders. They were considered a group, so to speak, because they each included some elements of 7th Brigade, CFA. An initial preparatory meeting was held at the 3rd Canadian Divisional Artillery Headquarters near Mount St. Eloi on February 10, and on February 14 each group dispatched an officer, accompanied by a telephonist, to establish themselves in the units they were relieving.

Each brigade was informed that it was to leave its ammunition wagons empty and take over the ammunition of 3rd Canadian Divisional Artillery upon their arrival. In some circumstances, the relieving troops would simply fall on the guns of the relieved unit, handing over their own guns to the now-departing troops. That wasn't to be the case in this move, however, as the troops were instructed that guns would not be taken over. In order to assist in being ready to fire as soon as possible, the aiming posts of the departing gunners would be left behind. These were poles that were planted equidistantly from each gun; each pole was used as a reference point with the site on the gun to ensure the gun was firing in the right direction. The guns were to move directly into the same gun pits used by the 3rd Canadian Divisional Artillery, and even use their gun-aiming data to align their cannons.[439]

The orders to move, designed to avoid congestion on the roads, were issued shortly thereafter in a tabular form that indicated the dates for units to move, where they were to start from, the route they were to take, and the time they were to begin. This was all with an aim to avoid traffic jams and ensure a smooth movement from one area to the next. The movement of the brigades was directed by the brigade major in the March Table, which was an early form of spreadsheet that listed the expected times of departure and arrival, and the routes for all of a brigade's batteries. In these particular orders, the brigade major directed each battery to maintain at least 50 yards between batteries and 500 yards between brigades, adding "[T]hese distances must be rigidly adhered to, as the route is congested. March discipline must bet strictly enforced." Notwithstanding this rather terse direction, the table nonetheless reflects some rather imprecise direction to the units; for example, the 4th Brigade was to follow the 6th Brigade once the latter unit wholly passed a bridge that lay three-quarters of a mile northwest of "D in Divon," referring to the name of a town as it was written on the map.[440]

As noted above, the British 5th Divisional Artillery was designated to support 2nd Canadian Division in its assault under the command of CRA, 2nd Canadian Divisional Artillery. An interesting story accompanies the arrival of the 5th Divisional Artillery. The 5th British Division was relieved by the 66th British Division in mid-March 1917 and then proceeded to the Vimy sector, where it fell under the command of the Canadian Corps; in fact, its 13th Infantry Brigade joined the 2nd Canadian Division for the assault. The 5th Divisional Artillery, however, was delayed in its previous sector as there was fear about a potential German offensive in that area, which was near the French town of Givenchy. The 5ᵗʰ British Division was eager to get is guns back, and some consternation arose as several orders for the 5ᵗʰ Divisional Artillery to be relieved and allowed to proceed to the Vimy sector were issued and subsequently rescinded. It got to the point that the men of the 5ᵗʰ British Division referred to their previous corps commander as the 'Pharaoh' because, in reference to the guns of the British 5ᵗʰ Divisional Artillery, "he would not let them go." Finally, on March 26, 1917, the 5ᵗʰ British Divisional Artillery left the Givenchy area and proceeded to link up with the 2ⁿᵈ Canadian Divisional Artillery. An advance party from the artillery brigades of the British 5ᵗʰ Divisional Artillery had actually deployed to the Vimy sector the previous month in order to prepare the gun positions and help to dump the 1300 rounds per gun that were allocated to the formation. By April 7, 1917, it was ready for the assault.[441]

The 3ʳᵈ Canadian Divisional Artillery headquarters relieved the Reserve Divisional Artillery and established itself at Camblain-l'Abbé on March 9, 1917, the same day its CRA, Brigadier-General Mitchell, had the opportunity to meet the visiting Canadian prime minister, Sir Robert Borden, at the 3ʳᵈ Canadian Division Headquarters.[442] Mitchell moved his headquarters forward on March 23, setting up shop in Villers-au-Bois after transferring the artillery responsibility for what would eventually be the 4ᵗʰ Canadian Division's frontage to the newly arrived Reserve Divisional Artillery. Despite moving into position on that date, the complete transfer of responsibility for the 3ʳᵈ Canadian Divisional frontage did not occur until March 26, 1917, when 3ʳᵈ Canadian Divisional Artillery fully relieved elements of 2ⁿᵈ Canadian Divisional Artillery who had, until that point, been covering the area that was designated for 3ʳᵈ Canadian Division. Three days later, the 3ʳᵈ Canadian Divisional Artillery was happy to welcome its erstwhile naval gunners of the 63ʳᵈ Divisional Artillery into the Vimy sector.[443]

As the 4ᵗʰ Canadian Divisional Artillery had not yet been formed, fire support for the 4ᵗʰ Canadian Division was provided by the Reserve Divisional Artillery. This formation had originated as the 3ʳᵈ Indian (Lahore) Divisional Artillery, and during the Great War it enjoyed a long history of fighting alongside the Canadian Corps, often filling the important role of a divisional artillery to one of the Canadian divisions whose formation often occurred weeks or months before its integral divisional artillery was created. The Lahore Divisional Artillery had initially supported the Indian Corps, but when the infantry of that formation was withdrawn in November of 1915 for service in Mesopotamia, the Lahore Divisional Artillery remained in France. When the 2nd Canadian Division arrived in France, without its divisional artillery, the Lahore gunners were assigned to support them. Likewise, when the 3rd Canadian Division was created, and the 2nd Canadian Divisional Artillery had assumed its role supporting its parent formation, the Lahore gunners took up the duty of supporting the 3rd Canadian Division. It made no sense to continue to refer to the organization as the Lahore Divisional Artillery, as its parent formation was abroad, so prior to the spring offensives of 1917, the formation was renamed the Reserve Divisional Artillery. As the assault on Vimy neared and the Canadian gunners of 3rd Canadian Divisional Artillery had moved into the fight, the 4th Canadian Division became the benefactors of the Reserve (Lahore) artillery support.

Of course, there was plenty to do to set the conditions for the fire plan to commence. Batteries and brigades had to move into their gun positions, and ammunition had to be brought forward and dumped for use. Accommodation for 12,000 rounds in every battery position had to be prepared.[444] These preliminary movements had to begin early, and the first two sheets of the war diary for the Headquarters, Royal Artillery Canadian Corps reveal a constant inflow of heavy and siege batteries.[445] Sixteen heavy batteries arrived in the Canadian Corps area in February, and another twenty-six in March. On March 20 alone five heavy artillery headquarters arrived in the area and fell under the command of Morrison.[446]

Such massive amounts of ammunition necessarily required enormous transportation resources. In Sir Douglas Haig's *Despatches*, he remarked that when the ammunition requirements for the Arras offensive were calculated, it was soon realized that the two single lines of railway that served the area could carry only half the estimated requirements.[447]

The preparation of gun positions was particularly important. Since most of the batteries of the reinforcing artillery brigades would not arrive until after the preliminary bombardment had begun, preparing the gun positions for the arriving batteries and brigades fell to the gunners of the Canadian Corps.[448] This included the preparation of gun pits for the cannons and howitzers, designating wagon lines, and digging ammunition dumps. This was no light work, and the Canadian gunners were constantly busy digging trenches and preparing gun positions. For example, the 23rd Battery, CFA, was required to dig defensive works for three batteries of reinforcing artillery in addition to its own.[449] Most work was done at night if possible, but given the time available the men sometimes had to work in the daylight, which of course exposed them to German fire. In fact, some of the Canadian gun lines were so close to the front lines, particularly the forward silent batteries in the 1st and 2nd Canadian Division areas, that German snipers were a genuine concern. Starting from its arrival in the area on March 29, the 5th Brigade, RHA, which was deploying well forward in support of 2nd Canadian Divisional Artillery, was constantly harassed by sniping fire from the German lines. The brigade's war diary attests to this, noting on April 1, 1917, that "work continues on new positions. Working parties much worried by a sniper." They were right to be nervous: on April 2, 1917 two men were wounded by the sniper, as was another on April 5.[450]

The Preliminary Bombardment

The initial phase of the preliminary bombardment began as scheduled on Z-20 – March 19, 1917 – in accordance with the gradual increase in fires articulated in the artillery instruction. Even as the guns of the Canadian Corps began their preliminary bombardment, the reinforcing heavy and siege batteries continued to slowly move into their new gun positions in the Canadian Corps area of operations and join in the shooting. As of March 23, 1917, the guns began to deliver a more deliberate volume of fire and increase their focus on wire cutting.[451]

On March 28, Morrison issued his Corps Artillery plan to the various brigades and batteries that had assembled to support the Canadian Corps. April 8, 1917, was originally designated Z-Day, the day of the attack, and the days preceding it were styled V-, W-, X-, and Y-day.[452] Morrison's plan was augmented four days later with the delivery of the *Canadian Corps Artillery Plan and Instructions* No. 2 and 3 on April 1, 1917.[453]

Activity along the Canadian Corps front increased in late March 1917 as the Canadian troops increased the frequency of their raids along enemy lines, hoping to develop a better picture of the enemy dispositions and layout. For example, on March 29 the 3rd Canadian Divisional Artillery fired a barrage in support of a raid conducted by 42nd Battalion.[454] Lieutenant John Newton, an officer with the CFA, went forward to the OP four days later, on April 3, 1917, to watch his brigade's trial barrage. After witnessing the withering fire directed at the German lines, he confided to his diary, "When the barrage came off it was most pretty to see. The Hun line is being battered to a pulp.

Watching the shells burst and seeing the upheavals of earth one wonders how the Hun can possibly exist."[455] Likewise, Joseph Hayes of Pictou, Nova Scotia's 85th Battalion in the 4th Canadian Division recalled that during the preliminary bombardment, it was common to have German soldiers wander toward the Canadian lines to surrender. In one instance, he recalled, "a lone Hun who appeared one dark night before a working party of the 85th with his hands in the air. He could speak a little English and when asked why he had given himself up this way replied 'Too much bombard.'"[456]

The Germans weren't sitting idly, however. The war diaries of the artillery brigades indicate that German artillery was active in both counter-battery and defensive fire roles, the latter in response to Canadian raids. Throughout the period, however, the tempo of enemy artillery activity varied over time, indicating that the effectiveness of the Canadian counter-battery fight often convinced the Germans to keep their guns silent lest they be located and exposed to fire from the Canadian Corps' heavy and siege artillery batteries.

If the first two weeks of the Canadian Corps artillery's preliminary fire had been bad for the Germans, it was about to get much worse. The fourth of April 1917 was V-Day, when the intensity of the bombardment increased substantially leading into the final week of the preliminary bombardment, which the Germans dubbed the "week of suffering."[457] Indicative of the scale of the increase in fire that occurred on V-Day, the 2nd Canadian Heavy Artillery Group, which consisted of 1st and 2nd Canadian Heavy Batteries, the 152nd Heavy Battery, RGA, the 2nd Canadian Siege Battery, and the British 12th Siege Battery, increased their daily rate of fire from a total of 714 rounds on April 3 to 2068 rounds on April 4, 1917.[458]

The Germans took note of the increase in fire. Generalleutnant Alfred Dietrich, commander of the 79th Reserve Infantry Brigade, noted that the artillery fire emanating from the Canadian Corps "soon put the fire of the Somme battle far into the shade."[459] Whereas the Germans had been able, for the first phase of the preparatory fire, to ascertain the rough strength of the guns opposing them by counting the number of rounds fired at them, as the Canadian Corps artillery increased its volume of fire this became impossible, as the rounds were arriving faster than anyone in the German lines could count them. Moreover, the intensity of the bombardment was such that the Germans could no longer attempt to repair wire or defensive works. Recall that one of the artillery effects designated for the preparatory period was the interdiction of resupply routes in the German back country. Interdicting fire, combined with the incessant bombardment of the German lines and the abysmal wet weather, turned the German defensive zone into a morass of mud and shell craters. The German eight-horsed ammunition resupply wagons were unable to get forward under such circumstances, even to the German batteries on the eastern slope of the ridge, so the German gunners had to carry the ammunition a very long distance by hand. The lot of the forward German troops holding the defensive lines was materially worse; they were essentially isolated due to the constant harassment of the Canadian artillery, and for the week leading up to the assault they survived only on bread and water that, Dietrich records, "they scooped out of the gas- and faeces-contaminated shell holes."[460]

The Canadian counter-battery program was enjoying success. Dietrich lamented that "the firing effect of our artillery was constantly interrupted through the destruction of the Battery Post and connections."[461] The result was that the German soldiers felt, according to Dietrich, that "they were without protection and at the mercy of the enemy's destructive fire."[462] Although Dietrich tries to make the best of the Germans' artillery response by stating that their guns kept up "their annihilating barrage" until 1900 hours on the day of the assault, he is forced to acknowledge that by the end of the day on April 9, only seventeen guns were still operational in the German defensive zone.[463]

The same day that the fire increased exponentially across the Canadian Corps front, the Headquarters, Royal Artillery Canadian Corps sent a message to all of the subordinate CRAs in the form of "Artillery Instructions No. 4," in which Morrison informed them that he had approved each of the fire plans they had submitted to support their respective divisional assaults.[464] The guns had now been pounding away at Vimy Ridge for two weeks, and results were starting to show. The CRA of 2nd Canadian Divisional Artillery reported that on the 2nd Canadian Division front all wire that could be observed appeared to be cleared.

Aggressive patrolling of the German lines by the Canadian infantry continued as March gave way to April. On April 4, 1917, the 52nd Battalion of 3rd Canadian Division conducted a raid of the German trench lines, supported by the fire of the 3rd Canadian Divisional Artillery guns. The support that they received was sufficient to prompt the CO, Lieutenant-Colonel W.B. Evans, to write the following missive via the artillery liaison officer, Captain Cook: "Kindly convey to [Officer Commanding]

Groups who cooperated this morning the thanks of myself and all ranks for their splendid assistance. All reports from those taking part in the raid and observing, that fire was well timed; splendidly pleased and very effective."[465]

Raids were also an important source of information for the artillery commanders, who had the responsibility to use their gunfire to cut wire so that the Canadian infantry could advance. As shown in earlier chapters, cutting wire by artillery fire was a laborious process, notwithstanding the increased efficiency wrought by the introduction of the 106 fuse to the imperial artillery arsenal. The report of the 15th Battalion in the 1st Canadian Division zone after a patrol on April 7, 1917, is indicative of how these forays into the enemy lines were so important to develop an understanding of the status of the wire obstacles: "The wire between No. 4 and No. 2 Craters is about 4 feet high and from 10 to 15 feet deep running up to [the enemy's] parapet. A few gaps were noticed but they are not sufficient to allow large parties to enter his lines."[466] Such information was critically important to allow the affiliated artillery commander to redouble his efforts to cut wire that posed an obstacle to the infantry's advance. Fortunately, the day after this report was recorded in the battalion's war diary, the diarist was able to write that "in the morning, our heavy artillery put on an intense bombardment of the enemy wire. In the afternoon two patrols went out and reported the enemy wire destroyed completely."[467]

In addition to the heavy workload, the gunners were further subjected to the despicable weather that came to the area in late March and early April 1917. *Cold, wet,* and *snowy* are the adjectives that figure prominently in the artillery war diaries of early March, and while temperatures rose somewhat throughout that month, the resultant thaw, combined with sleet and rain, caused the frost to come out of the ground and made the roads impassable for heavy traffic.[468] This, of course, had a negative influence on not only the men but also the horses who were being worked hard to get guns into position and move the ammunition forward. So busy were the batteries, and so crowded the assembly areas, that many horses were sadly left outside in the open during the lead-up to the assault. The 11th Canadian Field Brigade, at least, was able to build a rough stable in which to house their horses, but that only occurred on April 5, 1917, after several weeks of hard work under poor weather conditions.[469]

The weather also necessitated an extension of the fire plan. On April

ABOVE: Pack horses transporting ammunition to the 20th Battery, Canadian Field Artillery. (LAC 3194763)

6, 1917, Morrison issued another instruction, "Artillery Instructions No. 8," which announced the postponement of the assault by one day, the result of a request by flanking French forces. His instructions of April 6 therefore provided guidance on how to carry out the preliminary bombardment based on the revised schedule.[470] This necessitated a change in the alphabetical coding of the days. Thus, April 6, 1917, which had originally been designated as 'X' day, became 'Q' day, and the fire plan started anew with April 7, 1917, as X Day.[471] The same day, in the headquarters of the 4th Brigade, CFA, the anonymous unit diarist recorded the manner in which the FOOs were selected to go forward with the assault.

> *This morning the choice had to be made of an officer to go forward as FOO on the day of the [attack]. I volunteered as one and drew with the four batteries. I drew Zero day, 27th [Battery] Z+1, 13th [Battery] Z+2, D/21st [Battery] Z+3, 12th [Battery] Z+4. [Gunners] Mason, Gillis, Smith from HQ staff volunteered to go with me.[472]*

By April 7, 1917, preparations across the Canadian Corps front were starting to culminate as the Corps got closer and closer to going over the top on Z-Day. On April 7, 1917, the 3rd Canadian Divisional Artillery established its headquarters alongside the Battle Headquarters of 3rd Canadian Division, and by April 8, they were able to report that all of the wire on the 3rd Canadian Division front had been cleared or damaged to the extent it would not pose an obstacle to the assaulting infantry.[473] The same day, 1st Canadian Infantry Brigade carried out a large raid on German lines at 4:30 a.m. in one of the final efforts of the Canadian Corps to define the German defences prior to Z-Day.

In the final days leading up to the actual assault, the war diaries of the assaulting infantry battalions are replete with references to companies being pulled out of the line to a rearward area where they conducted rehearsals. To ensure close adherence to the schedule, a practice area was laid out where each unit of the Corps went through a full-scale rehearsal of the assault. The war diarist of the 2nd Canadian Divisional Artillery reported that in order to assist the infantry in understanding the pace of the advance of the barrage, the field artillery brigades of 2nd Canadian Division furnished men to represent the location of the barrage during the rehearsals, walking in front of the infantry while carrying flags.[474] Odell and Belton give an idea of what the tactical infantry assault plan was like when they recalled how they practised their assault prior to its execution:

> Our artillery was to lay a barrage on the first line of presumed German trenches…we were to keep within fifty yards of our barrage in diamond formation. This barrage was indicated by men on the right and left flanks of our battalion frontage, which was a lateral distance of 335 yards. Our battalion furnished four waves, each wave having its own mission to accomplish – the whole battalion having one final objective. Men with flags would continue waving them until the barrage was supposed to lift, then they would [run] forward and indicate by their flags where the barrage was then falling.[475]

The artillery required rehearsals as well. Morrison's staff at the Canadian Corps Artillery Headquarters planned two corps-level feint barrages. The first was scheduled for April 5, 1917, at 8:00 a.m., and the second on April 6, 1917, at 1:00 p.m. Recall from the previous chapter that the CRAs were each tasked to conduct at least two practice/feint barrages in their own zones of operation during the preliminary bombardment period. This allowed them both to practice their skills and to watch how the enemy reacted – and hopefully entice them to unmask their guns.[476]

The 2nd Canadian Divisional Artillery carried out one of these practice barrages on April 2, 1917, at 3:00 p.m. The orders for this practice barrage were issued on April 1, 1917, and they provide an excellent example of how the practice/feint barrages were planned and executed. In this case, both rolling and standing barrages were practised. Four barrage lines were created, A through D, and the firing units that were tasked to participate in the rolling barrage each spent two minutes creeping from one to the other. Once barrage line D had been fired, the fire returned to barrage line A for another two minutes of intense fire. Recall that this was done to convince the Germans that this was standard practice in the hope that, on the actual day of the attack, they would assume the barrage was going to return to the start line, and thus remain in their dugouts. In actuality, the barrage would continue rolling along and the assaulting infantry would close with the German defenders as they waited in their dugouts. The units firing standing barrages would likewise fire on the German support line followed by a deeper trench line and the Black Line objective, dwelling on each for two minutes, and then return to the initial support line.[477]

On the 3rd Canadian Division front, the CRA of 3rd Canadian Divisional Artillery went above and beyond, issuing orders on March 29, 1917, for both his own divisional artillery and the attached 63rd Divisional Artillery to fire three trial barrages each: both divisional artilleries would fire two on March 30 and 31, and the 63rd Divisional Artillery would fire their third on April 1, 1917, while 3rd Canadian Divisional Artillery would fire their third on April 2. Mitchell's orders specifically highlighted that no counter-battery fire was authorized as the intent of the trial barrage was to identify German batteries for future engagement.[478]

As the gunners pounded away at their targets throughout the preliminary bombardment, they had the best seats in the house to watch the aerial campaign being waged between the imperial and German air forces in the skies above the ridge. The Royal Flying Corps, providing the indispensable service of locating hostile batteries and reconnoitring the ridge, more often than not found themselves wanting in aerial combat with their German opponents, who counted among their number the infamous Baron Manfred von Richthofen, aka the Red Baron.[479] Perhaps this is who the war diarist in the 4th Brigade, CFA, was referring to when he wrote on April 5, 1917, "Our aircraft have not been able to stand up against the Hun machines to any extent. The Hun has a little red machine that has great speed and has already accounted for several of our machines, getting one today that came down in our lines."[480] The lack of success in the aerial campaign that was noted on April 5 seems to have been the rule, rather than the exception; on that date the war diarist of the 2nd Canadian Divisional Artillery noted: "Our planes [are] active. For the past three weeks enemy planes have had the best of every encounter on our front, [and] there have been many."[481]

Over the Top: The Barrage

As the planes jousted in the clouds and the guns pounded away at the mud, zero hour on Zero Day – the anointed time for the infantry to go "over the top" – crept closer and closer.

In the early morning hours on the day of the attack, the battalions of the Canadian Corps moved forward to assume their assigned positions, from which they were to begin their advance; by 4:40 a.m., the whole of the assaulting force was in place. In 3rd Canadian Division, the Princess Patricia's Canadian Light Infantry were able to enjoy a warm breakfast and a hot tot of rum in the Grange Tunnel, which had been constructed to shelter them as they advanced to their jumping-off point.[482] Frederick Howard of the 11th Canadian Mounted Rifles recalled that his battalion reached their jumping-off point at 4:30 a.m. Here, he and his colleagues waited nervously for what was to come, as "we all knew that there would be thousands of disasters and as the weary minutes dragged on," he wrote. "My heart seemed to turn to lead … [I]t was quite evident that within the next half hour or so many of us would be dead or permanently crippled."[483]

As the infantry waited in their jumping-off points, an interesting event occurred in the 102nd Battalion, one of the first-line assaulting battalions of 4th Canadian Division. The battalion's diarist recorded that at 2:00 am the unit headquarters received a message from one of the company runners, stating that there were "persistent" reports from the forward positions that one of the 18-pounders was consistently firing short. This was later confirmed by the battalion scout officer. The battalion notified its superior infantry brigade headquarters by wire, and the artillery liaison officer was sent for. Upon his arrival, he immediately contacted the supporting battery, and within thirty minutes the situation had been corrected. Sadly, a Lieutenant Frame in the forward trenches was wounded, due to this gun dropping short, before the artillery liaison officer's message could get through to his battery. Nonetheless, this is a good example of the important role played by the artillery liaison officer during the assault, and reflects the value of establishing a close connection between the assaulting infantry and the supporting artillery: with the two groups working together, a worse case of fratricide was avoided.[484]

It wasn't the infantry alone who moved into the tunnels to prepare for the advance; artillery officers and signallers, too, were detailed to move with the infantry in order to provide continuous fire support. This would be particularly important after cresting the ridge, as the Canadian Corps observers on the ground had no observation on the eastern slope of the hill. Harold Panabaker, an artillery signaller, explained in a letter to his friend Emily that four signallers from each battery of his brigade were detailed to accompany the observing officer during the advance; he had been chosen as one of them. He recounted that the detailed soldiers met at 11 o'clock on April 8 and moved forward over a mile of trenches, entering a long tunnel that they followed until they neared the opening, from which the assaulting infantry were to emerge. At the end of the tunnel was a telephone switchboard. Panabaker and his colleagues plugged the ends of their rolls of telephone wire into this and established contact with the battery command posts, after which they made themselves as comfortable as possible and awaited zero hour.[485]

At 5:29 and 56 seconds, all firing on the Canadian front ceased. For four seconds the land was silent, eerily silent, for the first time in weeks. It must have seemed surreal to both the Canadians and Germans, who had lived with the constant thump and crash of the massive preliminary bombardment. Then, at 5:30 all hell broke loose as the hundreds of guns supporting the Canadian Corps joined the thousands of flanking guns supporting the British assaulting armies to begin the bombardment in support of the assaulting infantry.[486]

Odell of the 24th Battalion recalled:

> *Exactly at 5:30 we hear the swish, swish, swish of our shells pass over our heads on their journey of destruction and defeat to the front line of the Germans. I had trouble to make the boys wait the one minute that was necessary. Finally, I blew my whistle, I knew they could not hear it, but I pointed in the direction of the enemy and everyone was over the top.*[487]

The Canadians climbed out of their trenches and tunnels and started their advance across no man's land, which separated the two trench lines.[488] This distance ranged from 300 yards in the south to only 150 yards in the north, where tunnels had been dug to allow the Canadians to debouche almost immediately on top of their adversaries.[489] Shortly after they went over the top, the barrage paused on the German front trench long enough to suppress them until the lead wave of Canadians could close up with it.

The Canadian Corps assaulted with all four divisions abreast. We've seen previously that the divisions were disposed from 1st to 4th, running from south to north. The 1st Canadian Division advanced with two brigades comprising six total battalions abreast: the 5th, 7th, and 10th on the right in the 2nd Canadian Infantry Brigade, and the 15th, 14th, and 16th Battalions of the 1st Canadian Infantry Brigade on the left. To the right of the 1st Canadian Division, the 2nd Canadian Division advanced with four battalions forward, including the 18th and 19th Battalions of the 4th Canadian Infantry Brigade, and the 24th and 26th Battalions of the 5th Canadian Infantry Brigade.[490] In the 3rd Canadian Division's area of operations, the 7th and 8th Canadian Infantry Brigades were in the lead. In the 4th Canadian Division, whose objective included the redoubtable Hill 145 from which observation of the whole ridge could be gained – and where, as a result, the German defences were particularly strong – the division attacked with the 11th and 12th Brigades in line, each brigade augmented with the addition of a battalion from the 10th Canadian Brigade.[491]

While advancing from objective to objective, the Canadian infantry moved in diamond or file formation, and when they arrived within fifty yards of the barrage that was pounding the German front line, the officer in command indicated to his men to spread out, as "the intense bombardment in front of us sent German limbs, bodies and earth all sky high."[492] Joseph Hayes of the 85th Battalion recalled that "the wicked bursts of overhead shrapnel and the sharp concussions of high explosive enveloped the Huns in a veritable rain of hell fire, lead and iron until their bodies were mangled and torn and bleeding and churned up with the mud of the once grassy fields of Vimy Ridge."[493] In a letter to his mother, Clifford Wells of the 8th Battalion wrote that "our artillery barrage was wonderful beyond description, lifting forward from objective to objective with clocklike precision, and practically obliterating the German trenches as it passed them." He later observed that when fresh troops passed through them to continue the advance, the barrage advanced "like a flock of dragons."[494]

Panabaker and his colleagues emerged from the dugout in one of the follow-on waves. "A couple hundred yards in front of us was the first wave of the attack, the figures of the men were outlined against the murk and the smoke of the most stupendous barrage the war has seen," he recalled. "We hurried on skirting large shell craters leaping over small ones, but bent on getting to a position where our officers would be able to observe the enemy and correct the fire of our brigade."[495]

After three minutes pounding away at the first objective, the barrage lifted off the German front line trench onto the supporting trench. The Canadians rushed forward and seized their first objective, the Black Line.[496] Both the 1st and 2nd Canadian Divisions reported the Black Line was secured at 6:15 a.m., forty-five minutes after zero hour. In the 4th Canadian Division zone, where the Black Line objective was much closer, the men of the 73rd Battalion occupied the recently evacuated German trenches at 5:37, a mere seven minutes after the attack began.[497]

The artillery had done its work. In the 4th Canadian Division, the assaulting troops found that the front-line wire was completely destroyed and there was very little of the German front line left intact.[498] But in some cases the artillery had been too effective. Colonel Nicholson recorded in his official history of the Canadian Army in the Great War that the prolonged preliminary bombardment and the barrage supporting the assaulting infantry had turned the ground into a near-impassable morass, writing that "the heavily laden infantry had to pick their way between deep shell-holes and negotiate a maze of shattered trenches and the torn remnants of wire entanglements… [E]verywhere the continuous shelling had pulverized the earth into vast puddles of clammy mud."[499]

After securing the first objective, the Canadians continued their advance toward the second line trench, which lay about 700 yards distant. In the 1st Canadian Infantry Division sector, the troops moved off at 6:45. Once again, they arrived within 50 yards of the barrage, which had paused on the second line, and had to wait while the artillery pounded their second objective for a further five minutes. Odell recalled that "at such a distance the air is hot and oppressive… I signalled to the boys not to go too fast for fear of moving into our own shell fire. As the barrage lifted, we doubled and jumped into the Fringe Trench, our second objective. There was no opposition. Quite a number of German [sic] lay about the trench."[500]

The suppressive effect of the artillery barrage was impressive. For example, Odell also recalled that when he was forced to pause his force while the barrage engaged their final objective, his soldiers were able to sit down and coolly smoke a cigarette while waiting for the barrage to lift.[501] In the 3rd Canadian Division zone the barrage halted on the intermediate objective for forty minutes, allowing the Princess Patricia's Canadian Light Infantry to mop up the trench: "the men could move back and forth overland without precaution behind Famine Trench [the intermediate objective.]"[502] In an ironic twist, in some circumstances the effectiveness of the bombardment obliterated German trenches and other points of reference and landmarks that were meant to assist the assaulting troops in navigation, causing some to wander into their own barrage.[503]

The 3rd Canadian Division arrived at the crest of the ridge at 7:30, while the 1st and 2nd Canadian Divisions, who had to travel farther due to the geographic shape of the ridge, arrived a half-hour later, at 8:00. In these two divisions, the reserve infantry brigades began to move up in order to continue the advance to the Blue and Black lines that lay beyond. By 9:00 these reserve brigades had taken up the advance and moved forward. In the 2nd Canadian Division, where the boundaries widened slightly after the Red Line objective, the 13th Brigade of the British 5th Division moved into a forward position alongside its Canadian confreres in order to compensate for the broader frontage the division was responsible for. After achieving the Blue Line objective, the 1st and 2nd Canadian Divisions paused for ninety minutes to allow their troops to bring machine guns forward.

Once the crest of the ridge had been achieved, the panoramic view beyond revealed a target-rich environment. In the 2nd Canadian Division area, "the Gunner F.O.O.'s...had the time of their lives switching their Batteries on to retiring columns and guns." The rout was so quick that one FOO "found a luncheon of stew and rice-pudding laid out for the Officers in a [German] Battery dug-out, which he at once availed himself of."[504]

Lieutenant Newton moved forward to act as a FOO and recorded in his diary the dangers associated with moving so close to the new German lines. He wrote,

> *Went forward to the O.P. in Counts Wood to act as F.O.O. The snipers were busy and got several of the infantry who were foolishly exposing themselves. In the afternoon the Hun commenced shelling the Wood so I & the telephonists decided to take refuge*

in an old German dugout about 100 yards in front. We carried our wire across this exposed place – snipers [sic] bullets whizzing around. Made it successfully and prepared to spend the night. We were then only 100 yards from our new front line which was on the far side of the steep hill. The view was magnificent – could see into Hun territory for several miles. It was a F.O.O.'s paradise.[505]

The unique geographical shape of the ridge meant that the final objective, the Brown Line, lay almost 3000 yards distant from the Blue Line in the 1st Canadian Division area of operations. In the 2nd Canadian Division it was much closer, eventually linking up with the Blue Line near where the British 13th Brigade had come into the line. By now, the troops of the Canadian Corps in the 1st and 2nd Canadian Divisions had outranged the guns that had supported them to this point, and the 'silent' batteries deployed forward now became the intimate direct artillery support to the advancing Canadians. The reduction in the number of guns available meant that instead of firing across the whole frontage of the assaulting battalions of the 1st and 2nd Canadian Divisions, the artillery concentrated its barrages in front of brigades and battalions in a series of successive advances from right to left.[506] By 2:40 in the afternoon, 1st Canadian Division had secured the Brown Line and the ridge had been captured in the 1st, 2nd, and 3rd Canadian Division sectors.

To the north, the 4th Canadian Division had a much harder fight. As we have seen, this division was given the unenviable task of securing Hill 145, also known as 'the Pimple,' which sat atop the northern end of the ridge and was strongly defended by the Germans, who fully understood its tactical importance. This zone was reinforced with concrete bunkers and tunnels, so its defenders had not suffered as monstrously from the preliminary barrage as had their colleagues in other sectors of the ridge.

The initial assault on the right of the 4th Canadian Division's line had gone relatively smoothly, but further north the Canadians encountered a trenchwork that had been left more or less unmolested by the bombardment, and from which the Germans poured a murderous machine-gun fire into the ranks of the assaulting infantry. The Canadians attempted to bypass the strong points and continue the advance, leaving the unsecured areas for the follow-on troops to mop up, but they were hampered in their efforts by Germans emerging from mine shafts and dugouts to harass them in the flank and rear.

The delay caused by the stubborn German defence provided

sufficient time for the Germans in their second line trench to prepare for the arrival of the Canadian assaulting wave, whereas in other areas of the Canadian attack the leading elements of the assault were able to exploit the suppressive effect of the protective barrage. Consequently, the men of the 4th Canadian Division were subjected to further murderous fire from the Germans ensconced in the second line trench. This caused the attack by the 11th Canadian Infantry Brigade to completely break down, and its commander was forced to bring up fresh troops and conduct a deliberate attack around 1:00 p.m. to regain the initiative.

The 12th Canadian Infantry Brigade also had an encouraging start to their assault, advancing with three battalions in line. They had had particular success in the 73rd Battalion's area of advance, where two mines had been detonated under the German trenches at zero hour, killing most of the German defenders in that sector.

The enemy artillery had been generally quiet, but did from time-to-time attempt to provide some defensive fire against the assaulting Canadians. At 9:10, German country battery fire landed among the batteries of 5th Brigade, Royal Horse Artillery, and put one gun out of action for half an hour.[507] Canadian heavy and siege guns did good work to try to suppress any hostile artillery that might have tried to interfere with the assault. On Zero Day, 2nd Brigade, CGA, supporting the 4th Canadian Division front, fired an astonishing 6,662 rounds of counter-battery fire.[508]

Bringing Up the Guns

The assaulting Canadian infantry eventually advanced beyond the range of the guns supporting the attack, and, as planned, while the silent batteries began hammering away at targets, the guns that had been supporting the assault since zero hour began displacing forward in order to ensure they could fire beyond the ridge and defeat any German counterattack that might develop. The spring rains, combined with the incessant shelling of the artillery, had turned the intervening ground between the original gun positions and the forward locations into a quagmire that seriously hampered the gunners' attempts to move forward. Guns, wagons, and limbers became mired in the mud, clogging routes of advance and delaying the forward movement of the artillery. It was the horses who suffered the most. The anonymous historian of the 18th Field Battery recalled one effort to dislodge a gun mired in the mud thus: "[O]ne glance

ABOVE: *Canadian Field Artillery bringing up the guns. Vimy Ridge, April, 1917.*
(LAC 3521867)

at the mud was enough to cause despair, and the horses, after many hard efforts to wade through, quietly laid down and died."[509] Likewise, the historian of the 23rd Battery described the battery's forward movement as "a terrible struggle, in which guns and horses threatened to disappear in a sea of mud, created by the terrific bombardment to which the ridge had been subjected."[510] The diarist of the 8th Brigade, CFA, recorded that when the 40th Battery moved forward on April 14, 1917, they found the roads to be in very bad condition, with so many blockages on the road on account of the mud that the battery took seventeen hours to move only a few kilometres.[511]

Not all brigades suffered the same. The commanding officer of the 3rd Brigade, CFA, supporting 1st Canadian Division had the foresight to make extensive preparations to move forward. On April 1, 1917, the brigade commander conducted an initial reconnaissance of the routes of advance for his guns, and then conducted a second survey on April 3, this time with his colleague from 1st Brigade, CFA. He made a final reconnaissance on April 6, 1917, to ensure the exact routes of advance were perfectly known. Then, on Z-Day, a large party under the guidance of Major Harry D.G. Crerar, who would later command First Canadian Army during the Second World War, immediately started building bridges over trenches as soon as the infantry had passed the first objective. Consequently, the brigade diarist was happy to report that "this work was so successfully carried out that every gun and howitzer of the 3rd Brigade, CFA was in action in vicinity of 500 Crater by 4:30 p.m."[512] Notwithstanding the fine preparatory work in 3rd Brigade, CFA, it was 3rd Battery in 1st Brigade who claimed the honour of moving their guns the farthest forward. Through sheer grit and determination, the gunners of 3rd Battery were able to move their guns 3,000 yards forward, a distance exceeding that achieved by any other battery of the Canadian Corps by 1,000 yards.[513]

The experiences of both 3rd Battery and the 3rd Brigade were the exception rather than the rule, however. The delay in bringing up the guns meant many opportunities to engage the Germans in the open plains east of the ridge were wasted due to the Canadian guns being out of range. Lieutenant Newton lamented in his diary that his battery was the only one from the division that managed to get forward, and consequently, although enjoying a spectacular view of a target-rich environment, he was unable to engage the Germans.[514]

Tactical success on Vimy Ridge brought with it some added risk: once the guns were forward, they were compelled to deploy in locations only recently abandoned by the Germans, who were therefore very well acquainted with the Canadians' precise locations and could direct accurate fire against the interlopers. Additionally, many of the defensive works occupied by the Germans until that point had been destroyed, either through the prolonged Canadian artillery bombardment or as a result of the infantry assault in which a liberal application of grenades and bombs had been used to clear out the German occupants, leaving the Canadians well exposed on the ridge. Consequently, German counter-battery fire at targets on the crest and eastern slopes of the ridge was far more accurate and effective than it had been prior to the assault. For example, a German shell struck the officers' mess shelter of the 120th Battery, 5th British Divisional Artillery, after it had moved forward, killing four officers including the battery commander. A similar event befell their sister battery, the 121st, who lost two officers.[515] On April 12, 1917, Newton and his signaller were driven out of their OP by intense German fire. He recalled:

> At 5 A.M. we decided to abandon this O.P. as Fritz had been shelling it all night, getting 3 hits on the Dugout [sic] which partially caved in the roof and sides, besides causing us to go out

in the midst of a blizzard to repair the wire, between 3 AM &
5 A.M. Believe me, it's not a very pleasant sensation, repairing
telephone wires with heavy shelling falling and bursting all
around. At 4.15 A.M. we "made a bunk" and landed up at the
dug out of a company of the 21st Bttn which is largely composed
of men from Sarnia and vicinity. Stayed there till 7:30 A.M. and
then came back to the Battery – pretty well fagged out but still
alive. Went to bed after breakfast and slept till 12 P.M.[516]

Resupply was difficult as well. Hussey recalls in his history of the 5th British Division, "All ammunition had to be supplied by pack horses, which could only cross the ridge by night, the load being eight 18-pr shells or four 4.5 shells to one animal; many horses succumbed to shellfire or were drowned in the shell holes."[517]

When ammunition resupply did make it forward, artillery dumps were attractive targets for the Germans. To throw the Germans off, dummy dumps were created under tarpaulins. One was so realistic that the Canadian Corps quartermaster, who had a dummy dump dropped near him, complained to the Corps headquarters staff about a dump being placed in such a dangerous location! Sadly, the Germans became quite adept at locating the Canadian ammunition dumps. In one instance, a dump of 10,000 60-pounder shells in Thélus was exploded by a German shell, causing a massive explosion.[518]

Once the guns were on the top of the ridge, the gunners had an excellent view of the back country they had been shelling for the previous three weeks. The men of the 23rd Battery took possession of two abandoned German 5.9-inch howitzers and, by turning the guns on their former owners, "proceeded to give the Hun a hot time in Mericourt and Acheville." The crowning achievement of this section of guns, as the battery's historian relates, was the destruction of a church spire in the town of Méricourt by direct hit fired over open sites. Sadly, once this impressive exercise of gunnery was accomplished, the Germans resolved to eliminate this nuisance and put both 5.9s out of action with direct artillery fire, wounding two of the 23rd Battery gunners. [519]

Eventually, the guns did reach their forward locations, but in some cases, it took days to accomplish. The 8th Brigade, CFA, for example, moved into a gun position in the town of Vimy itself on April 16, 1917, a full week after Z-Day, in some of the recently deserted houses of Vimy.

ABOVE: *Looking over crest of Vimy Ridge onto Vimy Village, which was captured by Canadians. (Canadian War Museum)*

They found, however, that despite their hasty retreat from their defensive positions on Vimy Ridge, the Germans had taken the time as they withdrew to poison most of the wells in the vicinity of the village with arsenic.[520]

With the withdrawal of the German defenders, Vimy was conquered by the Canadian Corps. While the majority of the ridge fell into Canadian hands on the first day, German resistance on the Canadian left flank lasted several days more before finally succumbing to repeated offensive actions by the 4th Canadian Division, supported by numerous barrages provided by the Canadian Corps artillery. Eventually, a calm fell over the ridge and, for the first time since the fall of 1914, it sat unsullied by German interlopers. Much blood had been spilled by French, British, German, and Canadian soldiers in repeated attempts to take or retain the ridge, so its capture, although undeniably important from a purely tactical perspective, was nonetheless equally impactful from an emotional perspective. Reflecting on the previously unsuccessful French assault on Vimy Ridge of 1915, French war correspondents Henry Ruffin and Andre Tudesq wrote of the Canadian Corps' victory of April 1917 that

"Nos morts de 1915 peuvent dormir en paix sur ce champ de bataille; les vainqueurs de Vimy viennent de les venger. / Our dead of 1915 can sleep in peace on that battlefield: the victors of Vimy have come to avenge them."[521]

CONCLUSION

It was a clear and calm day in February of 1918. Despite being winter, the sun was shining, and it was generally pleasant. A group of soldiers had gathered at a crossroads in the French countryside on the western slope of Vimy Ridge, called Les Tilleuls, also known as Thélus, after the copse of large linden trees that, before the war, had covered the place. Although the name persevered, the trees had long since been cleared away by three years of artillery fire. At the intersection rose an impressive stone cairn with a brilliant white cross atop it, surrounded by four large, inert German shells. The shells were situated at the four corners of the concrete base of the stone cairn; each sat on its base and stood upright. The base, shells, and cairn were all situated atop what had previously been a German dugout, one of the network of defensive emplacements scattered about the ridge prior to its capture by the Canadian Corps. On the south face of the cairn a Canadian Red Ensign hung lengthwise, concealing underneath it a large brass plaque. The cairn stood in terrain that was controlled by Allied forces, but which still lay precariously close to the front line; thus, the staccato of artillery fire could be heard echoing across the landscape.

The men had come for the unveiling of a memorial. As the area was so near the front lines, only a small number of participants had been allowed to congregate. The group consisted largely of dignitaries; the Canadian Corps Artillery's war diary recorded that the august troupe of luminaries who had braved the proximity to the front line included General Sir Julian Byng the commander of the Third British Army and former commander of the Canadian Corps; the commanders of the Canadian Corps and the British I, XIII, and XVII Corps; all four commanders of the Canadian divisions and their respective CRAs; and about one hundred staff and regimental officers.[522]

The same diarist recorded that the unveiling ceremony was brief but impressive, and was presided over by Lieutenant-Colonel The Reverend Cannon P.G. Scott, the senior chaplain of 1st Canadian Division. Scott led the assembly in a brief prayer and then turned the ceremony over to Lieutenant-General Arthur Currie, commander of the Canadian Corps. Currie stepped forward and lifted the Canadian Red Ensign to unveil the bronze plaque, which carried the following words embossed under the badge of the commonwealth artilleries:

> *Erected in memory of officers, non-commissioned officers and men of the Canadian Corps artillery who fell during the Vimy operations, April 1917. Canadian Field Artillery, Royal Field Artillery, Canadian Garrison Artillery, Royal Garrison Artillery, South African Heavy Artillery*

The unveiling ceremony at Thélus took place a mere ten months after the assault on Vimy Ridge itself. The speed with which the memorial was erected indicates that to those who had participated in the battle, it stood out as something different, something of note. Vimy had been more than just another battle: it was a watershed moment that necessitated some type of recognition. The fact that the unveiling drew the attendance of luminaries such as Byng and various British corps commanders also indicates that not only was the Battle of Vimy Ridge recognized as an event of intense importance, but the role of the artillery in that battle was likewise pivotal.

And it was indeed something to commemorate. The Battle of Vimy Ridge, as part of the broader Battle of Arras, was the first time in the war that the British and their imperial allies had a sufficient number of trained men, enough guns of the correct calibre, and the appropriate types and amount of ammunition to effectively enable ground manoeuvre. For the first time since the war had ground into the remorseless, immovable slugfest of trench warfare in the autumn of 1914, the British had found the solution to the hitherto intractable problem of the impenetrable defence. Of course, there had been local successes prior to Arras and Vimy Ridge, but none that were quite on the same scale. The Battle of Vimy Ridge truly was a turning point in the Great War.

Beyond the technical revolution that occurred on the slopes of Vimy Ridge, there was something more ethereal as well. Much has been made,

ABOVE: General Sir Arthur Currie, Canadian Corps commander, unveiling the memorial erected by Canadian Artillery in memory of artillerymen who fell during the taking of Vimy Ridge. February, 1918. (LAC 3379682)

both at the time of the battle and since then, of the importance of Vimy Ridge to the evolution of Canadian nationalism. It is oft repeated that the Battle of Vimy Ridge was the first time that all four divisions of the Canadian Corps had ever fought together. Some writers have even opined that Vimy Ridge was the birthplace of post-colonial Canada. However, even though many historians, politicians, commentators, and armchair generals have argued that Vimy Ridge was an event of massive historical importance to the concept of Canadian nationalism, there have always been detractors unwilling to accept this particular narrative. The ranks of the iconoclasts have swollen recently, fuelled, perhaps, by a post-modern revisionism that has given birth to a cottage industry of Vimy Ridge deniers. They do make some valid points, however. They are quick to point out the uncomfortable truth that, for an all-Canadian affair, there were numerous British officers in positions of substantial authority within the Canadian Corps, including no less than its commander, Sir Julian Byng. Moreover, the vast artillery park that supported the Canadian Corps was predominantly British in nature: for every Canadian Field

Artillery brigade there were four brigades of the Royal Field Artillery blasting away at the ridge. Finally, rarely remarked upon by those who hold up Vimy Ridge as a predominantly Canadian affair is the fact that the 4th Canadian Divisional Artillery had not yet been created at the time of the battle. As divisional artilleries were integral elements of infantry divisions in the Great War, from a purely technical perspective Vimy Ridge was *not* the first battle in which all four *complete* divisions of the Canadian Corps fought together; that honour goes to the Battle of Hill 70 in August 1917.

Despite all of these historical nuances, however, Vimy Ridge has ensconced itself in the Canadian national consciousness as a monumental event in the evolution of Canadian nationalism. And indeed it was. Notwithstanding the arguments above, one thing is certain: when the Canadian Corps seized Vimy Ridge after an unprecedented period of preliminary bombardment, advancing behind an exquisitely planned and executed barrage, new eras in both Canadian nationalism and the tactical employment of fire support began.

But as the echoes of the bombardment faded away, and the Canadian soldiers looked out from their recently conquered perches atop the Ridge – perhaps with a newfound sense of Canadian patriotism stirring in their bosoms, or perhaps not – the war was far from over. Nineteen months of bloodletting were still to come.

The months following Vimy Ridge were filled with substantial change in the Canadian Corps, especially among its artillery brigades. History was made on June 9 when command of the Canadian Corps passed from Sir Julian Byng, a British regular, to Lieutenant-General Arthur Currie, a Canadian militiaman and former gunner; Byng went on to command the Third British Army. Currie, having commanded the 2nd Canadian Infantry Brigade and the 1st Canadian Infantry Division, and having acted as Byng's emissary to collect lessons learned from the Somme and Verdun, brought an artillery-centric command philosophy to his new position. Having witnessed first-hand the ravages of trench warfare, his meticulous planning in preparing for battle was guided by a policy in which men would never be expended in doing work that could be accomplished with an artillery shell.[523]

An important reorganization of imperial artillery also took place after the Arras offensive. Up to that time, in order to bolster divisional artilleries with additional field artillery for offensives, the batteries of other divisions in reserve or holding a quieter zone of the battlefield were cut from their parent formation and attached to assaulting divisions as reinforcing artillery. This caused a large degree of confusion and extra staff work as divisional artilleries moved about the battlefield from one zone to another, falling under command of new formations and then returning to their own parent organization. In order to reduce the confusion caused by this practice, *army field brigades* were created in the summer of 1917. These, as the name implies, were field artillery brigades that fell under the command of a field army, and could be allocated as reinforcing artillery to assaulting corps and divisions without having to strip another division of its integral fire support.[524] Additionally, on June 20, 1917, the 4th Canadian Divisional Artillery was created by reallocating a brigade from each of the three extant Canadian divisional artilleries: the 3rd Brigade from 1st Canadian Division, the 4th Brigade from the 2nd Canadian Division, and the 8th Brigade from the 3rd Canadian Division. While the men of each of these brigades were doubtless disappointed to leave their colleagues with whom they had endured so much, the reformation ensured that when the 4th Canadian Divisional Artillery was established, it had the benefit of experienced, battle-hardened troops ready to support future offensive operations. They didn't have to wait long to do so.[525]

Currie's proclivity for using artillery, along with the doctrine of artillery destruction that had become de rigueur during the Arras offensive, continued during the first corps-level battle conducted by the Canadians under Currie's command, namely the Battle of Hill 70 in August of 1917. Currie and Morrison leveraged their supremacy in heavy artillery by using the big guns through all stages of the battle, experiencing significant success during the counter-battery fight in which 40 per cent of German batteries were neutralized. In a departure from the policy at Vimy Ridge, at Hill 70 almost all the counter-battery fires were executed through the use of predicted shooting.[526] Recall from the introductory chapter that predicted shooting is not ranged or adjusted on the target, but is rather fired without any adjustment, compensating for meteorological and other technical effects on the trajectory of the round.

This was the first major operation to be launched after Arthur Currie assumed command of the Canadian Corps, and it made full use of field and heavy guns in all stages of battle.[527] While the elements necessary for an all-predicted fire plan were in place by the time of Vimy Ridge, they were not yet regarded as wholly reliable and were not exploited. In fact, it was no less than Haig himself who vetoed the use of an all-predicted fire plan at Arras, reluctant to trust a new and untried methodology when so many lives were at stake.[528] Later, at the Battle of Cambrai, November–December 1917, which was executed by Byng and the Third British Army, Byng insisted on the use of predicted fire without any preliminary registration of targets. In the end, the new method of fire support was fully vindicated.[529]

In March of 1918 the Germans launched their last-gasp attempt at victory with a massive offensive designed to divide the British and French armies, drive through to the coast, and end the war before the recently mobilized forces of the United States could enter the conflict and tip the scales, massively, in favour of the Allies. The offensive had excellent initial gains, and the Germans recaptured much of the terrain lost to the Allies since the 1917 spring offensive; a critical exception was Vimy Ridge, which remained in Allied hands. Indeed, possession of the ridge was a key element in the Allied defensive scheme. The historian of the British 5th Division recalled that "[t]he capture of the Ridge had far-reaching results, for it remained in our hands all through the great German push of 1918, forming an impregnable barrier to their advance, and it was the hinge upon which all future operations hung."[530] In their victory of April 1917, the Canadian Corps contributed significantly not only to the Allied efforts to withstand the German onslaught of March 1918, but to roll it back. By April 29, the German offensive had ground to a halt; Ludendorff's great gamble had failed. By early June, the Canadian Corps was undertaking intensive training on open warfare. Four years of static warfare was coming to an end, and the phase of artillery destruction was soon to give way to that of artillery neutralization.

August 8, 1918, was the beginning of the Canadian Corps' "last hundred days," the period of massive offensive operations carried out not only by the Canadians but by many Allied forces that culminated in the Armistice of November 11, 1918. General Erich von Ludendorff, the chief of staff of the German army, would later look back on that date and refer to it as the "black day of the German army."

On August 8, 1918, the Canadian Corps launched its assault against Amiens. Unlike the assault on Vimy Ridge, there was no lengthy preliminary bombardment. Like Byng, Currie chose to forego the preliminary bombardment and meticulous registration of the artillery, focusing instead on the use of predictive fire with meticulously calculated compensation for meteorological and technical conditions. The effects spoke for themselves. The Germans were caught completely by surprise; their wire defences were smashed by the plentiful and much more effective

106 fuse. The era of artillery neutralization, whereby the intent of the artillery was not to destroy the German wire defences and emplacements, but rather to neutralize them and keep the defenders suppressed as the assaulting troops advanced, had arrived. Moreover, as the Canadians had established a vast superiority in artillery, many guns were left out of the initial fire plan and held in readiness to advance with the infantry in order to provide continuous fire support. And it worked like a charm. By the end of the first day, the Canadian Corps had advanced over seven miles and had captured 15,000 men and 400 artillery pieces.

A month later, a similar plan was executed when the Canadian Corps assaulted the Drocourt-Quéant Line, a section of the infamous Hindenburg Line, on September 2, 1918. Once again, a preliminary bombardment was forgone in favour of an all-predicted fire plan focused on neutralization instead of destruction. One more change in the doctrinal paradigm was undertaken when, instead of beginning at dawn, which had often been the case, the attack began at 3 o'clock in the morning. Like the attack at Amiens, guns were once again left in reserve to advance with the infantry and provide continuous fire support.[531]

A sequel to the assault on the Drocourt-Quéant Line was the Canadian Corps' assault on the Canal du Nord, launched on September 27, 1918, with the goal of carrying on the successes they had enjoyed earlier. Once again, a heavy bombardment was avoided and neutralizing fire was maximized. In a bit of trickery, the Canadian gunners also planned to fire a reverse creeping barrage, in which the fire, rather than creeping forward and leading the infantry, would begin at deeper German targets and creep toward the assaulting Canadians. The intent was to make the German defenders believe their own artillery was firing short, confuse them, and, hopefully, make them call on their own guns to cease firing.

Not long after the Canal du Nord was secured, the guns finally fell silent on November 11, 1918 – the eleventh hour of the eleventh day of the eleventh month. The war to end all wars had finally come to an end, with the blood of the better part of a generation spilled on the fields of Flanders and Northern France. In its four years of grisly violence, the role of the artillery had changed remarkably. At the outset, the guns were expected to manoeuvre with the infantry, close with the enemy, and engage in direct fire over open sights. The war was never meant to last for four years, so the ammunition available was that which had been deemed necessary for the style of manoeuvre warfare everyone predicted.

As we've seen, this was not to be. Manoeuvre ground to a halt and the war transformed into a protracted siege. Hundreds of miles of barbed wire and thousands of machine guns conspired to keep both sides from moving the line very far at all, and when they tried, the result was carnage. A new approach was required, with new and more numerous guns and more effective ammunition, all controlled in a more efficient and effective manner.

The ranks of imperial formations swelled with recruits. British industry churned out more and more guns to support them. British scientists experimented with new technology to make the rounds more effective, and imperial soldiers learned through costly, bloody trial and error how best to return mobility to the battlefield. By the spring of 1917 and Haig's great offensive, the British and imperial armies finally had sufficient men, guns, and ammunition, along with the correct command-and-control organization, to plan and direct their employment and finally break the stalemate. For the Canadian Corps, the end results of the transformative first two and a half years of bloody battle became manifest on April 9, 1917, on Vimy Ridge. The era of artillery destruction had begun.

Its life cycle, however, would be short. The Germans, too, learned to adapt and in the succeeding months both the imperial and German antagonists modified their doctrine and tactics in response to each other. Still, the destructive power of the artillery continued to be used, and at every instance the lessons learned at Vimy and Arras were improved upon until, finally, in August of 1918 the Allied armies, their ranks bolstered by late-coming Americans, reaped the benefits of their overwhelming fire superiority and their effective use of it. The Germans had been sufficiently bloodied – their ranks culled, their guns depleted by counter-battery fire – that the Allied leaders could now forego the long, costly, and slow preliminary bombardments of artillery destruction. For the last one hundred days of the war, the Allies employed the technical and tactical lessons of the spring of 1917 to neutralize the German defenders, restore manoeuvre to the battlefield, and eventually secure victory.

I have attempted by this work to craft a narrative of how, during the Great War, the artillery evolved to become the battle-winning arm that it was in the spring of 1917; an evolution that was only achieved at great cost in lives lost and dollars spent. Moreover, I have attempted to demonstrate in these pages that the artillery narrative of the great war, and subsequent conflicts, is much more than just the number of guns that were deployed and the number of rounds that were fired, but rather something more profound, far reaching, and worthy of dedicated study. The artillery system of early 1917, as I have demonstrated here, was massive, intricate, and integrated. It consisted of thousands of mortars, howitzers, guns, men, horses, and projectiles all working synergistically towards a common end in the face of inclement weather and a determined and resourceful foe. I have endeavoured to demonstrate how all these pieces, and the millions of individual actions involved, came together in a coordinated whole for the Canadian Corps at Vimy Ridge. I have sought to shed light on the myriad components of the artillery system ranging from life in a dug out, to life at the OP, to the challenges of leading a horse to water and the millions of other individual actions that lamentably go unreported and undocumented in the majority of historical studies. I have attempted to shed light on the individual gunner's experience, and how he contributed to the Allied war effort as a small part of a massive enterprise. I hope, from exploring and illustrating these details, to allow the reader to extrapolate from the Canadians' experience at Vimy Ridge and thus gain a better understanding and appreciation for the millions of similar experiences that occurred in vast imperial and allied armies on the Western Front.

The success of artillery operations during the 1917 spring offensive depended on detailed planning and coordination to ensure the multitude of independent elements, from brigades to batteries to individual guns, ended up where they needed to be, with the ammunition they required, and the technical and tactical orders necessary for the gunners to execute their mission. Most importantly, its success depended on the sheer grit, courage, and determination of the legions of gunners who served the guns, and who did so whilst perpetually hungry, cold, tired, and fearful. Thanks to their efforts, and the efforts of millions of their allies, victory in the spring of 1917 was secured, setting the conditions for total victory nearly two years later. This book is their story.

ENDNOTES

1 "Vimy," in '*Tchun! The Canadian Corps Training School*, Volume 1, Number 3 (June 30), 1917, 9.

2 Sir Arthur Conan Doyle, *The British Campaign in France and Flanders, 1917* (London: Hodder and Stoughton, 1919), 39–40.

3 John Keegan, *The First World War* (Toronto: Vintage Canada, 2000,;originally published 1998), 326.

4 Stevenson, "The Field Artillery Revolution and the European Military Balance, 1890–1914," *The International History Review*, Volume 41, Number 6 (2019), 1316.

5 Ibid., 1314.

6 J.B.A. Bailey, *Field Artillery and Firepower* (London: Routledge, 2016), 267.

7 Shelford Bidwell and Dominick Graham, *Fire-Power: British Army Weapons and Theories of War* (Barnsley: George Allen & Unwin Ltd., 1982), 63.

8 Colonel H.A. Bethell, *Modern Guns and Gunnery: A Practical Manual for Officers of the Horse, Field and Mountain Artillery* (Woolwich: F.J. Cattermole, 1913), 169.

9 Royal Regiment of Canadian Artillery website, *Standing Orders for the Royal Regiment of Canadian Artillery Volume 1 – Customs and Traditions*, file:///C:/Users/user/Downloads/rca-standing-orders-2015-vol1.pdf, last accessed April 25, 2017.

10 Forces War Records website, *Unit History: Royal Artillery*, https://www.forces-war-records.co.uk/units/4980/royal-artillery/, last accessed April 25, 2017.

11 Dale Clark, *British Artillery 1914–1919: Heavy Artillery* (Oxford: Osprey Publishing, 2005), 3.

12 Shelford Bidwell, *Gunners at War* (London: Arrow Books, 1972), 35.

13 G.W.L. Nicholson, *Gunners of Canada: The History of the Royal Regiment of Canadian Artillery, Volume I, 1534–1919* (Toronto: McClelland and Stewart Limited, 1967), 245.

14 Bidwell, *Gunners at War...*, 36.

15 WHF Webster, "The Development of Mobile Artillery, 1914–1918," *Journal of the Royal United Services Institute* (63: 453, 49–58), 1919.

16 David Hutchison, *The Young Gunner: The Royal Field Artillery in the Great War* (Leicester: Matador, 2016), 97.

17 Nicholson, *Gunners of Canada, Volume I...*, 159.

18 Ibid., 162–3.

19 Ibid., 165.

20 Ibid., 169–72.

21 Ibid., 190.

22 Ibid., 182.

23 Nicholson, *Gunners of Canada, Volume I...*, 190.

24 Ibid., 190.

25 Lord Hankey, *The Supreme Command 1914–1918, Volume 1* (London: George Allen and Unwin Limited, 1961), 68.

26 Ibid.

27 Ibid., 82; Paul Guinn, *British Strategy and Politics 1914–1918* (Oxford: The Clarendon Press, 1965), 26

28 Nicholson, *Gunners of Canada, Volume I...*, 191–2.

29 Desmond Morton, *Army Headquarters Historical Report Number 98: The Command of the Overseas Military Forces of Canada in the United Kingdom, 1914–1918,* available at ahq098.pdf (canada.ca), 4.

30 GWL Nicholson, *Official History of the Canadian Army in the First World War: Canadian Expeditionary Force 1914–1919* (Ottawa: Queen's Printer, 1962), 7

31 Canada, Militia Department, *The Quarterly Militia List of the Dominion of Canada (Corrected to 30th June 1914) and Appendix* (Ottawa: King's Printer, 1914), 11–33; "Every Unit Ready to Go to Colors," *Manitoba Free Press*, August 5, 1914, 20.

32 Nicholson, *Official History of the Canadian Army in the First World War...*, 7.

33 A. Fortescue Duguid, *Official History of the Canadian Forces in the Great War, Volume I* (Ottawa: King's Printer, 1938), 8

34 Ibid., 6.

35 "German Beaten at Edmonton," *Manitoba Free Press*, August 5, 1914,

3.

36 "Regina Relieves Itself," *Manitoba Free Press*, August 5, 1914, 3.

37 Chris Sharpe, "Enlistment in the Canadian Expeditionary Force 1914–1918," *Canadian Military History*, Volume 24, Issue I, Article 23, 19.

38 *Official History of the Canadian Forces in the Great War, Volume 2*, xxii; *Official History of the Canadian Forces in the Great War, Volume I*, 2–3.

39 *Official History of the Canadian Forces in the Great War 1914–1919, Volume 1…*, 30–35.

40 Sharpe, "Enlistment…," 20.

41 *Official History of the Canadian Forces in the Great War, Volume 2…*, xxii; *Official History of the Canadian Forces in the Great War, Volume I…*, 24.

42 Ibid., 26.

43 Ibid., 45.

44 *Official History of the Canadian Forces in the Great War, Volume 2* xxii; *Official History of the Canadian Forces in the Great War, Volume I*, 20–21.

45 Ibid., 67.

46 Nicholson, *Gunners of Canada, Volume I*, 197–9.

47 *Official History of the Canadian Forces in the Great War, Volume I*, 110.

48 Sharpe, "Enlistment…," 20.

49 Ibid., 20–21.

50 C.P. Stacey, *Canada and the Age of Conflict Volume 1: 1867–1921* (Toronto: University of Toronto Press, 1984, o.p. 1977), 198.

51 Ibid., 109.

52 Nicholson, *Official History of the Canadian Army…*, 109.

53 George F.G. Stanley, *Canada's Soldiers. The Military History of an Unmilitary People.* 3rd Ed. (Toronto: Macmillan of Canada, o.p. 1954), 318.

54 Stevenson, "The Field Artillery Revolution…," 1316.

55 Lord Kitchener, "Instructions for General Sir D. Haig Commanding the Expeditionary Force in France," in *Official History of the Great War Based on Official Documents, Military Operations in France and Belgium, 1916: Appendices* (London: Macmillan and Co. Ltd.), 40.

56 Bidwell and Graham, *Fire-Power…*, 94.

57 Ibid., 95–96.

58 E.W.B Morrison, *Morrison: The Long-Lost Memoir of Canada's Artillery*

Commander in the Great War. Susan Raby-Dunne, ed. (Victoria: Heritage Books, 2018), Kindle edition, Chapter 3.

59 Nicholson, *Official History of the Canadian Army...*, 40.

60 Ibid., 49.

61 Ibid., 53.

62 Nicholson, *Gunners of Canada, Volume I...*, 214.

63 Ibid., 215.

64 Nicholson, *Official History of the Canadian Army...*, 60.

65 Ibid., 61–62.

66 Mark Humphries and Lyndsay Rosenthal, "Sir Richard Turner and the Second Battle of Ypres, April and May 1915," *Canadian Military History*, Volume 24, Issue 1, Article 14.

67 Nicholson, *Gunners of Canada, Volume I...*, 225.

68 Humphries and Rosenthal, "Sir Richard Turner...," 397.

69 Nicholson, *Official History of the Canadian Army...*, 67; Nicholson, *Gunners of Canada, Volume I...*, 227.

70 Nicholson, *Gunners of Canada, Volume I...*, 230.

71 Nicholson, *Official History of the Canadian Army...*, 133.

72 Ibid.

73 Tim Cook, "The Blind Leading the Blind: The Battle of the St. Eloi Craters," *Canadian Military History*, Volume 5: Issue 2 (1996) Article 4.

74 Ibid.

75 Ibid.

76 Nicholson, *Official History of the Canadian Army...*, 147.

77 Ibid., 149.

78 Ibid., 149.

79 Ibid., 149.

80 Ibid., p 150.

81 Nicholson, *Gunners of Canada, Volume I...*, 253–4.

82 Nicholson, *Official History of the Canadian Army...*, 161.

83 Ibid., 160.

84 Ibid., 162.

85 Ibid., 161–2.

86 Ibid., 162.

87 Mark Humphries, "The Myth of the Learning Curve: Tactics and Training in the 12th Canadian Infantry Brigade, 1916–1918," *Canadian Military History*, Volume 14, Issue 4 (April 16, 2012), 15–29.

88 Nicholson, *Official History of the Canadian Army…*, 163.

89 Ibid., 163.

90 The Entente representatives included the following: Belgium – General Wielemans; Great Britain – General Sir William Robertson and General Sir Douglas Haig; Italy – General Porro; Romania – Colonel Rudeanu; Russia – General Palitzine; Serbia – General Rachitch; and France – General Joffre.

91 United Kingdom, "Resolutions of the Chantilly Conference (Translation)," *History of the Great War Based on Official Documents, Military Operations in France and Belgium, 1917: Appendices* (London: Macmillan and Co. Ltd.), 1.

92 Field-Marshal Sir Douglas Haig, *The Private Papers of Douglas Haig 1914–1919*, Robert Lake, ed. (London: Eyre and Spottiswoode, 1952), 180.

93 United Kingdom, "GHQ Letter OAD 258, 2nd January 1917," in *History of the Great War Based on Official Documents, Military Operations in France and Belgium, 1917: Appendices* (London: Macmillan and Co. Ltd.), 10.

94 Canada, Library and Archives Canada (hereafter LAC), *The Artillery Preparation for the Attack on the Vimy Ridge by the First Army*, found at http://data4.collectionscanada.ca/netacgi/nph-brs?s1=1s t+army&s13=&s12=&l=20&s9=RG9&s7=9-52&Sect1=IMAGE &Sect2=THESOFF&Sect4=AND&Sect5=WARDPEN&Sect6= HITOFF&d=FIND&p=1&u=http://www.collectionscanada.ca/ archivianet/02015202_e.html&r=5&f=G, last accessed November 3, 2014.

95 Ibid., 10.

96 United Kingdom, "London Convention of 16th January 1917 (Translation)," *History of the Great War Based on Official Documents, Military Operations in France and Belgium, 1917: Appendices* (London: Macmillan and Co. Ltd.), 16.

97 United Kingdom, "GHQ Letter OAD 286, 26th January 1917," *History of the Great War Based on Official Documents, Military Operations in France and Belgium, 1917: Appendices* (London: Macmillan and Co. Ltd.), 18.

98 Ibid., 18; War Diary (hereafter WD) General Officer Commanding Royal Artillery Canadian Corps (hereafter GOC RA), "Canadian Corps: Artillery Instructions for the Capture of Vimy Ridge," 38.

99 Alan English et al., eds., *The Operational Art: Canadian Perspectives,*

Context and Concepts (Winnipeg: Canadian Defence Academy Press, 2005), 8–9.

100 Ian McCulloch, "A Study in Operational Command: Byng and the Canadian Corps," in *Changing Face of War: Learning from History*, 51.

101 Ibid., 42, 57.

102 Ibid., 58

103 Ibid., 247.

104 LAC, *Report, Canadian Corps Operation, Vimy*, RG9-III-D-3, 1–2.

105 Ibid., 2.

106 Ibid., 3.

107 Ibid., 3.

108 Alexander McClintock, *Best o' Luck; How a Fighting Canadian Won the Thanks of Britain's King* (Toronto: McClelland, Goodchild & Stewart, 1918), 123–5.

109 For Morrison's biography, please see the website of the Museum of the Royal Regiment of Canadian Artillery at http://www.rcamuseum. com/English/Great per cent20Gunners/morrison.htm, last accessed March 17, 2016.

110 WD, GOC RA, December 16, 1916.

111 Morrison, *The Long-Lost Memoir...*, Chapter 17.

112 Nicholson, *Official History of the Canadian Army...*, 213.

113 William Ogilvie, *Umty-Iddy-Umty: The Story of a Canadian Signaler in the First World War* (Erin: Boston Mills Press, 1982), 10.

114 Hugh R. Kay, *Battery Action! The Story of the 43rd Battery Canadian Field Artillery 1916–1919* (Ottawa: CEF Books, 2002), 6.

115 Canadian Letters Website, "Letter from Gunner Bertram Cox, 18 Sep 17," document 41694 | Canadian Letters, accessed June 2, 2022.

116 Kay, *Battery Action!...*, 4.

117 Edgar Wallace, *Kitchener's Army and the Territorial Forces: The Full Story of a Great Achievement* (London: George Newnes, 1915), 103.

118 Ibid., 103.

119 Ibid., 39

120 R.B. Talbot Kelly, R.G. Loosmore (ed.), *A Subaltern's Odyssey: Memoirs of the Great War 1915–1917* (London: William Kimber, 1980), 68.

121 Andrew Iarocci, "Engines of War: Horsepower in the Canadian Expeditionary Force 1914–18," *Journal of the Society for Army Historical Research*, Volume 87, Number 349 (Spring 2009), 59–83.

122 Major J.S. Hammond, "Report on Remount Depot at Lachine, Near Montreal, Canada," *Field Artillery Journal*, Volume VII, Number 4, October–December 1917.

123 David Sobey Tamblyn, *The Horse in War and Famous Canadian War Horses* (Kingston: Jackson Press, 1920), 16.

124 Major J.S. Hammond, "Report on Remount Depot at Lachine, Near Montreal, Canada," *Field Artillery Journal*, Volume VII, Number 4, October–December 1917; Tamblyn, *The Horse in War...*, 9.

125 E.L. McColl, *6th Battery, 2nd Brigade Canadian Field Artillery* (Bonn: Charles Georgi, 1919), 19.

126 Ogilvie, *Umty-Iddy-Umty...*, 11.

127 Ibid., 103.

128 Ibid., 100.

129 Ogilvie, *Umpty-Iddy-Umpty...*, 10.

130 Raymond Edward Priestly, *The Signal Service in the European War of 1914–1918 (France)* (Chatham: W&J Mackay, 1921), 6.

131 F.H. Cooper, *Khaki Crusaders: With the South African artillery in Egypt and Palestine* (Cape Town: Central News Agency, 1919), 46.

132 Cecil W. Longley, *Battery Flashes* (New York: E.P. Dutton, 1916), p. 4.

133 Hugh. R. Kay, *Battery Action...*, 16.

134 C.A. Rose, *Three Years in France With the Guns: Being Episodes in the Life of a Field Battery*, 52.

135 Priestly, *The Signal Service in the European War...*, 144.

136 A.L. Pemberton, *The Development of Artillery Tactics and Equipment* (London: United Kingdom War Officer, 1950), 1.

137 Charles Bormann, *The Shrapnel Shell in England and in Belgium, with Some Reflections on the Use of the Projectile in the Late Crimean War: A Historic-Technical Sketch* (Brussels: Louis Truyts, Printer, 1862), 15.

138 Ian V. Hogg and L.F. Thurston, *British Artillery Weapons and Ammunition 1914–1918* (London: Ian Allan Ltd., 1972), 217.

139 United Kingdom, War Office, *Treatise on Ammunition, 10th Ed* (London: War Office, 1915), 266

140 Ibid., 266–7.

141 Bidwell and Graham, *Fire-Power...*, 98.

142 Alexander Haig, *Haig's Final Dispatch: Review of the Whole War as One Great and Continuous Engagement –British March to the Rhine [First Half]* (Bell & Howell Information and Learning Company, 2000), 549.

143 Anon., *60ᵗʰ Canadian Field Artillery Battery Book 1916–1918*, n.p., 1918, 41–2.

144 *Treatise on Ammunition: 10ᵗʰ Ed...*, 268?

145 Bailey, *Field Artillery and Firepower...*, 233.

146 Bethell, *Modern Guns and Gunnery...*, 154.

147 A. Marshall, "The Invention and Development of the Shrapnel Shell," *Field Artillery Journal*, 13.

148 Ibid.

149 Leslie W.C.S. Barnes, *Canada's Guns: An Illustrated History of Artillery* (Ottawa: Canadian War Museum, 1979), 74.

150 Vivian B. Lewes, "Fothergill Lectures – Modern Munitions of War," *Journal of the Royal Society of Arts*, Number 3272, Volume LXIII, 1915, 824.

151 Ibid., 827.

152 R.B. Talbot Kelly, *A Subaltern's Odyssey...*, 180.

153 Bethell, 266.

154 Colonel H.C.B. Rogers, *Artillery Through the Ages* (London: Seely Service and Co. Ltd., 1971), 157.

155 Barnes, *Canada's Guns...*, 69.

156 Grant, *SOS! Stand To!...*, 236–7.

157 *Artillery in Offensive Operations*, 14.

158 Cecil Street, *The Making of a Gunner*, 205.

159 Hogg and Thurston, *British Artillery Weapons...*, 9–10.

160 Bidwell and Graham, *Fire-Power...*, 44.

161 In imperial artilleries, guns were often named according to the weight of the shell they fired.

162 Stevenson, "The Field Artillery...," 1302.

163 Ibid., 1302.

164 Ibid., 1302–03.

165 Ibid., 1304.

166 Ibid., 1305–06.

167 Edward M. Spiers, "Rearming the Edwardian Artillery," *Journal of the Society for Army Historical Research*, Volume 57, Number 231 (Autumn 1979), 171.

168 Ibid., 168.

169 Major General Sir John Hedlam, *The History of the Royal Artillery From the Indian Mutiny to the Great War, Volume II, 1899–1914* (Woolwich: The Royal Artillery Institution, 1937), 72–3.

170 Stevenson, "The Field Artillery Revolution...," 1302.

171 Hedlam, *The History of the Royal Artillery...*, 422.

172 Bruce I. Gudmundsson, *On Artillery* (Westport: Praegar, 1993), 12.

173 Barnes, *Canada's Guns...*, 68–9

174 Ibid., 69.

175 Nicholson, 172.

176 Wainwright Merrill, *A College Man in Khaki: Letters of an American in the British Artillery* (New York: George H. Doran Company, 1918), 114.

177 Nicholson, 167.

178 Barnes, *Canada's Guns...*, 70.

179 United Kingdom, War Office, *40/3124 18-Pr Q.F. Gun, Gun Drill, 1916* (London: His Majesty's Stationery Office, 1916), 3.

180 Bidwell and Graham, *Fire-Power...*, 13.

181 Hedlam, *The History of the Royal Artillery...*, 81–2; Hoggs and Thurston, *British Artillery Weapons...*, 102.

182 Nicholson, *The Gunners of Canada, Volume I...*, 195.

183 Ibid., 209, Barnes, *Canada's Guns...*, 74.

184 Bidwell and Graham, *Fire-Power...*, 20.

185 Johnathon Spain, "Frederick Turner: An Artillery Officer in Flanders, 1918–10," *Journal of the Society for Army Historical Research*, Volume 84, Number 337 (Spring 2006), 34.

186 Stevenson, "The Field Artillery Revolution...," 1314.

187 Bailey, *Field Artillery and Firepower...*, 243.

188 Hogg and Thurston, *British Artillery Weapons and Ammunition...*, 125.

189 Bidwell and Graham, *Fire-Power* ..., 68.

190 Hogg and Thurston, *British Artillery Weapons and Ammunition...*, 124.

191 Ibid., 95–96.

192 Barnes, *Canada's Guns...*,78; Hogg and Thurston, *British Artillery Weapons and Ammunition...*, 127.

193 Hedlam, *The History of the Royal Artillery...*, 83.

194 Hogg and Thurston, *British Artillery Weapons...*, 116.

195 Ibid., 160.

196 Barnes, *Canada's Guns...*, 80.

197 Hogg and Thurston, *British Artillery Weapons...*, 160.

198 Barnes, *Canada's Guns...*, 80.

199 Canadian Letters Website, *George Kempling Diary, 27 July*

1916, https://www.canadianletters.ca/document-5081 (accessed September 15, 2022).

200 Anon., "The Work of the Heavies," in *Trinity War Book: A Recital of Service and Sacrifice in the Great War* (Toronto: Trinity Methodist Church, 1921), 210.

201 Anon., "My First Trip to the Firing Line," in *Trinity War Book: A Recital of Service and Sacrifice in the Great War* (Toronto: Trinity Methodist Church, 1921), 178–9.

202 Spain, "Frederick Turner…," 35.

203 A.D. Harvey, "Trench Mortars in the First World War," *The Royal United Services Institute Journal*, Volume 157, Number 4 (August/September 2012), 86–92.

204 Bidwell and Graham, *Fire-Power…*, 17.

205 Gudmundsson, *On Artillery…*, 74

206 Harvey, "Trench Mortars….,"86.

207 Bailey, *Field Artillery and Firepower…*, 242.

208 Gudmundsson, *On Artillery…*, 76.

209 United States, War Department, *Manual for Trench Artillery United States Army, Part V The 58 No. 2 Trench Mortar* (Washington: July 1918), 9.

210 Wilfrid Stokes, "The Stokes Gun and Shell, and their Development," *Professional Memoirs, Corps of Engineers, United States Army, and Engineer Department at Large*, Volume 10, Number 54 (November–December 1918), 766.

211 A.D. Harvey, "Trench Mortars in the First World War," *The RUSI Journal*, Volume 157, Number 4 (2012), 87.

212 Gudmundsson, *On Artillery*, 79–80.

213 United Kingdom, War Office, SS 139/6, *Artillery Notes No. 6 – Trench Mortars*, March 1917, 3.

214 Harvey, "Trench Mortars…," 86–7.

215 United Kingdom, War Office, *40/3124 18-Pr Q.F. Gun, Gun Drill, 1916* (London: His Majesty's Stationery Office, 1916), 10.

216 Kay, *Battery Action…*, 10–11.

217 Wallace, *Kitchener's Army…*, 115–16.

218 Cecil W. Longley, *Battery Flashes* (New York: E.P. Dutton, 1916), 30.

219 United Kingdom, War Office, *40/3607 Notes on the Technical Reconnaissance of an Artillery Position and the Training of the Headquarters of a Battery* (London: His Majesty's Stationery Office, 1917), 7–8.

220 Longley, *Battery Flashes*, 38.

221 Ibid., 2, 11.

222 Ibid., 9–11.

223 Ian Ronayne, *Amateur Gunners: The Great War Adventures and Observations of Alexander Douglas Thorburn* (Barnsley: Pen and Sword Military, 2014), 35–6.

224 Ibid., 12.

225 Ibid., 135.

226 Henry Augustus Butters, *Harry Butters, Royal Field Artillery, an American Citizen, Life and War Letters* (New York: John Lane Company, 1918), 136.

227 Reginald Grant, *S.O.S. Stand to!* (New York: D. Appleton and Company, 1918), 51–2.

228 Ibid., 122.

229 Ibid., 260.

230 John Macartney-Filgate, *The History of the 33rd Divisional Artillery in the War 1914–1918* (London: Vacher, 1921), 16.

231 Great Britain, War Office, *Field Artillery Training 1914* (London: Her Majesty's Stationery Officer, 1914), 360–62.

232 Hutchinson, *The Young Gunner...*, 10–11.

233 Ronayne, *Amateur Gunners...*, 40.

234 C.A. Rose, *Three Years in France with the Guns Being Episodes in the Life of a Field Battery* (Kirkaldy: The Allen Lithograph Company, 1919), 3.

235 Longley, *Battery Flashes*, 38.

236 D.C. MacArthur, *The History of the Fifty-fifth Battery, Canadian Field Artillery* (Hamilton: H.S. Longhurst, 1919), 27.

237 Ronayne, *Amateur Gunners...*, 36–37.

238 Anon, *The 60th Canadian Field Artillery Battery Book 1916–1919*, n.p., 1918, 39.

239 *Notes on the Technical Reconnaissance of an Artillery Position....*, 1.

240 *Field Artillery Training 1914*, 316.

241 Hutchinson, *The Young Gunner...*, 72.

242 Ibid., 87.

243 D.C. MacArthur, *The History of the Fifty-fifth Battery, Canadian Field Artillery* (Hamilton: H.S. Longhurst, 1919), 26–7.

244 R.J. Manion, *A Surgeon in Arms* (New York: D. Appleton and Company, 1918), 63–4.

245 McNaughton, "Counter-Battery Work," 389.

246 Jeffrey E. Marston, *Servants of the Guns* (London: Smith, Elder, & Co., 1917), 41.

247 Hutchinson, *The Young Gunner…*, 129.

248 Coningsby Dawson, *Carry On: Letters in War-time* (New York: John Lane Company, 1918), 115–16.

249 C.A. Rose, *Three Years in France with the Guns, Being Episodes in the Life of a Field Battery* (Kirkaldy: The Allen Lithograph Company, 1919), 51.

250 Ibid., 51–5.

251 *Field Artillery Training 1914…*, 296–7.

252 Hector MacQuarrie, *How to Live at the Front: Tips for American Soldiers* (J.B. Lippincott, Philadelphia, 1917), 186.

253 MacQuarrie, 188.

254 Pemberton, 1.

255 Bidwell and Graham, *Fire-Power…*, 20.

256 Bidwell and Graham, *Fire-Power…*, 24.

257 Brooke, "The Evolution of Artillery…," 258.

258 Colonel G.W.L. Nicholson, *Gunners of Canada, Volume II*, 251.

259 Hutchinson, *The Young Gunner…*, 161.

260 Ibid., 177.

261 Colonel G.W.L. Nicholson, *Gunners of Canada, Volume II*, 276.

262 Ibid., 275.

263 H.D. Clark (ed), *Extracts from the War Diary and Official Records of the Second Canadian Divisional Ammunition Column* (St. John: J&A MacMillan, 1921), 8.264 Lt.-Col. (later Field Marshal) Alan Francis Brooke (hereafter Alan Brooke), "The Evolution of Artillery in the Great War," *Royal Artillery Journal*, Volume LI, Number 5; Alan Brooke, "Evolution of Artillery," *Royal Artillery Journal*, Volume L1, Number 5, 261.

265 Col. H.A. Bethell, *Modern Artillery in the Field* (London: Macmillan and Co. Limited, 1911), 272.

266 J.A.B. Bailey, *Field Artillery and Firepower* (Annapolis: Naval Institute Press, 2004), 240.

267 Bethell, *Modern Artillery…*, 281.

268 Ibid., 281.

269 Bethell, *Modern Artillery…*, 285.

270 Weber, "The Development of Mobile Artillery," 50.

271 Gudmundsson, *On Artillery…*, 33.

272 Brooke, "The Evolution of Artillery…, 261; Shelford Bidwell and

Dominick Graham, *Fire-Power: The British Army Weapons and Theories of War 1905–1945* (Barnsley: Pen & Sword Military Classics, 2004), 68–9; Bailey, *Field Artillery...*, 240.

273 Bidwell and Graham, *Fire-Power...*, 62.

274 Lewes, "Fothergill Lectures – Modern Munitions of War...," 821.

275 Major-General A.G.L. McNaughton, "Development of Artillery in the Great War," *Canadian Defence Quarterly*, Volume 6, Number 2, 162.

276 Bidwell and Graham, *Fire-Power*, 96.

277 Ibid., 96.

278 Bailey, *Field Artillery and Firepower*, 244.

279 Bidwell and Graham, *Fire-Power*, 96.

280 McNaughton, "Development of Artillery in the Great War," 161.

281 Ibid., 169.

282 Nicholson, *Gunners of Canada, Volume I...*, 242.

283 Ibid., 242.

284 Marble, "Preparing the Attack"; Nicholson, *Gunners of Canada, Volume I...*, 243.

285 Brooke, "The Evolution of Artillery...: II – Factors Effecting the Evolution of Artillery," *Royal Artillery Journal*, Volume LI, Number 6, 374–7.

286 *Artillery notes...,*" 13.

287 Brooke, "The Evolution of Artillery...: II – Factors Effecting the Evolution of Artillery," 376.

288 War Department, SS 139/3, *Artillery Notes Number 3 – Counter-Battery Work*, February 1917, 17.

289 Ibid., 242–3.

290 J.A.B. Bailey, *Field Artillery and Firepower*, 250.

291 War Department, SS 139/4, *Artillery Notes Number 4 – Artillery in Offensive Operations*, 27.

292 J.A.B. Bailey, *Field Artillery and Firepower...*, 250, n27.

293 Major-General A.G.L. McNaughton, "Development of Artillery in the Great War," *Canadian Defence Quarterly*, Volume 6, 164.

294 Nicholson, 312.

295 F.W. "Artillery and the General Staff," *Journal of the Royal United Services Institute* (Feb. 1919), 470.

296 United Kingdom, War Office, *SS 139/4 Artillery Notes Number 4 – Artillery in Offensive Operations* (London: His Majesty's Stationery Office, 1917), 5.

297 Ibid., 15–31.

298 Ibid., 15.

299 Bailey, 59.

300 Gudmundsson, *On Artillery*…, 130.

301 Ibid., 38.

302 Bidwell and Graham, *Fire-Power*, 110.

303 McNaughton, "The Development of Artillery," 161.

304 Brigadier-General A.G.L. McNaughton, "Counter-Battery Work," *Canadian Defence Quarterly*, Volume 3 (1926), 380.

305 *Artillery Lessons Drawn from The Battle of the Somme, c. December 1916*, Montgomery-Massingberd Papers, LHCMA, file 7/4.

306 McNaughton, "Counter-Battery Work," *Canadian Defence Quarterly*, Volume 4 (1926), 380.

307 McNaughton, "Counter-Battery Work," 380.

308 Brooke, "The Evolution of Artillery in the Great War Number IV – The Evolution of Artillery Organization and Command," *The Royal Artillery Journal* (Volume LII, Number 3), 378–9.

309 McNaughton, "Counter-Battery Work," 381.

310 McNaughton, "Counter-Battery Work," 390.

311 McNaughton, *The Development of Artillery*, 160.

312 Walter Raleigh, *The War in the Air. Being the Story of The part played in the Great War by the Royal Air Force, Volume I* (Oxford: Clarendon Press, 1922), 260.

313 McNaughton, "Development…," 164.

314 Lieutenant-Colonel D.L. Fromow, *Canada's Flying Gunners: A History of the Air Observation Post of the Royal Regiment of Canadian Artillery* (Ottawa: Air Observation Post Pilots Association of Canada, 2002), 17.

315 Ibid., 17.

316 Bidwell and Graham, *Fire-Power*…, 102.

317 Ibid., 102.

318 Fromow, *Canada's Flying Gunners*, 20.

319 Raleigh, *The War in the Air*…, 341.

320 Ibid., 341–342.

321 McNaughton, *The Development of the Artillery*, 164.

322 Silviu Baluta, Gehorghe Andrei, "Determining the Coordinates of Hostile Gunfire by Using the Sound Ranging Method," AFASES 2012, 1.

323 Arthur R. Hercz, *A Trinaural Method for Sound Ranging Volume I*

(Ann Arbor: The University of Michigan, 1965), 1.

324 Nicholson, *Gunners of Canada, Volume I…*, 314.

325 Baluta, Andrei, "Determining the Coordinates….," 1; Nicholson, *The Gunners of Canada, Volume I…*, 314.

326 L.C.L Oldfield. "ARTILLERY and the Lessons We Have Learnt with Regard to it in the Late War (Lecture)." Journal of the Royal United Service Institution 67 (1922): 579. ProQuest. Aug. 17, 2016.

327 Nicholson, *Gunners of Canada, Volume I…*, 314.

328 John T. MacCurdy, MD, *War Neuroses* (London: Cambridge University Press, 1918), 14.

329 *Artillery in Offensive Operations…*, 15.

330 Ibid., 16.

331 Sanders Marble, "Preparing for the Attack: Part I, 1914–1916," in *"The Infantry Cannot Do with a Gun Less": The Place of the Artillery in the British Expeditionary Force, 1914–1918* (New York: Columbia University Press, 2003), http://www.gutenberg-e.org/mas01/mas01.html, last accessed June 17, 2015.

332 War Department, SS 98/5, *Artillery Notes Number 5 – Wire Cutting*, June 1916, 7

333 Marble, "Preparing for the Attack…."

334 *Artillery in Offensive Operations*, 16.

335 Hutchinson, *The Young Gunner…*, 123.

336 Bidwell and Graham, *Fire-Power…*, 111.

337 Nicholson, *Gunners of Canada, Volume I…*, 268.

338 *Artillery in Offensive Operations*, 16.

339 Ibid., 17–18.

340 Ian V. Hogg, *Barrage: The Guns in Action* (New York: Ballantine Books, 1970), 8.

341 United Kingdom, War Office, *40/4406 Barrages* (London: His Majesty's Stationery Office, 1917), 2.

342 McNaughton, *The Development of Artillery*, 168.

343 Weber, "The Development of Mobile Artillery," 53.

344 Bidwell and Graham, *Fire-Power…*, 73.

345 Ian V. Hogg, "The Birth of the Barrage," in *Barrage: The Guns in Action* (New York: Ballantine Books, 1970), 8–33.

346 *40/4406 Barrages*, 2.

347 Weber, "The Development of Mobile Artillery," 53.

348 Ibid, 53.

349 Ibid.,3.

350 McNaughton, *The Development of Artillery*, 168.

351 *40/4406 Barrages*, 3.

352 *Artillery Notes Number 4 – Artillery in Offensive Operations*, 9.

353 Ibid, 21.

354 Bidwell and Graham, *Fire Power...*, 111.

355 Archibald Montgomery, *The Story of the Fourth Army in the Battles of the Hundred Days, August 8th to November 11th, 1918* (London: Hodder and Stoughton Ltd., 1919), 269.

356 *40/4406 Barrages*, 5.

357 Ibid., 20.

358 Ibid., 6.

359 Ibid., 6.

360 Oldfield, *Artillery and the Lessons Learnt in the Late War*, 584.

361 Ibid., 583–84

362 *Artillery Notes Number 4 – Artillery in Offensive Operations*, 9.

363 United States, War Department, *Field Artillery Notes Number 2* (Washington: Government Printing Office, 1917), 26–7.

364 E.W.B. Morrison, "Impressions – Canadian Artillery," *Lethbridge Herald*, October 5, 1918, 3.

365 Hutchinson, *The Young Gunner...*, 150.

366 Bailey, *Field Artillery and Firepower...*, 240.

367 United Kingdom, *History of the Great War Based on Official Documents: Military Operations France and Belgium, 1917: Appendices* (London: Macmillan and Co. Ltd., 1949), 19.

368 Ibid.

369 E.W.B. Morrison, *The Long-Lost Memoir...*, Chapter 17.

370 Hussey, *The Fifth Division...*, 151.

371 WD, GOC RA, March 28, 1917.

372 Ibid., 41.

373 Ibid., 40–41.

374 Gudmundsson, *On Artillery...*, 29.

375 Stevenson, "The Field Artillery Revolution...," 1311.

376 Ibid., 1311.

377 Gudmundsson, *On Artillery...*, 22, 25.

378 Ibid., 34.

379 Ibid., 36.

380 Alfred Dietrich, "The German 79th Reserve Infantry Division in the Battle of Vimy Ridge, April 1917," *Canadian Military History*, Volume 15, Issue 1 (2006), 72.

381 Ibid., 72.

382 Ibid., 75.

383 WD, GOC RA, March 28, 1917, 42.

384 Ibid., 44.

385 Ibid., 45.

386 *Artillery Notes Number 4 – Artillery in Offensive Operations*, 21

387 WD, GOCRA, "Canadian Corps: Artillery Instructions...," 141–44.

388 "Artillery Communication Letter Codes," located at http://www.1914–1918.net/artillerycodes.html, last accessed November 5, 2014.

389 WD, GOC RA, "Canadian Corps: Artillery Instructions...," 46.

390 WD, GOC RA, "Canadian Corps: Artillery Instructions...," 47.

391 War Department, SS 139/3, *Artillery Notes Number 3 – Counter-Battery Work*, February 1917, 11.

392 WD, GOC RA, "Canadian Corps: Artillery Instructions...," 48.

393 Ibid., 48.

394 Ibid., 49.

395 Ibid., 49.

396 Canadian Letters Website, *Gilroy, Wilbert H., Letter: 1917 September 24th*, https://www.canadianletters.ca/document-4987, accessed August 5, 2022.

397 WD, GOC RA, "Canadian Corps: Artillery Instructions...," 51.

398 Ibid., 51.

399 Ibid., 51–2.

400 Ibid., 52.

401 Ibid., 52.

402 Ibid., 53–4.

403 E.W.B. Morrison, "Impressions – Canadian Artillery," *Lethbridge Herald*, October 5, 1918, 4.

404 WD, 1st Canadian Divisional Artillery, April 2, 1917.

405 WD, GOC RA, "Canadian Corps: Artillery Instructions...," 55.

406 Ibid., 39.

407 Ibid., 55.

408 WD, 1st Canadian Divisional Artillery, April 3, 1917; WD, 5 RHA, April 3, 1917.

409 WD, 1st Canadian Divisional Artillery, April 3, 1917.

410 WD, GOC RA, Canadian Corps, "Artillery Instructions for the Capture of Vimy Ridge. Appendix A – Distribution of Div'l. Artilleries Army Field Artillery Brigades and Trench Mortars."

411 The Royal Regiment of Canadian Artillery Website, "Major General HA Panet" http://rca-arc.org/major-general-ha-panet-cb-cmg-dso-1869-1951/, accessed October 5, 2020.

412 WD, 2nd Canadian Divisional Artillery, "Operation Order Number 114," dated April 6, 1917.

413 Ibid.; LAC, RG9-III-D-3, Volume 4967, Field 536. WD 4th Brigade, Canadian Field Artillery, Message from 2nd Canadian Divisional Artillery to 2nd Canadian Division, dated March 31, 1917.

414 WD, GOC RA, Canadian Corps, "Artillery Instructions for the Capture of Vimy Ridge. Appendix A – Distribution of Div'l Artilleries Army Field Artillery Brigades and Trench Mortars."

415 Nicholson, *Gunners of Canada, Volume I...*, 251.

416 WD, 3 Canadian Divisional Artillery, "Reorganization Order 3rd Canadian Divisional Artillery."

417 LAC, RG9-III-D-3, Volume 4970, File 547, WD 8th Brigade, Canadian Field Artillery, April 8–12, 1917.

418 WD, 3rd Canadian Divisional Artillery, "Report on Operations Leading up to the Attack Upon and Capture of the Vimy Ridge."

419 WD, GOC RA, Canadian Corps, "Artillery Instructions for the Capture of Vimy Ridge. Appendix A – Distribution of Div'l Artilleries Army Field Artillery Brigades and Trench Mortars."

420 LAC, RG9-III-D-3, Volume 5067, WD Lahore Divisional Artillery, April 9, 1917.

421 WD, GOC RA, Canadian Corps, "Artillery Instructions for the Capture of Vimy Ridge. Appendix A – Distribution of Div'l Artilleries Army Field Artillery Brigades and Trench Mortars."

422 Nicholson, *Gunners of Canada, Volume. I...*, 281.

423 Royden History Website, *Coddington: Remembering the Fallen of the First World War.* http://www.roydenhistory.co.uk/farndon/warmemorial/coddington/massie_roger_john/massie_roger_john.pdf, accessed 11 October 2020; Nicholson, *Gunners of Canada, Volume I...*, 244.

424 WD, GOC RA, "Canadian Corps: Artillery Instructions...," 39.

425 Website, *The Long, Long Trail. Researching Soldiers of the British Army in the Great War of 1914–1919*, "Heavy Batteries of the Royal Garrison Artillery." https://www.longlongtrail.co.uk/army/regiments-and-corps/the-royal-artillery-in-the-first-world-war/the-heavy-batteries-of-the-royal-garrison-artillery/, accessed October 12, 2020.

426 Nicholson, *Gunners of Canada. Volume I...*, 248.

427 WD, GOC RA, "Canadian Corps: Artillery Instructions...," 56.

428 WD, GOC RA, Canadian Corps, "Artillery Instructions for the Capture of Vimy Ridge. Appendix B – Distribution of Heavy Artillery."

429 Website, *The Long, Long Trail. Researching Soldiers of the British Army in the Great War of 1914–1919,* "Army Service Corps Mechanical Transport Companies." https://www.longlongtrail.co.uk/army/regiments-and-corps/the-army-service-corps-in-the-first-world-war/army-service-corps-mechanical-transport-companies/, accessed October 12, 2020.

430 Colonel Puckle, "The Organization of the Transport and Transportation at the Front in France. May 9, 1917," in *The Army Service Corps of the British Army and the Organization of the Transport and Transportation at the Front in France. Lectures delivered before the Officers of the Quartermaster Corps and Quartermaster Reserve Corps at Washington, D.C. on May 2 and May 9, 1917, Respectively* (Washington: Government Printing Office, 1918), 20.

431 Nicholson, *Official History of the Canadian Army in the Great War,* 248.

432 J. McCartney-Filgate, *The History of the 33rd Divisional Artillery in the War 1914–1918* (London: Vacher & Sons, 1921), 78.

433 James Belton and Ernest Gregory Odell, *Hunting the Hun* (New York: D. Appleton and Company, 1918), 32, 35–36.

434 WD, 1 Canadian Divisional Artillery, March 7–9, 1917.

435 WD, 2 Canadian Divisional Artillery, March 11, 1917.

436 WD, 1 Canadian Divisional Artillery, March 25, 1917.

437 WD, 2 Canadian Divisional Artillery, December 21, 1916.

438 Ibid., February 14, 1917.

439 Ibid., "Operation Order Number 98," dated February 6, 1917.

440 Ibid.

441 A.H. Hussey, *The Fifth Division in the Great War* (London: Nisbet & Co. Ltd., 1921), 149–50.

442 WD, 3 Canadian Divisional Artillery, March 9, 1917.

443 WD, 3 Canadian Divisional Artillery, "Operation Order Number 7," dated March 25, 1917.

444 McCartney-Filgate, *History of the 33rd Divisional Artillery...*, 80.

445 War Diary (WD), General Officer Commanding, Royal Artillery, Canadian Corps, LAC, RG9, Militia and

Defence, Series III-D-3, Volume 4958, Reel T-10775.

446 Nicholson, *Gunners of Canada, Volume I...*, 280.

447 Sir Douglas Haig, *Sir Douglas Haig's Despatches (December 1915– April 1919)*, J.H. Boraston, ed. (London: J.M. Dent and Sons, Ltd., 1919), 85.

448 E.W.B. Morrison, *The Long-Lost Memoir...*, Chapter 17.

449 Anon., *From Otterpool to the Rhine with the 23rd Battery Canadian Field Artillery* (London: Charles and Son, 1919), 13.

450 WD, 5 RHA, April 1–5, 1917.

451 WD, 1st Canadian Divisional Artillery, LAC RG9, Militia and Defence, Series III-D-3, Volume 4958, Reel T-10775 .

452 McCartney-Filgate, *The History of the 33rd Divisional Artillery....*, 81.

453 WD GOC RA, Canadian Corps, April 1, 1917.

454 WD, 3 Canadian Divisional Artillery, March 29, 1917.

455 Canadian Letters and Images Project Website, "Newton, John. MC: Diary." https://canadianletters.ca/content/document-8689?position =6&list=ivjmj5OziZgdTWgWGNLZxmRR4zf8RWGuOMTxpYy MBiw, accessed 15 October 2020.

456 Joseph Hayes, *The Eighty-fifth in France and Flanders; Being a History of the Justly Famous 85th Canadian Infantry Battalion (Nova Scotia Highlanders) in the Various Theaters of War, Together With a Nominal Roll and Synopsis of Service of Officers, Non-Commissioned Officers and Men Who Served with the Battalion in France* (Halifax: Royal Print and Litho., 1920), 49.

457 Nicholson, *Gunners of Canada, Volume I...*, 282.

458 LAC, RG9-III-D-3. Volume/box number 4975, file number 565, WD, 2nd Brigade, Canadian Garrison Artillery, April 1–9, 1917.

459 Dietrich, "German 79th Reserve...," 74.

460 Ibid., 74–5

461 Ibid., 74.

462 Ibid., 75.

463 Ibid., 79, 82.

464 WD General Officer Commanding, Royal Artillery, Canadian Corps, "Artillery Instructions Number 4," LAC RG9, Militia and Defence, Series III-D-3, Volume 4958, Reel T-10775.

465 WD, 8th Canadian Field Artillery, April 4, 1917.

466 LAC, RG9-III-D-3, Volume: 4924, File 391, WD 15th Canadian Infantry Battalion, April 7, 1917.

467 Ibid., April 8, 1917.

468 E.W.B. Morrison, *The Long-Lost Memoir...*, Chapter 17.

469 WD, 11th Canadian Field Artillery, April 5, 1917.

470 WD General Officer Commanding, Royal Artillery, Canadian Corps, "Artillery Instructions Number 8," LAC RG9, Militia and Defence, Series III-D-3, Volume 4958, Reel T-10775.

471 McCartney-Filgate, *The History of the 33rd Divisional Artillery...*, 81.

472 WD, 4 Canadian Field Artillery, April 6, 1917.

473 WD, 3 Canadian Divisional Artillery, April 7–8, 1917.

474 WD, 2nd Canadian Divisional Artillery, April 5, 1917.

475 Belton and Odell, *Hunting the Hun...*, 19.

476 WD, Reserve Divisional Artillery, "G.581," dated April 4 1917.

477 WD, 2nd Canadian Divisional Artillery, "Operation Order Number 113," dated April 1, 1917.

478 WD, 3 Canadian Divisional Artillery, "Operation Order Number 75," dated March 29, 1917.

479 Major Bill March, "Air Power and the Battle for Vimy Ridge," *Esprit de Corps*, *http://espritdecorps.ca/army-articles/air-power-and-the-battle-for-vimy-ridge*, accessed August 29, 2022.

480 WD, 4th Brigade, Canadian Field Artillery, LAC, RG9, Militia and Defence, Series III-D-3, Volume 4967, Reel T-10788-10789, April 5, 1917.

481 WD 2nd Canadian Divisional Artillery, LAC, RG9, Militia and Defence, Series III-D-3, Volume 4959, Reel T-10776-10777, April 5, 1917.

482 Ralph Hodder-Williams, *Princess Patricia's Canadian Light Infantry* (Toronto: Hodder and Stoughton, 1923), 217.

483 Fred Howard, *On Three Battle Fronts* (New York: Vechten Waring Company, 1918), 161.

484 LAC, RG9-III-D-3, Volume: 4944, File 456, WD 102nd Battalion, CEF, April 9, 1917.

485 Harold Panabaker, Canadian Letters and Images Project Website, "Hager, Emily Letter: 1917 May 17th," https://www.canadianletters.ca/document-4997, accessed May 17, 2022.

486 Nicholson, *Gunners of Canada, Volume I...*, 282.

487 Belton, Odell, *Hunting the Hun...*, 55.

488 Ibid., 43.

489 Nicholson, *Official History of the Canadian Army...*, 259.

490 Nicholson, *Official History of the Canadian Army...*, 254.

491 Ibid., 259.

492 Belton and Odell, *Hunting the Hun...*, 56.

493 Hayes, *The Eighty-fifth in France...*, 51.

494 Clifford Wells, *From Montreal to Vimy Ridge and Beyond. The Correspondence of Lieut. Clifford Almon Wells*, O.C.S. Wallace, ed. (Toronto: McClelland, Goodchild & Stewart, 1917), 304–05.

495 Harold Panabaker, Canadian Letters and Images Project Website, "Hager, Emily Letter: 1917 May 17th." https://www.canadianletters.ca/document-4997, accessed May 17, 2022.

496 Belton and Odell, *Hunting the Hun...*, 57.

497 LAC, RG9-III-D-3, Volume: 4943, File 451, WD 73rd Battalion, CEF, April 9, 1917.

498 WD, Reserved Divisional Artillery, April 9, 1917.

499 Nicholson, *Official History of the Canadian Army...*, 253.

500 Belton and Odell, *Hunting the Hun...*, 58.

501 Ibid., 61.

502 Hodder-Williams, *Princess Patricia's...*, 219

503 Ibid., 218.

504 Hussey, *The Fifth Division...*, 154.

505 Canadian Letters and Images Project Website, "Newton, John. MC: Diary." https://canadianletters.ca/content/document-8689?position =6&list=ivjmj5OziZgdTWgWGNLZxmRR4zf8RWGuOMTxpYy MBiw, accessed October 15, 2020.

506 Nicholson, *Official History of the Canadian Army...*, 257.

507 WD, 5 RHA, April 9, 1917.

508 WD, 2 CGA, April 9, 1917.

509 Anon., *Overseas Service of the 18th Battery Canadian Field Artillery*, n.p., 1918, 5.

510 *From Otterpool to the Rhine...*, 13.

511 WE, 8 Canadian Field Artillery, April 14, 1917.

512 LAC, RG9-III-D-3, Volume: 4966, File 533, WD, 3rd Canadian Field Artillery, April 1–9, 1917.

513 Nicholson, *Gunners of Canada, Volume I...*, 285.

514 Canadian Letters and Images Project Website, "Newton, John. MC: Diary." https://canadianletters.ca/content/document-8689?position =6&list=ivjmj5OziZgdTWgWGNLZxmRR4zf8RWGuOMTxpYy MBiw, accessed October 15, 2020.

515 Hussey, *The Fifth Division...*, 156.

516 Canadian Letters and Images Project Website, "Newton, John. MC: Diary." https://canadianletters.ca/content/document-8689?position

=6&list=ivjmj5OziZgdTWgWGNLZxmRR4zf8RWGuOMTxpYy MBiw, accessed October 15, 2020.

517 Hussey, *The Fifth Division…*, 156.

518 Ibid., 157.

519 *From Otterpool to the Rhine…*, 14.

520 WD, 8 Canadian Field Artillery, April 16, 1917.

521 Henry Ruffin, Andre Tudesq, *Notre camarade Tommy, offensives Anglaises de Janvier à Juin 1917* (Saint-Germain : Librairie-Hachette et Cie, 1917), 125–6.

522 WD, GOC RA Cdn Corps, Feb. 19, 1918.

523 Nicholson, *Gunners of Canada, Volume I…*, 292.

524 Ibid., 291.

525 Ibid., 291.

526 Ibid., 297.

527 Ibid., 292.

528 Bidwell and Graham, *Fire-Power…*, 91–3.

529 Ibid., 93.

530 Hussey, *The Fifth Division…*, 151.

531 Nicholson, *Gunners of Canada, Volume I…*, 349.

ABOUT THE AUTHOR

David Grebstad was born in Dryden, Ontario and has served as an officer in the Royal Regiment of Canadian Artillery for over thirty years with operational tours of duty in Afghanistan, Italy and Egypt. He is a graduate of the University of Manitoba, the University of New Brunswick and the Royal Military College of Canada, as well as the Canadian Army Command and Staff College, and the Joint Command and Staff Program of the Canadian Forces College. He is a qualified Instructor-in-Gunnery and had the very great honor to command Y "Forward Observer/JTAC" Battery of the 2nd Regiment, Royal Canadian Horse Artillery. An avid amateur historian, he has been published in several peer-reviewed academic journals, often writing on the history of the Canadian Artillery at war. He and his wife, Colleen, a Health Services Officer in the Canadian Armed Forces, reside in Ottawa.

DOUBLE ‡ DAGGER
— www.doubledagger.ca —

Double Dagger Books is Canada's only military-focused publisher. Conflict and warfare have shaped human history since before we began to record it. The earliest stories that we know of, passed on as oral tradition, speak of war, and more importantly, the essential elements of the human condition that are revealed under its pressure. We are dedicated to publishing material that, while rooted in conflict, transcends the idea of "war" as merely a genre. Fiction, non-fiction, and stuff that defies categorization, we want to read it all.

Because if you want peace, study war.